The Business HANDBOOK

A Guide To Building Your Own Successful Amway Business

D1376452

AUTHOR OF THE MILLION-COPY BEST-SELLER
DON'T LET ANYBODY STEAL YOUR DREAM

DEXTER R. YAGER, SR.
WITH DOYLE YAGER

Published by
InterNet Services Corporation, USA

Printed in the United States of America.
ISBN 0-9328-77-26-5

Cover photography by Dennis Nodine, Charlotte, North Carolina;
Writing by Darryl E. Hicks, High Point, North Carolina;
Illustrations by Burt Mader, Sudbury, Massachusetts;
Cover and Complete Design by Craftsman Printing, Charlotte, North Carolina

DEDICATION

This book is dedicated to **you** and **your future**. Thousands of successful people started their Amway business the same way you are beginning, and this network marketing system has helped transform their lives for the better through financial flexibility, travel opportunities, long-lasting friendships and more time to enjoy all these benefits. We believe that with the information you have in your hands right now, you can achieve your highest dreams.

Success can be yours through an uncommon dedication to the high goals of personal liberty and through your consistent pursuit of preservation of the American free enterprise system.

You can achieve great things by replacing the word "try" with the winner's creed, "It will be done!"

As you read each chapter in this book, realize YOU CAN DO IT!

Above all, "Don't let anybody steal your dream!"

**Build yourself a
SUCCESSFUL NETWORK MARKETING
AND DISTRIBUTION BUSINESS!**

THIS BOOK CAN CHANGE YOUR LIFE!

Often when reading a book, we fully decide to apply what we need to our lives. All too often though, weeks later, we have forgotten our good intentions. Here are 5 practical ways to turn good intentions into practical habits.

1. **READ THIS BOOK MORE THAN ONCE.**
   Let me encourage you to personalize and internalize these principals which have generated a turning point in the lives of many people by reading from cover-to-cover, then at least once again.

2. **UNDERLINE AND MAKE NOTES**
   Have a pen and a highlighter in your hand. Underline specific lines and paragraphs—a simple act that will triple your retention rate. Write your own thoughts in the margins and make it your book.

3. **RE-READ YOUR UNDERLINES**
   By underlining and highlighting, you can quickly review key items and portions of this book. Then re-read your key items over and over.

4. **APPLY THE MATERIAL IMMEDIATELY**
   There is an old saying, "Hear something… you forget it. See something… you remember it. Do something… you understand it." Apply what you learn as soon as you possibly can… it helps you understand and remember it.

5. **PRIORITIZE WHAT YOU WANT TO LEARN**
   Select 3-5 things from the book you need to begin with. Apply them faithfully and make them a habit.

Remember every person struggles with turning their good intentions into habits. Using these 5 points will turn wishing into doing and doing into habits.

As I mentioned earlier, many successful people in the past have traced a new, exciting, profitable chapter in their lives to the reading of a specific book. I want that to happen to you!

Write the date you start reading this book: May 28, 1994 RB
May the date you have just written be the beginning of incredible blessings, rewards and growth!

—Dexter R. Yager, Sr.

Dec. 7, 1994 SB

We want to thank all those who have encouraged and applauded our efforts in putting the knowledge we have gained and developed into this book for the benefit of others.

First, we want to thank Jeffrey Yager, President of InterNet, Yager Enterprises and ICCA, and Steven Yager, Vice President of the same companies. They are vital to every aspect of our partnership, including this book.

We also want to extend our appreciation to several key individuals who have worked with us on *The Business Handbook*. Darryl E. Hicks has greatly assisted us in transforming our thoughts and message to paper and therefore making this book eminently more readable than it might have been otherwise. Burt Mader has helped make this book more easily understood through his illustrative excellence. Both are professionals in their fields; combining that with their insight as distributors has contributed greatly to the success of this book.

We are deeply indebted to so many wonderful people at Amway Corporation headquarters who have provided us with a wealth of information and encouragement. Specifically, in addition to Rich, Jay, Dick and the all the DeVos and Van Andel family members, we want to thank Tom Eggleston (Chief Operating Officer), Bob Kerkstra (VP—Sales Plan Administration), Sharon Grider (Legal), Kim Bruyn, Beth Dornan and Mark Longstreet (Public Relations), Ken McDonald (Communication), Matt Rumpsa, Gary VanderVen and Kevin McNees (Distributor Relations), Pat Nasser (Print Communications), Bob Bogacz (Creative Resources, Inc.), Judy Jones (International Public Relations), and Beth Ballard (International).

In addition, we want to express our gratefulness to numerous Diamonds and above for their invaluable comments, editing suggestions and overall impact toward the success of this book.

Finally, we would sincerely like to thank our dedicated InterNet staff members and the wonderful people at Craftsman Printing for their help in the preparation of the manuscript and design work.

CONTENTS

Chapter Thirteen
VIEWS 336
...*Your Long-Distance and
International Sponsoring Efforts*

Chapter Fourteen
THE TIME CLOCK 358
...*Your Personal and Professional Management Skills*

Chapter Fifteen
WADING THROUGH THE RED TAPE 380
...*Your Legal and Ethical Policies*

Dexter Yager is more than another Horatio Alger story. His name is well known to hundreds of thousands of business people throughout the world. As a popular speaker, consultant, motivator and dreambuilder, he spends a great deal of time with people in counseling individuals, consulting with small groups and in addressing large conventions both in the United States and abroad.

He is also the sponsor and host of several large "Free Enterprise" and "Weekend of the Diamond" Celebrations. He has a personal commitment to re-establish—in the hearts and minds of all people—the traditional values and successful business principles upon which the foundation of America and the free world was built.

He and his wife, Birdie, have attained the top level of Crown Ambassador Direct Distributor in the Amway business.

Being the father of seven children and grandfather of twelve, Dexter realizes the importance of teaching principles which make America great for everyone—regardless of age, race, sex or nationality.

The Yager name seems synonymous with success, as this Christian businessman has greatly contributed to or been responsible for the development of many businesses including a classic group of restaurants and a beautiful racquet club resort in southern Florida. He is also responsible for developing a long list of family-owned businesses—real estate development, real estate acquisition and management, construction, publishing, manufacturing and distribution.

He is an author whose books have sold in the millions. One of those, *Don't Let Anybody Steal Your Dream*, has sold over one million copies.

To political leaders, business insiders, knowledgeable networkers, bankers and entertainment celebrities and peers who are among his devotees, he is one of a handful of motivators whose achievements are equal to his advice.

When the subject is how to make money and build lasting success, some people may speak more eloquently and clearly than Dexter Yager, but few can relate to people better. When it comes to having money or attaining wealth, few have his down-to-earth style.

To use his own terminology, Dexter Yager is a "doer."

Doyle Yager is not only a fast-track success story, but his ability to influence people positively is becoming legendary. For starters, he has been nominated to some of the most prestigious groups in the world, including "Who's Who in Sales and Marketing" (1987), "Outstanding Young Men of America" (1989), "Who's Who in United States' Executives" (1990), "Who's Who Among Rising Young Americans" (1991) and "Who's Who Worldwide" (1993).

Why so much acclaim, even though he is in his mid-thirties?

Although his parents, Dexter and Birdie Yager, are considered by industry insiders to be among the nation's leading businesspeople, Doyle has never been content to merely follow in his parents' footsteps.

Instead, he has taken many opportunities given to him and found innovative new ways to carve out his own success:

• He conceptualized a private, trend-setting bi-monthly magazine, *Dreambuilders Review*, which continues to be distributed to readers throughout North America and Europe.

• Soon afterward, he developed and has successfully marketed a custom-targeted advertising program which has been a bonanza to the entire network marketing industry.

• With his insight, instinct and sweat equity, his father's business acumen and marketing organization, and with his brothers' commitment and dedication (Jeff is president and Steven is vice president), co-founded a family-owned and operated distribution company of self-help materials—cassettes, books and customized sales aids. That company, InterNet Services Corporation, now has offices or affiliates in Canada,

Australia, Mexico, Central America and throughout Europe.

• I.C.C.A., a cassette duplication plant he also co-founded, has become a leader in the industry.

He has produced over 100 large business meetings and corporate conventions with attendances reaching above 100,000. Featured speakers have included Presidents Ronald Reagan and George Bush, former Vice President Dan Quayle, bestselling authors Zig Ziglar and Norman Vincent Peale, former Miss America Cheryl Prewitt, Colonel Oliver North, General H. Norman Schwarzkopf, Jr., and entertainers such as Alan Thicke, Louise Mandrell, Pat Boone, Johnny Cash, the Smothers Brothers, the Everly Brothers and the Oak Ridge Boys.

• Today, he serves as CEO and an officer of the board of directors for Internet Services Corporation, Yager Enterprises and Intercontinental Communications Corporation of America (ICCA)—a company which has been named among the top ten fastest growing companies in the Southern Piedmont area of North Carolina.

• He is founder of Americorp (American Influence Corporation), a growing company which develops and distributes positive living cassettes and training materials to churches, businesses and individuals.

Last, but certainly not least, Doyle is the loving father of two children, Aaron and Justin.

Definitely, the most exciting and successful trend in today's business world is a concept called NETWORK MARKETING.[1]

As we move toward the 21st century, informed people no longer listen to those who would mis-label true network market ing companies as illegal pyramids or chain letter-variety schemes. Instead, more and more enlightened free-enterprise entrepreneurs are optioning for this ingenious concept as an opportunity to own a potentially profitable, booming business with minimal risk and initial investment.

It is no wonder that this free enterprise phenomenon is considered to be one of the fastest growing, most dynamic new ways to own a personal business in today's turbulent marketplace.

Amway Corporation is expanding at a whopping 30% average each year for nearly 35 years (with peaks of 50% during some recent years). The network marketing industry accounts for some 12-million distributors and the number expected to rise to 40-million by the year 2000[2]. According to the Direct Selling Association (DSA), network marketing continues to be the dominant player in the $13-billion direct sales industry. Economic analysts already say home shopping is already a $175.6 billion industry.

This form of business is being taught and discussed in numerous prestigious institutions of higher learning. *Success* Magazine says, "Network marketing is the most powerful way to reach consumers in the 1990s."

Industry analysts project that by the year 2000, one out of every two American households will be involved with network marketing, and at least half of all goods and services will be made available through network marketing methods.

---

1. The term, "Network Marketing," has been used to describe such distribution systems as Amway. Earlier, such terms as "direct sales" and "multi-level" were used. Today, this business approach is sometimes called "interactive distribution," "referral marketing," "mutual-benefit marketing" or "worldwide distribution systems." Refer to the GLOSSARY OF TERMS in the back of this book for more information. Chapter Four also provides a more thorough discussion of these terms.
2. Richard Poe, "Network Marketing: The Most Powerful Way to Reach Consumers in the 90s," *Success*, May 1990, p. 74.

In other words, you are on the right team at the right time with the right success-building system!

YOUR PART ON THE TEAM

By reading a book with such an obvious title, you are showing a serious interest in the Cadillac of all network marketing companies. By all comparisons, Amway is the proven leader in this industry's explosion.

We must admit that our preceding remarks are somewhat biased, since performance and bonus checks from Amway have been coming to the Yager household for three decades.

Let us congratulate you for taking steps to learn, grow and improve—whether you are merely considering a future as a networking professional, or if you are already building a successful marketing and distribution system.

Your life can change for the better through this business!

There is no question that the concept works. However, since you have little experience or knowledge in this area, you still probably have a number of questions. To overcome those doubts and concerns, the best way to start is by acquiring business-building knowledge as rapidly as possible. The more information you possess, the less susceptible you will be to the uninformed opinions of others who might like to "keep you from getting hurt or being disappointed if it doesn't work out." (Whether you announce your decision to enter a tennis tournament, learn a foreign language or start your own business, those dream-stealers always seem to be around, don't they?)

It is our desire that this book helps speed your learning process. By applying the principles illustrated throughout this book, you will learn from the mistakes and the triumphs of those who have blazed the success trail ahead of you.

It is also our desire that the information in this book helps speed your business-building process. It is more fun and definitely more profitable to build it fast, as opposed to going more slowly. Even if you have a shortage of time, as most successful people do, the most effective way to duplicate your time is to quickly sponsor some people who have a need and will make the time. A healthy 90-day target would be to earn the prestigious QUICKSILVER pin, which represents the fact that you understand both how to sponsor personally and how to build depth.[3] Ninety percent of the people who go QUICKSILVER also go Direct. You can, too!

Above all, what you do with the experience-based lessons throughout this book can revolutionize your thoughts and actions. These principles will show you how to apply what you are learning to achieve a life filled with happiness, accomplishment and success.

A BUSINESS-BUILDING FRAMEWORK

We believe that a distribution system and network marketing guidebook is crucial. We are more convinced than ever that the vast majority of people have absolutely no idea how to begin to make their dreams come true. You probably already have all the potential necessary to build your own business, but what good is potential if you don't know how to use it? And how can you build a life worth living without workable plans or blueprints?

By making your first move to become a part of network marketing and interactive distribution, you have started your own success-journey. You may not know all the business-building steps, but you can make your dreams come true by applying what you learn.

By using this knowledge and adding fuel to it by exercising your right to choose—you can begin to establish priorities, develop self-confidence, generate enthusiasm, organize your goals, accumulate wealth, handle challenges, and continue to be the person you were meant to be. We believe this business can enable you to be a winner IN THE GAME OF LIFE!

---

3. Refer to the GLOSSARY OF TERMS in the back of this book for more information on the QUICKSILVER pin.

INSTRUCTIONS

Why this book?

With 500,000 new titles rolling off the world's presses this year—80,000 of them in the United States alone—why one more?

Why *The Business Handbook?*

Well, we believe that theories are fine, but we have sought to put together the most comprehensive, practical material which is designed to help you accelerate your business.

You will be challenged to achieve your highest potential as a network marketing professional.

You can achieve the best results as you read *The Business Handbook* by following these seven tips:

(1) Make the book YOURS.

Have a pen and "highlighter" in your hand. Underline specific lines and paragraphs—a simple act that will triple your retention rate.

(2) Keep a notebook handy.

Many of our thoughts should trigger foundations for your own creative insights. Personalize what we have written. Prepare a brief summary of the highlights for future references. You also may want to jot notes in order to help you recall important points.

(3) Realize that some specific information or illustrations may not apply specifically to you.

Attempt to tailor general topics to your situation. If you have any questions, your upline will be happy to counsel with you.

(4) When possible, counsel with others in your line of sponsorship who are reading and learning from this book.

Counseling and discussing with your upline about the principles you learn in this book can be a tremendous assistance as you seek practical ways to maximize your business.

(5) As you read this book, consider yourself not only a student, but also as a future teacher.

The better student you are of this business, the better teacher you can become.

(6) Don't let your education end when you complete this book.

Re-read the chapters. Your upline can suggest books, *Dreambuilder* Magazine articles and tapes on related subjects.

(7) Most importantly, apply what you have learned as soon as possible.

This business is what the corporate world refers to as OJT—On the Job Training. Therefore, the concepts presented throughout this book are most useful as you actively build your business. When in doubt, do something positive that you have gleaned from these pages—the sooner the better.

Success is fueled by knowledge. We will provide you with the best knowledge gained in building this business to the Crown Ambassador Direct level which has hundreds of downlines at the Diamond Level.

We know that network marketing works. That's why we encourage you to personalize and internalize these principles which have generated a new lifestyle for many people. Read this book from beginning to end, many times. Everything can change for you when you do the right things, do them often enough and do them with the proper attitude.

THE BEGINNING

Many successful people in the past have traced a new, exciting, profitable chapter in their lives to the reading of a specific book.

We want that to happen to you!

May the date you have written earlier be the beginning of incredible blessings, rewards and growth as you BUILD YOUR OWN SUCCESSFUL NETWORK MARKETING BUSINESS!

A WORD TO WISE BUILDERS

Do not mistake or misuse the information in this book. The principles offered are to serve as guidelines, but should not be interpreted as engraved-in-stone laws in every situation.

In addition, since this book is not published by Amway Corporation, it carries no formal or legal corporate endorsement. It is simply an organizational distributor training manual based on our successful methods.

Again, as you have questions relating to this book or to building your distributorship, especially with one technique or another (and you will!), consult your upline.

Dexter R. Yager, Sr.   Doyle L. Yager

My dad and mom were there when Amway was born. I watched them help pioneer the way. I've been around Dexter and Birdie as they have continued to blaze the trail with their proven success system.

After over three decades of seeing the business grow, I know that there is nothing else out there that can compare to the Amway opportunity. It is truly an equal opportunity business—for men and women of all backgrounds. The only barrier is yourself and the size of your dreams.

JODY VICTOR
Former Corporate Certified Public Accountant
Second Generation Crown Direct Distributor (USA)
Past ADA Board President ('84–'85 & '90–'91) and Advisor ('91–'92)

Blueprints

...Your Opportunity for Success

If our travels to various places around the world have taught us anything, that one thing would be how wonderfully blessed free people are.

Millions of people in many other areas of the globe would gladly exchange places with those of us who live in free market countries. Most envy the opportunities we enjoy, and many have given up their material possessions, left their friends and some even left family behind—all just to live in a free country of unlimited opportunities.

Most people, if asked to name the greatest single benefit in life, outside of life itself, would probably say "freedom." That desire for liberty has been a major reason why many of the wars have been fought.

Yet even in the great lands of the free market world, many men and women live in economic and occupational slavery. Their lifestyles, hours, working conditions, vacations, and other conditions of employment are determined by someone else.

Sadly, most "free" people are working for the profits of someone else. Simply stated, many of us are building someone else's business and fulfilling others' dreams.

THE 45-YEAR PLAN

Quite frankly, though some might argue, entrepreneurs feel there are no great jobs. A person could search lists of occupations in vain, trying to find the one job which gives great opportunities and freedom to determine one's own working hours, the type of

working conditions, the amount of pay, promotions and retirement benefits. There are no jobs which offer equal amounts of both time and money.

The standard 45-year plan is hardly ideal. Usually a man or woman is 18 to 25 before finishing all the preparation for a vocation or profession. Filled with dreams and youthful expectation,

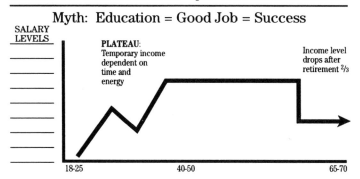

THE STANDARD 45 YEAR PLAN

Myth: Education = Good Job = Success

SALARY LEVELS

PLATEAU:
Temporary income
dependent on
time and
energy

Income level
drops after
retirement $^2/_3$

18-25   40-50   65-70

most people quickly reach an income plateau. Even if the economy and workplace stay steady, they do well merely to stay ahead of inflation.

Faced with built-in plateaus, most people have to eventually do one of two things:

(1) Scale down their dreams,

or

(2) Increase their income.

Since the income made in most professions and vocations is dependent upon one's time and energy, and since all of us have a limit as to what we can produce in a day—no matter what our income level—the vast majority of men and women have to settle for scaled-down dreams.

That is unfortunate, for what it clearly means is that generally when people reach retirement age, thereby reducing income even more, dreams for the so-called "golden years" must also be altered.

How ineffective are the results of the typical 45-year plan?

For starters, today's younger workers are losing the race

for prosperity. Clifford M. Johnson, director of family support at the Children's Defense Fund in Washington, was quoted in a *BusinessWeek* article titled "What Happened to the American Dream?" Johnson said: "Young families are in an economic free-fall despite the longest boom since World War II.[1]" In fact, added Frank Levy, an economics professor at the University of Maryland, "The baby busters may never match their parents' living standards.[2]"

Not only do all workers face economic uncertainties, but most simply do not make enough money to live as well as they desire. One indicator of this fact is moonlighting. A record 7.2 million people—6.2% of all workers, have more than one job. That is up from 5.7 million in 1985.[3]

The average family headed by middle-agers has just $2,300 in financial assets, not including the equity in their home. That middle-aged couple who plans to retire at age 65 should be saving $11,500 each year for the next 20 years in order to meet projected retirement expenses.[4]

It gets worse during the so-called "golden years." One-third of all Americans work after retirement—primarily because they need the money.[5] In fact, according to the Social Security Administration, of those people who do reach the age of 65, 45% have to depend upon relatives and 30% are forced to depend on charity. Only 2% are actually able to enjoy financial freedom.

In addition, according to a recent study by the Department of Health, Education and Welfare, for every 100 people starting their careers, only 71 are still alive at 65. Of those, 55 have annual incomes between $5,200 and $33,000 (the median income is $7,900), 13 have annual incomes under $5,200 (below poverty level), and 3 have annual incomes over $33,000 and are considered financially successful.[6]

1. Paul Grange, "What Happened to the American Dream?" *BusinessWeek*, August 19, 1991, p. 80.
2. *Ibid.*
3. "Moonlighting On the Rise," *USA Today*, December 14, 1989.
4. "A Rude Awakening from the American Dream," *The Fourth Annual Merrill Lynch Retirement Planning Survey*, 1992, p. 20.
5. "One-third of Americans Work After Retirement," High Point (NC) *Enterprise*, February 7, 1993, p. 4E.
6. U.S. Department of Health, Education and Welfare, Income and Resources of the Aged, January 1980. The study has been adjusted for consumer price index changes through 1993.

In the United States, the average monthly Social Security benefit for ALL retired workers is $653.[7] In Canada, the basic pension is $373.32 per month.[8] That figure dwindles throughout most of the world. It is no wonder that the median cash reserve for most retiring men and women is less than $500.

THE 5-10 YEAR PLAN

There is a better way—one that could involve a 5 to 10 year plan of economic flexibility. It is the way known as network marketing and personal business ownership.

You see, we believe that our economic system should reward people in direct proportion to their efforts. Obviously, that condition exists best when a person owns his or her own business within our free enterprise framework.

The free enterprise system has been called the "ultimate wealth-creating program." In fact, the ability to create profit through private enterprise has been built entirely due to that entrepreneurial spirit.

YOUR DESIRE TO OBTAIN FREEDOM

The Amway Sales and Marketing Plan itself is a good example of what free enterprise is all about. The plan provides equal opportunity to all people (regardless of background, nationality or other differences) to further their own achieve-

---

7. *1993 Social Security Manual*, Globe Communications, p. 16.
8. *Ibid.*

ment through personal effort and initiative. It is an opportunity which is not limited to those who have special skills, education, or large amounts of capital to invest. Success in network marketing is possible wherever there are people in free societies who are willing to commit themselves to conscientiously build their businesses.

You have decided to build your own network marketing and distribution business. Congratulations! You are joining a great, growing multitude of people who place a tremendous value upon that free enterprise system.

You are becoming a part of that segment of society who believes we must continue to recognize performance and to preserve our personal freedoms (the right to own property, the right to worship as you choose, the right to express your opinions, the right to unchecked progress). In fact, you are now

involved with people who believe that the freedoms we enjoy are completely tied up in the freedom to build our own business.

Liberty consists of the ability to choose. One of the great benefits of living in a free society is that we have the right to make our own important decisions. We can obey the law, or we can disobey it, but we must then be prepared to reap the results of either decision. We can work, or we can depend on others to work for us. We can build our own business, or we can use our labors to help somebody else reach his or her dreams.

We decide.

BEYOND MEDIOCRITY

Even with such opportunities available, a large percentage of people refuse to make the decisions which could turn everything around. Instead, they retreat to live in society's comfort zones—those stagnant places with little room for growth.

As mentioned before, some call this the 45-year plan. This means, for most men and women, working at a job with hopes of retiring at 65 or 70. Unfortunately, most people have to retire on less than they couldn't live on before retirement.

There has to be a better way.

There has to be something else "out there" for people like you who want MORE out of life than a dead-end job and a gold watch at the retirement party.

We feel that one of the most foolish concepts in our world is the idea that we should all settle for mediocrity instead of striving for excellence, for reaching outstanding levels of performance, for achieving great feats and for carving our own niches in the marketplace.

It was not always so. Free nations were built by pioneers who believed in attempting great things. Leading countries became major positive forces in the free world because their citizens loved freedom and achievement. All of us have advanced because we are believers and builders.

It is time that more people join in that pursuit of excellence and greatness once more. You, too, can band together with free people around the world who believe in building an exciting future.

Rich DeVos, Co-founder of the Amway Corporation, said the following:

> *I see America as the horizon of human hopes. To those who say that the design defies our abilities to complete it, I answer: To act with enthusiasm and faith is a condition of acting great.*
>
> *It is time more and more of us became builders, encouragers, believers, doers, and motivators-all joined together with the common bond of freedom and achievement.*

Freedom—enough time and money to do what you want to do—must be a prime motivation for building your own business. Motivation is the inner urge which can incite you into positive action. The greatest achievements throughout history have started from that God-given urge— that dream to achieve.

But the greatest, most motivating dreams will have little lasting effect unless you determine a specific plan of action.

A FINAL NOTE

In this network marketing system, there are certain success patterns which many men and women have already followed on their own freedom trail, and this book is a compilation of those principles which have helped scores of people become exciting, secure, loving and sharing business-builders.

You can be great in the world of Amway, too. You have so many opportunities before you. The time to build a large, successful business is better NOW than ever before! Your horizons can stretch as far as you will allow yourself to dream.

Take advantage of your God-given dreams and freedoms. You can do the "impossible."

**Your opportunity for success
is absolutely possible through
NETWORK MARKETING
AND DISTRIBUTION!**

BUILDING BLOCKS

Every country has achieved its greatness because of small business men and women, and I'm concerned that we maintain the climate that made it possible for me and millions of others to start a business and build it.

RICH DEVOS
Co-Founder, Amway Corporation
Bestselling Author and Speaker
Owner of the Orlando Magic NBA
Team

Free Enterprise is so much a part of our free way of life that, when it is restricted, it is just a matter of time before other basic freedoms are threatened...the role of government is not to try to guarantee happiness, but to provide the opportunity for people to work out their happiness for themselves.

JAY VAN ANDEL
Chairman of the Board
& Co-Founder,
Amway Corporation
Past Chairman of United States
Chamber of Commerce

I am very optimistic about the future of Amway. There are many tremendous opportunities ahead. In fact, even though we have spread throughout the free world, there are still over two billion people in countries who have yet to be introduced to Amway.

We have a strong support structure in place. We have the most wonderful products and services. We have a far-reaching vision. And, most of all, our goals are to bring value, to make a real difference and to make this world a better place to live.

DICK DEVOS
President, Amway Corporation
Co-founder, Windquest Group
President, Orlando Magic NBA Team

The vision for the future of Amway, shared between the corporation and distributors, is to become most admired among all businesses. Our shared commitment is to secure the future by actions which are admirable in every way by our distributor family.

TOM EGGLESTON
Chief Operating Officer and
Executive Vice President of
Worldwide Direct Sales, Amway Corporation

Not long after we got involved in this Amway business, we heard the phrase, "You can have anything in this world that you want if you help enough other people get what they want." This business has proven that statement to be true over and over, and it's more true today than ever—regardless of your background, the color of your skin, your age or your business experience.

RUTH HALSEY
Former School Teacher
Triple Diamond Direct Distributor (USA)

Let's talk about the power of personal example. People are watching you and listening to you to see if you will win. You can't let them down.

You have no idea whom you are helping by becoming a winner. Your own children are watching you. If you become a winner, they will become incredibly encouraged. If you quit, they will quit. If you make it, they will get up and try again. Why? Because you did it first.

Remember, you have no idea whom you are influencing. Give people hope. Don't ever quit. Don't let rejection win. Instead, become the winner of your dreams.[1]

RON BALL
Author, Minister,
Speaker and Direct
Distributor (USA)

Whether you are a businessperson or someone earning a salary, you should never apologize for trying to earn more money. Never feel guilty for wanting to keep more of it for you and your family. Do not accept the silly notion that there is poverty and suffering because you are greedy and aren't paying enough in taxes. Realize that regardless of the job you have, you are helping to create other jobs. The goods and services you consume help create employment for people who wouldn't otherwise have it.[2]

RUSH LIMBAUGH
Broadcaster, Speaker and
Bestselling Author

1. From the Ron Ball cassette, *Keep the Steam in Your Dream (How Winners Overcome Rejection)* (Marietta, GA: Ron Ball Association, 1993).
2. Rush Limbaugh, *The Way Things Ought to Be* (New York: Simon & Schuster, 1992), p. 78.

The best way to build this business is by focusing your attention on other people and their dreams. That isn't as easy as it sounds, because so many people simply have grown afraid to dream. Too many men and women have let their dreams die. But you have the opportunity to make a difference in their lives.

As you help people start dreaming again, you will affect not only each of them—as individuals, but will also affect their families, their friends and their community. In a very real sense, your ability to help people achieve their dreams can eventually touch the entire world.

TIM FOLEY
Former All-Pro Miami Dolphins
Professional Football Player
and Broadcaster
Triple Diamond Direct
Distributor (USA)

Small opportunities are often the beginning of great enterprises.

DEMOSTHENES (385-322 B.C.)
Greek Orator and Statesman

One of the best parts of building the Amway business is the association you have with such high-quality people. I've seen such a profound effect from these associations and friendships—not only for Annette and me, but also for our children.

Take advantage of these relationships. They will change your life!

STEVE WOODS
Former Police and Drug
Enforcement Pilot
Diamond Direct Distributor (USA)

The reason so many people around the world yearn for America is that they see something here which we Americans often lose sight of—because it surrounds us and pervades our society. What they see, that we miss, is our freedom.

JEANE KIRKPATRICK
Co-founder of Empower America;
Former Ambassador to the
United Nations

When Hank and I first got involved in building our Amway business, I started hearing people talk about dreams. We were suddenly surrounded by men and women who loved freedom and were willing to do whatever it took to achieve their dreams. That appealed to me, both then and now, because I know that dreams do come true!

You see, when I was six, my family and I were shipped as slaves from my native Poland to a labor camp in Siberia. We dreamed of freedom and were eventually released and reunited. We dreamed of going to America and that came true in 1951. I dreamed of marrying a handsome, wise man, and Hank is living proof that dreams really do come true. When we dreamed about getting more out of life than the traditional corporate career could afford, this business came along.

Your dreams can come true, too. You are in a business where your leaders understand the power of vision, and where you will find others who believe in you and your dreams.

ALICIA GILEWICZ
Former Homemaker
Diamond Direct Distributor (USA)

The spirit of America is strong and its future is great! The entrepreneurs, the self-reliant, those with personal initiative, optimism and courage are leading America to take freedom's next step.

We've made a new beginning, a dramatic and far-reaching step for a much better tomorrow. We've come too far, struggled too hard, and accomplished too much to turn back now.

We can make our beloved country the source of all the dreams and opportunities she has placed on this good earth to provide. We need only to believe in each other and in a God who has so blessed our land.

RONALD WILSON REAGAN
Former Actor and Governor of California
Fortieth President of the United States,
Statesman, Speaker and
Bestselling Author

I hear people talking about the Amway business as if it were something so incredibly difficult—even impossible. Nothing could be farther from the truth. Using the Yager system of books, tapes, functions and upline support, this is one of the best, most simple things I've ever been involved with, especially compared with the so-called "real" business world. The income potential is superb, but you don't have so many of the challenges, red tape and hassles associated with more traditional businesses. The hard part is staying focused and being willing to change your attitude.

JIM RICHARDSON
Inventor and Former Builder
Diamond Direct Distributor (USA)

Five areas of management constitute the essence of proactive performance in our chaotic world: (1) an obsession with responsiveness to customers, (2) constant innovation in all areas of the team, (3) partnership—the wholesale participation of and gain sharing with all people connected with the organization, (4) leadership that loves change (instead of fighting it) and instills and shares an inspiring vision, and (5) control by means of simple support systems aimed at measuring the "right stuff" for today's environment.[3]

TOM PETERS
Bestselling Author of
In Search of Excellence,
A Passion for Excellence and
Thriving on Chaos

In the very beginning of Amway, it was faith that kept us going—faith in the fact that what we were doing was necessary and right.

JOE VICTOR, SR.
Former Milkman
Charter Amway Distributor
Crown Direct Distributor (USA)
Former ADA Board President
(1977-78, 1987-88)

When shallow critics denounce the profit motive inherent in our system of free enterprise, they ignore the fact that it is the economic support of every human right we possess and without it all rights would soon disappear.[4]

DWIGHT D. EISENHOWER (1890-1969)
U.S. Military Leader, Statesman and
Thirty-fourth President

3. Tom Peters, *Thriving on Chaos* (New York: Harper & Row, 1987), p. 45.
4. "Thoughts on the Business of Life," *Forbes,* July 22, 1991, p. 336.

When we first saw this business, it was vastly different from my life in the armed forces and Peggy's experience as a special education teacher. We really didn't understand what we had in our hands because we had nothing to compare it to.

Even though we didn't use the word "paradigm" back then, we realized that we had to change our way of thinking to a new, more productive mindset.

As we plugged into the proven success system, and as we began building a relationship with Dexter and Birdie Yager, we started seeing that this network marketing and interactive distribution business has virtually all the best elements of other personal ownership methods, but without all the things such as oppressive overhead and employees costs which are connected with traditional businesses. With the Amway opportunity, we have something so unique that when people really understand it, they almost always get involved and start building it for themselves.

In fact, here's the phrase I've had rooms and coliseums full of distributors repeat with me for some time: "I've never shown this to an ambitious person who was looking for something, who took the time to check this out, who didn't get excited about it."

BILLY FLORENCE
Former Air Force Officer and Pilot
GM Automobile Dealership Owner
Diamond Direct Distributor (USA)
ADA Board President, '93-94

Marketing & Distribution Paradigms

...Your Key to New Business Concepts

In 1900, Harvey Firestone saw the emerging need for a solution to a problem related to the automobile. Turn-of-the-century cars were becoming more popular, but there seemed to be a problem with wheels. Roads were bumpy, at best, and treacherous, at worst. The old, stiff rubber tires made riding tortuous, and the jolting action often broke parts of the chassis.

The old solutions were simple. Tires and wheels had been the same for a number of years. But Harvey Firestone had a new solution. When he began telling people that he was going to build tires that had air inside, he was instantly branded as a crazy zealot. But he persisted with his outlandish idea. Nearly a century later, anyone who enjoys the "give" and wearability of inflated tires can thank the man whose company still boasts his name.

Where might the tire industry have gone if Harvey Firestone had not been open to the unknown? What if he, as other people of his day did, kept looking for known solutions?

HARVEY FIRESTONE

SOLUTIONS

The truth is: All of us need fresh solutions to the unprece-dented challenges—personal, career-wise and corporate—that we face. That need is nothing new; it is just more urgent. But so often we become so adept at digging ruts and building comfort-able boxes for ourselves, that we allow ourselves to accept a life of non-creativity and self-made prisons. In doing so, we cheat ourselves from reaching our highest potential. We also tend to blind ourselves from the best opportunities.

How?

John Sculley, former CEO of the Apple Computer Corporation, now Chairman and CEO of Spectrum Information Technologies, has said:

> *The future seems less predictable today. We have never lived in a time of so much volatile change. It makes planning for the future incredibly complex and difficult, and many companies have lost millions of dollars placing bets on the wrong horses.*[1]

Joel Arthur Barker, author of *Future Edge*, talks about one of the most telling wrong-horse bets by the Swiss. In 1968, they held 65% of the world's watch market share and between 80% and 90% of all the profits. But 10 years later, both market share and profits had dropped below 20%. In 1968, Japan had virtually no share of the watch market, but 10 years later, they led the world. In a capsule, in ten years the Swiss were dethroned as watch kings, and the Japanese rose to the top.

Why? How could something like this happen?

It is all due to the quartz movement watch, which is totally electronic and 1000 times more accurate than its spring prede-cessors. It is such a brilliant idea, and the most amazing part of all is that the quartz movement watch was invented by the Swiss. Yet when the inventors and researchers presented the new watch to company leaders in 1968, it was rejected. Watch

---

1. John Sculley, *Odyssey: Pepsi to Apple… A Journey of Adventure, Ideas and the Future* (New York: Harper & Row, 1987), p. 292.

moguls were so unimpressed that they never even bothered to protect the idea with a patent. When researchers presented this new idea to the Annual World Watch Congress, at least two companies took great notice: Seiko of Japan and Texas Instruments of the United States. The rest, as they say, is history. Tens of thousands of Swiss watch workers have since been laid off. The country's economy may never rebound.[2]

Why?

After all, the new quartz movement watch had no main-spring, no bearings, required few moveable parts, was battery-powered and electronic. How could that possibly be the watch of the future?

After all, hadn't the Swiss led the world in finding new and innovative ways to manufacture the innerworkings of modern watches? They had introduced waterproofing and self-winding watches. But they were blinded by the fact that they were

---

2. Joel Arthur Barker, *Future Edge: Discovering the New Paradigms of Success* (New York: Morrow, 1992), pp. 15-17.

already so successful at what they were doing. They assumed, wrongly, that what had been successful in the past would continue to be successful in the future.

How wrong that assumption continues to be. There will always be high-end watches such as Rolex, but the marketplace now belongs to low-end watches such as Armitron or Timex. If anything, more and more of today's buyers continue to shy away from the mid-range Swiss-made watches.

False assumptions are the reasons why so many people will be unable to keep up with tomorrow's trends. You see, change is everywhere, and it is happening faster than ever—at an accelerated pace.

During the 1960s, Bob Dylan's warbling words touched a generation's heart. He sang:

> *Come writers and critics who propheticize with*
> *your pens,*
> *And keep your eyes wide for the chance won't*
> *come again.*
> *And don't speak too soon for the wheel's still*
> *in spin,*
> *And there's no telling who that it is naming.*
> *For the loser now will be later to win,*
> *For the times they are a-changin'.*[3]

If the times were a-changin' during the Sixties, the times are many times more turbulent now. Based on trends on the horizon, we join many others in the belief that during the coming decade the marketplace will be more unpredictable than ever—much more so than most industry analysts are forecasting.

Financial, technological and marketplace changes will come fast and furiously, and only the most flexible people and organizations, those who can learn to change quickly and live with the confusion, will survive.

Yet, during the coming chaos, there will also be a growing number of people and corporations who will flourish, despite the obstacles.

PARADIGMS

Change is a fact of life. All people and businesses will face many changes, both unexpected and on many different levels. But the problem is that we often don't anticipate the right changes because we are blinded by our **PARADIGMS.**

"Paradigm" is one of those words which is often used, and misused, with little understanding of what the word really means. It is a word with a rich heritage that has evolved through the Greek, Latin and French languages. It is defined as a **pattern, example** or **model.**

Contemporary behaviorists and sociologists use "paradigm" to describe any idea or set of ideas that provides the basis for a framework of beliefs and actions. Simply put, it is a **controlling perception.**

Adam Smith, the noted futurist, explains paradigms as shared assumptions. He goes on to say:

> *The paradigm is the way we perceive the world; water to the fish. The paradigm explains the world to us and helps us to predict its behavior.*[4]

The problem is that our assumptions—or paradigms—often keep us from predicting the future very well. What do we mean?

Consider the paradigms—or assumptions—that caused some of these famous people to make very bad predictions:[5]

- Thomas Edison, back in 1880, put down his own invention, the phonograph. He said, "It is not of any commercial value." Okay, maybe record players aren't as commercial today as CD or cassette players, but what an amazing run phonographs have enjoyed through the 20th century. Who could imagine life without them?

- President Grover Cleveland, in 1905, said, "Sensible and responsible women do not want to vote." History

---

4. Adam Smith, *Powers of the Mind* (New York: Ballentine Books, 1975), p. 19.
5. Barker, pp. 88-9.

has proven quite different, hasn't it?

- Think of this one: Back in 1920, Robert Millikan, a Nobel Prize winner in physics, insisted, "There is NO likelihood man can ever tap the power of the atom."

- Or consider this forgettable phrase that slipped the lips of Tris Speaker, a Hall of Fame baseball player, about Babe Ruth, one of the greatest homerun hitters of all time: "He made a big mistake when he gave up pitching."

- If you think that was an unwise statement, consider this one in 1927 from Harry Warner, powerful studio head of Warner Brothers Pictures. "Who wants to hear actors talk?"

- Let's skip ahead a few years to 1943. Thomas Watson, Sr., chairman at the time of the company that would eventually be called IBM, said, "I think there is a world market for about five computers."

- And if you think that one could cause embarrassment, think about this one from 1977. Ken Olsen, president of Digital Equipment Corporation, said, "There is NO reason for any individual to have a computer in their home."

Let us also give you a couple more quick ones from the world of pop music:

- Did you know that during the early 1950s a young Elvis Presley was turned down by a well-known Gospel singing group because, "He didn't have a very good voice!"[6]

- Or did you know that during the early 1960s American record companies passed on the offer to record the Beatles; in fact, one Capitol Records executive stated flatly, "Groups with guitars are definitely on their way out."[7]

Elvis and the Beatles, of all singers! But they were turned

---

6. Steve Landis and Bob Posten, *The New Gold Rush: Brand Equity & Product Positioning Strategies for the '90s and Beyond* (Jupiter, FL: Sutter Mill Publishing, 1990), p. 51.
7. *Ibid.*

down by sincere, knowledgeable people, unfortunately, made faulty assumptions based on soon-to-be-outdated paradigms.

Again, we keep referring to paradigms. You see, whatever your stage of life, you bring your collection of paradigms—your basis for actions and opinions—to every decision. Dr. Carl Sorensen, a professor at Stanford University, says it best:

> *There's an old expression, 'Seeing is believing.' But it is more accurate to say that 'believing is seeing.' That is, you tend to see what you believe you're going to see. You bring to a situation what you expect you're going to experience.*

Believing is seeing! The point is this: Your view of the world is shaped by your preconceptions.

PARADIGMS—GOOD OR BAD?

What about these paradigms? Are they bad or good? The answer is **both**. The truth is, everyone in the world works within a given number of paradigms. Therefore, paradigms are neither bad nor good, of themselves. In fact, paradigms help you determine some sort of framework for your life. They help provide guidelines for success and failure. Paradigms help you screen the thousands of information scraps which bombard you every day. Paradigms are a common, everyday part of everyone's life.

The problem occurs when you allow your paradigms to become imprisoning boxes, and when you are unable—because of your paradigms—to adapt to change.

So what's the answer?

If each of us has certain paradigms, and paradigms tend to blind us to the future, what is the answer? Can our paradigms be changed to adapt to new ideas?

The answer is, of course, a resounding YES! You can choose to change your paradigms. Take a look at history. Some controlling perceptions, once tightly held, have been shifted. Let us give you a few examples:

- People used to believe that the world was flat. Nearly everyone believed this until 1492. Even today a group that calls itself "The Flat Earth Society" refutes the notion that the earth is spherical.

Basically, however, most people whom you ask will say that they believe the earth is round. A major paradigm has been changed.

• Here's another: Not many years ago, most medical and scientific experts believed that smallpox would reach epidemic proportions and eventually destroy humanity. As late as 1967, there were two million deaths documented around the world.

But because of a shift in thinking during the past half-century, largely due to improved inoculation procedures, smallpox has effectively been controlled. In fact, smallpox was officially declared to have been eradicated in 1979.[8] Another paradigm was shifted.

• How about this one: It is not technologically possible to put a man on the moon. That was a controlling paradigm throughout the world. In fact, The New Scientist Magazine even printed this idea in its April 30th, 1964, issue, by reporting: "The odds are now that the United States will not be able to honor the 1970 manned-lunar-landing date set by Mr. Kennedy."

The refutation of this paradigm was broadcast to the world when on June 20, 1969, at 4:18 EDT, Neil Armstrong and Edwin Aldrin landed the lunar module Eagle in the Sea of Tranquility on the moon. Then, at 10:56 EDT, Armstrong took man's first step on the moon and spoke those now-unforgettable words, "One small step for man; one giant step for mankind."[9]

You can add your own paradigms that have been shifted.

These mindset changes occur constantly. Look back at your life. You have probably gone through a number of para-

---

8. *Webster's Family Encyclopedia* (New York: Arrow, 1990), p. 2376.
9. *The World Book Yearbook* (Chicago: Field Enterprises Educational Corporation, 1970), p. 13.

digm shifts that would have seemed impossible a year or two before. That is necessary. We must either make paradigm shifts, or we will be obsolete. Larry Wilson, best-selling author and founder of the Pecos River Learning Center, has written:

> *Our options are to learn this new game, the rules, the roles of the participants and how the rewards are distributed, or to continue practicing our present skills and become the best players in a game that is no longer being played.*[10]

To be truly successful, you must get past ditches and rut-prisons. Then you can discover new highways of creativity and freedom.

UP-AND-COMING PARADIGMS

"If I can shift my paradigms and begin anticipating changes in the directions business is headed, and if I can do it ahead of time," you may ask, "what ones should I be looking for?"

Let us share a few major trends gleaned from Joel Barker's book, *Future Edge*[11] and from such other futurists as John Naisbitt:

- One is the regionalization of world economics. Barker believes, rather than one equilateral global market-place, we will probably see real strength coming from such separate blocks as North, Central and South America, as well as Europe and the Pacific Rim.

- A second is the greening of industry, meaning the leading businesses of the world will be involved in such environmentally-friendly programs as recycling, pollution control and searching for new energy sources.

- Quality everywhere is another paradigm that will shape leading-edge companies.

- Fiber Optics is another fast-growing trend, and will be used to carry all kinds of messages. Virtually every

---

10. Tom Peters, *Thriving on Chaos: Handbook for a Management Revolution* (New York: Harper & Row, 1987), p. 50.
11. Barker, pp. 171-197.

type of business and personal communications will be influenced by this paradigm.

• New forms of energy use will change the way we view our resources.

• Education will be influenced even greater by industry's cry for competent entry-level employees.

But what do these paradigms mean for you, in terms of business opportunity?

To answer, we refer to an article entitled, "Seize the Future," which appeared in a 1990 issue of *Success* Magazine.[12] The writers focused on ideas from futurist and bestselling author John Naisbitt, primarily from his pacesetting book, *Megatrends 2000*.

The article stated flatly:

Every day there are hundreds of trends being born, spawned by the collision of social, technological and economic forces. More than ever, the entrepreneur's special eagerness and curiosity about change will help him see opportunities others have overlooked.[13]

Readers were urged to use the article as a guide to the future. Let us quickly sketch nine of the most powerful megatrends from that article:

(1) Computers will continue to shift the advantage to smaller companies and entrepreneurs.

(2) The marketplace will continue to flatten and democratize. In fact, by the year 2000, 85% of Americans will work in a company of 200 or fewer employees, and this will create niche opportunities for thousands of start-up entrepreneurs.

(3) Information will continue to be the hottest commodity. In fact, 20 million of the 21 million new jobs generated by the year 2000 will be in the information and service sector.

---

12. "Seize the Future (Make Top Trends Pay Off Now)," *Success* Magazine, March 1990, pp. 39-45.
13. *Ibid*, pp. 39-40.

(4) The hottest industries will include health-care services, hospitality, personal services, niched entertainment and environment-friendly enterprises.

(5) International opportunities for business will flourish for all companies and entrepreneurs who have the foresight to tap into worldwide networks.

(6) People will network more intensely to problem-solve and develop common strategies.

(7) The number of home-based businesses will skyrocket. There may be as many as 40 million home-run enterprises by 2000. As many as 40% will be started by visionary women.

(8) Innovation will accelerate, thereby increasing the need for cutting-edge, ear-to-the-ground research and development in companies of all sizes.

(9) Marketing will be more crucial than ever, since consumers will be more demanding and specialized. Common forms of tomorrow's marketing will include multimedia public relations video conferences, interactive television, advertisements on video disks and home-video catalogs.

Obviously, from the article and book, the **entrepreneur** is tomorrow's champion today.

A FINAL NOTE

Think back. If you could have been one of the Swiss watch company owners, and could have known the dramatic paradigm shift that would occur almost overnight because of the quartz movement watch. What would that have meant for you?

Or what if you could have known about the fast-rising popularity of an Elvis or the Beatles—and could have tapped financially into that paradigm?

And can you imagine how different your decisions would be if you could have tomorrow's information available today?

You can join this ongoing experiment. You can profit from one of the best emerging business concepts!

**As you expand the boundaries
of your mind and alter your paradigms,
you open new doors to business success
in NETWORK MARKETING AND
INTERACTIVE DISTRIBUTION!**

BUILDING BLOCKS:

We started on the road to financial flexibility when we realized that the only realistic way for us to achieve it was to get into a business of our own. Because of that decision—and all the choices we've made since then to back up our original decision—we have been able to accomplish so many more goals than we could have imagined back then.

Here's the thing: Opportunity brings responsibility. Anyone who lives in a free market country has an obligation to be as productive as possible. The greatest part of this business is that it allows you to be responsible, productive and fulfilled— and rewarded!

BILL CHILDERS
Former Sales Representative
Executive Diamond Direct
Distributor (USA)
Past ADA Board Officer

We can easily forgive a child who is afraid of the dark; the real tragedy of life is when men are afraid of the light.

PLATO (427-347 B.C.)
Greek Philosopher

A lot of people have a lot of reasons for building this business, but a lot more have excuses for not doing what it takes to succeed. Here's one major fact that is true for any area of life, especially for this business: If you don't start, it's certain you won't arrive. Get rid of the excuses. Get your "Why?" Then don't stop.

RANDY HAUGEN
Former Automotive
Parts Manager
Executive Diamond Direct Distributor (USA)

Football is a growing thing. The game develops. It doesn't stay the same. It changes and it has nuances. It's one of the things that makes it exciting. It's a dramatic evolutionary thing. You have to change to meet the challenges.

When a football team or a group can work together and, in effect, rub off on one another, it's a real human experience that can only be understood if you've been through it. When the players have trust, faith and belief as a whole, they are better able to inspire one another.[1]

CHUCK NOLL
Former Head Coach of the
Pittsburgh Steelers
("Team of the Decade of the Seventies"
who won four Super Bowls in six years)
NFL Hall of Fame Member (USA)

The best rewards come from the greatest commitments. There will always be challenges, especially when you decide to go after your dreams, but anything worthwhile seldom happens overnight or without a struggle. Every success in life carries its own price tag. If you understand this, especially in this business, you can proceed with confidence—no matter what happens.

CRIS COSTA
Former Secretary
Diamond Direct Distributor (Spain)

---

1. Quoted from Jim O'Brien, *Whatever It Takes* (Pittsburgh, PA: O'Brien Publishing, 1992), p. 58.

. . .whether they shift us in positive or negative directions, whether they are instantaneous or developmental, paradigm shifts move us from one way of seeing the world to another. And those shifts create powerful changes. Our paradigms, correct or incorrect, are the sources of our attitudes and behaviors, and ultimately our relationships with others.[2]

STEPHEN R. COVEY
Bestselling Author
Chairman of the Covey
Leadership Center (USA)

The best part about building our Amway business is that our freedom is just the beginning. Now we get to help others win their freedom, too!

PILAR AGUADO
Former Government Employee
Diamond Direct Distributor (Spain)

We tend to meet any new situation by reorganizing, and a wonderful method it can be for creating the illusion of progress while producing confusion, inefficiency and demoralization.

PETRONIUS (First Century A.D.)
Roman Satirist, Novelist
and Philosopher

---

2. Stephen R. Covey, *The Seven Habits of Highly Effective People* (New York: Simon & Schuster, 1989), p. 30.

I've seen the plaque that says, 'The person who dies with the most toys wins.' In this business, the saying is changed to, 'The person who has the most choices wins.' And the ironic thing is that getting lots of choices begins with your decisions about building this business. Will you do whatever it takes? Will you follow the success system? Will you keep going when you feel like quitting? It all comes down to choices.

TOM PAYNE
Former Dentist
Triple Diamond Direct
Distributor (USA)

Many people have asked how I kept myself motivated, especially when times were tough. When I was growing up, I didn't have a mother or father to encourage me. There was no one person pushing me, although there were many who helped me and influenced my thoughts. I guess I just had a burning desire to make something of myself. In the beginning it was a matter of survival. Then it became something I just couldn't shake off even after I'd been a financial success.[3]

DAVE THOMAS
Founder of Wendy's International
and Bestselling Author (USA)

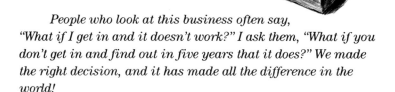

People who look at this business often say, "What if I get in and it doesn't work?" I ask them, "What if you don't get in and find out in five years that it does?" We made the right decision, and it has made all the difference in the world!

PHILIP SMART
Former Commercial
Real Estate Agent
Diamond Direct
Distributor (Australia)

---

3. R. David Thomas, *Dave's Way* (New York: Berkley Books, 1991), p. 213-4.

Old money, inherited money, is not the path to riches. Most millionaires, I have found, are self-made and hard-working. Who am I talking about? People in commercial and investment banking, insurance and real estate are at the top. Doctors and lawyers do well, but they're not at the top of the scale. The best way to become a millionaire is to be an entrepreneur.

Most millionaires are inner-directed, not outer-directed. Most other people put themselves in a position where someone else has defined for them where they will work and what they will do with their spare time. Entrepreneurs are different. They are, to a large extent, contrarians, and that's why they are so successful.[4]

DR. THOMAS J. STANLEY
Bestselling Author of *Selling to the Affluent, Marketing to the Affluent* and *Networking to the Affluent;*
Professor of Marketing at Georgia State University

When we first saw this business, we were interested, but we also had a lot of questions. At the time, it looked as if our country was headed for a downturn in the economy. If we wanted to continue our medical research, we needed to develop other forms of income.

This business has proved to be everything we dreamed of—and so much more. It continues to offer so many opportunities, not only for Roland and me, but for anyone who makes the commitment to build a large organization.

JENNY MCGREADY
Medical Research Scientist
Diamond Direct Distributor
(Australia)

---

4. Excerpted from interviews with NBC News (March 4, 1986) and *Georgia Trend* Magazine (March 1986).

Now then, I say again that the opportunity to get rich, to attain unto great wealth, is here in Philadelphia now, within the reach of almost every man and woman who hears me speak tonight, and I mean just what I say. I have not come to this platform even under these circumstances to recite something to you. I have come to tell you what in God's sight I believe to be the truth, and if the years of life have been of any value to me in the attainment of common sense, I know I am right; that the men and women sitting here, who found it difficult perhaps to buy a ticket to this lecture or gathering tonight, have within their reach "acres of diamonds," opportunities to get largely wealthy.[5]

RUSSELL H. CONWELL
Bestselling Author

The greatest help in achieving your dreams is the element of business support materials, as well as upline support and functions. I've heard the phrase—"Cake without eggs ain't cake!" It's especially true with this system. This system works best when you use all the ingredients—books, tapes and meetings. We decided quickly that we didn't need to reinvent the wheel. The system was already in place and had been proven over and over with all the heroes of the business.

BOB COVINO
Former Real Estate Developer
Diamond Direct Distributor (USA)

---

5. Russell H. Conwell, *Acres of Diamonds* (Old Tappan, NJ: Fleming Revell, 1960), p. 19-20.

Here's a basic fact: The Amway business can change your life. The opportunity is available to anyone who desires to make a better life. It works!

For over two decades, Susan and I have seen what people from all walks of life can do with this business when they get a big enough dream.

*Sure, people everywhere talk about business ownership in terms of traditional businesses. I went that route for several years. But what I found is that **no** other business—from traditional retail stores to franchises, or from mall spaces to discount outlets—can compare to the advantages of the Amway business.*

As with most other business methods, you have to have a pattern to be able to succeed. With our system, we not only have that pattern, but we now have hundreds of examples of Amway Diamonds who have made this pattern work in their lives.

The best part is that this opportunity is better today than ever before. How many other businesses that have been around this long can say that?

HAL GOOCH
Former Furniture Manufacturing Business Owner
Double Diamond Direct Distributor (USA)
Past ADA Board Officer

*S*tructures

...Your Own Business

Obviously, based on information in Chapter Two, new business trends are at the forefront of changes that are being felt nearly everywhere. And the most exciting part of all is that you can be part of what many experts are now heralding as the "wave of the future."

During this chapter we want to share these hot entrepreneurial trends and the profitable, exciting role you can play in this economic groundswell.

WAYS OF DOING BUSINESS

There are several primary means to do business. One of the best-known is retailing.

Every neighborhood has clothing stores, grocery markets, car dealerships, and gasoline stations; with each, the owner/manager buys products from a manufacturer/supplier at wholesale costs, and sells these products to customer/clients at retail (marked-up) prices.

This concept of marketing, of course, evolved from direct sales into the small merchandisers, then during the nineteenth century into general stores and department stores. Even today's sophisticated "discount" stores fall into this category.

The majority of business done around the world is through retail sales, but there can be tremendous problems with overhead, building, upkeep, storage, personnel, advertising, security and so much more.

The many costs involved—from manufacturers to distributors, and from wholesalers to retailers—all add up to decreased profits for the retailer and increased prices for the consumer.

RETAILING

For years, retail giants such as Sears, J. C. Penneys, Saks, Bloomingdale's, Macy's, Ben Franklin, Dillards, Neiman-Marcus, Speigels and Montgomery Ward reigned supreme.

But those times are changing. IBM and General Motors have laid off thousands. Sears has laid off tens of thousands of employees during the past few years and have began dismantling its once-flourishing $57-billion financial and merchandising empire, closing its 97-year-old catalog business, 113 retail stores and 2,000 catalog stores as part of a massive restructuring plan.[1]

Many former top retail leaders have gone out of business. All it takes is a look down Main Street USA or through the malls in most towns or cities throughout the world, and the empty stores are ample evidence that something drastic has happened to the world of retailing.

Today, alternatives to traditional retailing have changed the way the world sells and buys. In fact, of the top retailers in America during the late 50s and early 1960s—when today's giants such as Wal-Mart, K-Mart and Amway started—most are gone now. That is how things have changed so dramatically.

---

1. Betty Joyce Nash, "Rise and Fall of a Retailing Giant," Greensboro (NC) *News & Record*, January 26, 1993, p. C1.

Today, despite some gloomy forecasts for the retail industry, there are many who still dream of owning their own business. A quick look into this aspect of retailing can be a staggering reality check!

A community grocery store, a cozy restaurant, a fast-food franchise, an auto parts store—all require a substantial investment of money and time (translation: blood, sweat, and tears) before the accountants can begin to use anything but red ink.

In fact, the Small Business Administration estimates that 65% of all new businesses that begin each year will be but a tragic memory within five years.

Not only does staggering overhead cause the downfall of so many businesses, but the starting costs of most enterprises defeat most new businesspeople even before they begin. Figure 2-1 gives you an idea of the considerable amount of money needed just to start up your own business.

FIGURE 2-1[2]

Business	Starting Costs (X 1000)	Business	Starting Costs (X 1000)
Appliance Store	$ 48-70	Health Food	$ 25-50
Auto Parts	55-110	Hardware	55-85
Auto Repair	42-105	Ice Cream	28-80
Bakery	28-60	Imports	35-67
Barber	17-30	Jewelry	55-200
Bar (Cocktail)	65-115	Liquor	75-120
Bookstore	46-60	Men's Wear	45-100
Beauty Salon	15-60	Motel (medium)	190-400
Coin Laundry (44-unit)	115-138	Paint	30-100
Car Wash	65-72	Pants/Jeans	25-75
Camera Shop	65-110	Pet Shops	30-75
Crafts	35-70	Photo Studio	25-45
Campground	35-110	Plants	10-25
Day Care	28-85	Printing (quick copy)	30-60
Deli	30-105	Restaurant (medium)	50-150
Donut Shop	26-85	Sandwich Shop	30-150
Dry Cleaner	75-110	Service Station	45-75
Electronic Shop	45-175	Shirt Outlet	20-65
Florist	40-50	Shoe Store	48-140
Furniture	50-500	Sporting Goods	50-75
Family Clothing	65-110	Tire Dealer	40-75
Gift Shop	25-65	Toy Store	70-120
Garden	28-60	Travel Agency	5-35
Grocery (convenience)	40-85	Tune Up	25-60

2. The figures reflect estimated national industry averages. Statistics are based upon research by the High Point (NC)-based INNOVEX MEDIA GROUP.

You have heard the phrase, "It takes money to make money." This is true, most of the time, especially in today's retailing world. Obviously, beginning any business which requires such a substantial amount of upfront money can be risky at best.

Finances aside, in addition to traditional retailing, there are other ways of owning a business. Here are the most common:

DIRECT SALES: This is the oldest, most personal form of marketing. From the earliest days where one person bartered goods or services with another person, to today's polished professionals armed with their flip-chart and multi-media presentations, this form of one-to-one contact has accounted for a tremendous amount of product flow.

With this method, the salesperson generally buys merchandise at wholesale (or discounted) prices, then presents his or her wares directly to the consumer.

From the dedicated ten-year-old who shows up at your front door with those boxes of tempting cookies, to the most suave insurance, cosmetic, and home products representatives— all are people who are employed in the often profitable realm of direct sales.

There are inherent advantages and disadvantages with this marketing system. The latter includes the fact that with most direct sales companies, profits depend solely on one's own ability to move merchandise personally, as opposed to the geometric potential through network marketing, to be discussed further. Also, when the direct salesperson decides or is forced to change areas or territories, he or she normally needs to start developing his clientele or consumer routes all over again without the benefit of maintaining proper contact with those previous clients/consumers.

Direct marketing is a $13-billion industry in the U.S., with some 5 million people working for nearly 700 companies nationwide. According to the Direct Selling Association, almost half of all direct marketing companies sell home or family care products. Together, they make about 50,000 sales calls daily.[3]

MAIL ORDER: Another long-standing form of merchandizing is handled through those catalogs, pamphlets, and advertisements to which nearly everyone has responded.

Whether it is the Alaskan fisherman who sends his check and order to Maine for a new pair of thermal underwear, or the housewife who requests the "amazing" 43-piece set of kitchen gadgets (all for 19.95!), mail ordering has proven to be a convenient method of obtaining merchandise.

Add to this genre the high-tech world of home shopping clubs, and you have a sometimes-glitzy, sometimes unexceptional phenomenon. Despite the demise of such once-heralded catalogers as Montgomery Wards and Sears, this method of distribution continues to flourish.

There are some inherent problems, such as the postal and delivery system, but Americans have grown up enjoying the convenience of shopping at home-enough, at least, to put up with the week to month delay.

In fact, a few of the network marketing companies (Amway is the industry leader) have added the beneficial elements of mail ordering from catalogs, and they have ingeniously been able to maintain the profit and bonus system with at-home catalog convenience.

Thus far in this chapter, we have primarily looked at methods of retailing. Let's move on. As you probably already know, non-traditional ways of doing business have become today's hottest concepts.

---

3. Carol Kleiman, "Direct Selling Attracts Job Seekers," High Point (NC) *Enterprise*, September 6, 1992, p. F1.

BUSINESS DIRECTIONS

What worked well yesterday doesn't mean that it will survive today or tomorrow. Consider, for example, some of today's most-advanced marketplace trends:

DISCOUNT STORES: Industry leaders, Wal-Mart & K-Mart started back in 1962. Within the next few years, they led the way in overshadowing their top competitors—to the tune of $75-80 billion a year!

Of the top ten retailers when Wal-Mart and K-Mart opened for business, all are gone now. That is how much things have changed.

During recent years, profits for Wal-Mart, now the nation's top chain, have increased as much as 28%. Obviously, discount stores will continue to be a prominent force in the marketplace.

WAREHOUSE CLUBS: A very-visible offshoot from the discounting phenomenon is what began as big-box, bulk-buying stores.

The warehouse club industry grew at hyperspeed during the 1980s, from 15 warehouse club stores in 1983, and by 1992, the number grew to 577 outlets, reaching a $34 billion total revenue by 1993.[4]

Leading clubs include Sam's (owned by Wal-Mart), Price, Costco and BJ's Wholesale. Some still think of these places as vast caverns of generic products, but the industry is being forced to change. As competition has increased, most stores have started adding products and services. Sam's, for example, has added produce, meats and bakery items. Pace now earns 30% of its revenue from food. Costco is rolling out photolabs. BJ's Wholesale is testing eyeglass centers. And several clubs are expanding internationally.[5]

FRANCHISES: Just as the discount phenomenon began during the early 1960s, so the franchise sensation started during that time.

The McDonald's chain was one of the first. Later came such giants as Lerners Clothing, Kentucky Fried Chicken, Wendy's and Midas Muffler shops—to name only a few.

Presently, franchises do a whopping $758.5 billion worth of business throughout America alone—that accounts for approximately one-third of all goods and services currently being bought.[6]

Franchises are obviously here to stay.

IN-HOME SHOPPING: Right now, there are 80-100 million homes throughout America which are involved in some form of in-home shopping. QVC, an industry leader in the area of cable TV-based in-home shopping, boasts nearly 100,000 new subscribers per month![7] Hundreds of companies and dozens of celebrities—from baseball's Reggie Jackson to NASCAR's Richard Petty, from weight-loss guru Richard Simmons to

---

4. Ellen Neuborne, "Warehouse Clubs Diversify to Survive," *USA Today*, p. 4B.

5. *Ibid.*

6. Carol Steinberg, "World of Franchising," *USA Today*, October 8, 1992, p. 4B.

7. "QVC Is Shopping And a Whole Lot More," QVC Publications, June 1993, p. 6.

designer Bob Mackie, and from soap opera's Susan Lucci to Broadway's Carol Channing—have joined this marketing parade.

How profitable is it? Consider country comedian Ray Stevens. The silly-song serenader, who made us laugh at "Ahab the Arab," "Gitarzan" and "The Streak" during the 60s and 70s, rose to the top of music video charts in 1993 because of in-home shopping. Says Susan Wloszczyna, writing in *USA Today:*

> *Despite the reluctance of today's radio program-*
> *mers to take him seriously, the singer felt the appetite*
> *for his country-fried corn never went away. So the*
> *king of novelty records hit on a novel idea. He assem-*
> *bled videos of eight songs, including "The Streak" and*
> *"It's Me Again, Margaret," and began selling the cas-*
> *sette via cable-TV commercials last year.*
>
> *TV sales took off like a streaker—1.7 million videos*
> *so far. Since reaching stores in early April, the tape*
> *has sold an additional 100,000-plus copies. A second*
> *TV-promoted video, Ray Stevens Live!, is moving at*
> *an even faster clip.*[8]

Stevens' popularity continues to skyrocket. His Branson, Missouri, theater puts on two shows a day for 4,000 people, six days a week. Many of those concerts overflow with youngsters who have "discovered" Ray's comic genius through the videos. What is Stevens' response to this in-home shopping phenomenon?

> *I have a whole new generation of fans. People send*
> *me Polaroids of their kids watching the video.*[9]

In-home shopping—specifically in the form of interactive technology—is going to be the next great shopping move.

Corporate America is waking up to the fact that people want the convenience of in-home shopping. Since the 1980s, cable channels such as QVC and the Home Shopping Network opened the doors to this phenomenon. Then IBM and Sears joined forces to form a new company called PRODIGY. They

---

8. Susan Wloszczyna, "Stevens' New Ray of Pop Popularity," *USA Today*, June 17, 1993, p. D1.
9. *Ibid.*

quickly developed nearly 500,000 subscribers. That was just the beginning.

In England, a grocery company called Supershop allows customers to order a full-range of groceries 24 hours a day using an interactive TV system. The groceries are then delivered within hours.

Now, Saks Fifth Avenue and Macy's have entered the world of interactive marketing. Even speciality retailer Nordstroms, known for top-notch customer service, has joined the in-home shopping trend, creating a Direct Sales Division, which will handle projects such as a national mail-order catalog program and potential television shopping broadcast channels. Says the company's co-chairman James Nordstrom:

We see a future in interactive television in particular. It's a format that closely matches the Nordstrom style of personalized service. It is our intention to be a major player in this new arena.[10]

The future of interactive distribution was trumpeted by an April 12, 1993, *Time* cover story under the headline, "The Info Highway: Bringing a Revolution in Entertainment, News and Communication." Using glitzy graphics, the story mapped the soon-to-be-in-your-home information network: TV networks, TV & video producers, movie collections, interactive video games, record companies, broadcast stations, long-distance phone services, interactive shopping channels, television archives, libraries and data banks, news and information services, financial services, classified advertisements and video catalogs.[11]

John Sculley, Apple Computer chairman, estimates that the revenue generated by this mega-industry could reach $3.5 trillion worldwide by the year 2001. By contrast, the entire U.S. gross national product today is about $5.9 trillion![12]

Amway Corporation—along with such major players as MCI, Time Warner, TCI, MicroSoft, Intel, HBO and AT&T—remains on the cutting edge of putting interactive media at distributors' and customers' fingertips.

10. Ellen Neuborne, "Nordstrom Turns to Home Shopping," *USA Today*, May 18, 1993, p. B1.

11. Nigel Holmes, "Mapping the Information Highway," *Time*, April 12, 1993, p. 52.

12. Philip Elmer-DeWitt, "Take a Trip into the Future on the Electronic Superhighway," *Time*, April . 1993, p. 53.

Soon, most cable TV customers are able to order movies, do banking, make phone calls through their TV sets and enter the world of electronic malls. In one form or another, this is already happening in the United States, in England and other places around the world.[13]

Tom Eggleston, Amway's Chief Operating Officer, points to a bold new future:

> *Imagine Amway as part of an interactive TV network which links every television in every home by one of 500 channels back to Ada, Michigan. Whether that linkage is by cable TV or by telephone lines is unimportant to us. Whether the black box is made in the U.S. or Japan, let's put it aside. Even how long it may take for this tomorrow to become reality is at best a guess. But make no mistake, that tomorrow is near. Amway has devoted considerable resources to understand and capitalize on this technology. It will help us become so much better than we are.*
>
> *Imagine that each evening you can preview a variety of video messages sent to your TV that day. Perhaps it is footage of Jay Van Andel donating $6 million as the Grand Rapids Museum is named for him that day. Perhaps it is Dick DeVos opening Amway Argentina with President Menem that day. Perhaps it is my meeting in China with their top economic development official that day. Perhaps it is a dynamic demonstration of Satinique hair care products introduced that day. In sum, it is visual, it is immediate and it is powerful!*
>
> *Before your meeting each night, you select ten minutes of video shorts. You add video comments from your upline EDC or your Diamond's comments during his trip to Warsaw, Poland—all made that day. Maybe you want to capture comments of women in New York on a shopping spree that was earned from Amway retail volume; maybe the testimonial from the Atlanta Braves about their use of SA8 to clean their uniforms.*

---

13. John Schneidawind, "Cable Deal Focuses on Interactive Information," *USA Today*, May, 18, 1993, p. B1

Now, instead of carrying the audience on your words alone for the next hour or two, you have added to your arsenal powerful television images, to which your audience of the 90s is conditioned to respond—timely, dramatic, memorable sights and sounds.

The real power comes in Step Two. Everyone you send home that night can turn on a TV channel and try to stump Amway. Through the power of interactivity, any question would be indexed through key words to prompt a three- to five-minute video answer on the questioner's TV screen. "I heard Amway was an illegal pyramid." Up pops sections of the 1979 FTC decision. If the questioner wants more, he could get commentary from court decisions, followed by commentary from lawyers. Another question: "Amway's products seem overpriced. What is the truth about concentration?" Up pops performance comparisons with competitors, price comparison on a per-dose basis—real research data powerfully presented.

The most explosive power comes in Step Three. Everyone who becomes a distributor is linked to Ada and to their line of sponsorship through interactive TV. Do you want to see the price list? Up it pops. Do you want to learn more about the potency of Double X, up pops the expert Amway scientist explaining it in lay person's terms. Since you have already entered your sizes into the TV memory, if you want to check for clothing in stock, it finds and models for you the exact item in your size. Ordering is automatic by touching the screen. Bonuses are calculated the same way. What is your volume this month? Up pops the answer. What is happening in each leg of your business? Up it pops. What is my volume in Poland? Bingo!

We must get ready for this revolution of high tech. The second part is high touch, the rhythm, the heart of the business. The Company and distributor leaders are so closely linked that the human element will always be emphasized.

*Visual, interactive TV technology will propel us into
the 21st Century. Together, we must be united to celebrate the freedoms of this business. What a bright
future we share!*[14]

The next hot trend is A MOVEMENT TOWARD SMALLER
AND NICHE BUSINESSES.

The majority of new jobs created in the United States
are now being created by small businesses with under 25
employees.

These small businesses are emerging on virtually every
corner of free market countries' neighborhoods.

Why?

The computer has shifted the advantage to the small company. With so much computer technology available today, small,
agile firms are able to spot emerging market trends quickly and
move into niches before bigger rivals even notice the possibilities.

Referring to widespread computer technology, economist
George Gilder says:

*This will mean an enormous magnification of the
power of entrepreneurs. Small companies will be able to
communicate, organize and manufacture all around
the world. They will compete against big bureaucracies
and large hierarchies that try to control them.*[15]

HOME-BASED ENTERPRISES—Home-based businesses have
grown remarkably in the past few years—from 14.9 million
income-generating households in 1988 to over 24 million homes
today.[16] Already 28% of America's population presently has a
business in their home generating annual revenues of $382.5 bil-
lion. Yes, $382.5 billion![17] This same phenomenon seems to be
happening around the world.

These enterprises run the gamut from small craft and
artists shops to the high-tech world of faxes, modems and com-
puter-based consultants.

---

14. Edited and condensed from Tom Eggleston's June 11th speech during the 1993 Amway
Convention in Ada, Michigan.
15. "Seize the Future (Make Top Trends Pay Off Now)," *Success Magazine*, March 1990, p. 40
16. Reiva Lesonsky, "Think Home Based Business," *Entrepreneur*, September 1993, p. 8.
17. *Ibid.*

How big will this groundswell become? According to a study done by AT&T, at least 50% of the population in the United States will be working at home by the turn of the century—that is 40 million households!

Though home-based business owners still run the gamut of age and experience, two of the fastest-growing segments are former corporate workers and recent college graduates. Sarah Edwards calls these people "propreneurs." She says:

> *They don't think of themselves so much as starting businesses in the classic sense as simply creating their own jobs.*[18]

According to futurist John Naisbitt, the best home-based businesses include financial, consulting, training and information-type services. He says:

> *When you have fax machines, computers, Federal Express and world-wide telephone service, it doesn't really matter where you are.*[19]

Add voice-mail messaging (such as AMVOX) to that list, and the world of home-based businesses is obviously different today than ever before. Tomorrow will be more exciting than ever.

---

18. *Ibid.*
19. "Seize the Future," p. 44.

DISTRIBUTION

The movement away from retailing and the simultaneous dismantling of traditional distribution systems was foretold several years ago by futurists such as John Naisbitt in *Megatrends 2000* and Alvin Toffler in *The Third Wave.*

At the same time retail giants are floundering, discount houses such as Wal-Mart, K-Mart and Target stores continue to flourish. In a very real sense, they are changing the marketplace landscape forever.

Also, franchises—such as McDonald's, Pip Printing, Wendy's, Snelling Employment Services and Priority Management executive trainers—are also booming, taking away more of the traditional retail market.

But the future does not belong just to the up-and-coming giants of discounting and franchising. Far from it!

Consider for a moment the words of one of the world's most-read economists.

Paul Zane Pilzer is the best-selling author of two books and has served as advisor to both Presidents Reagan and Bush. A Wharton graduate, he became the youngest officer at Citibank (age 22) and their youngest Vice President (age 25). While at Citibank, he started several entrepreneurial businesses and earned his first $1 million before he was 26. In 1985, he testified before the U.S. Congress, warning that the Savings & Loan problem would grow to a $200 billion disaster; his words went largely unheeded at that time, but in 1989 he wrote about the growing scandal in the critically-acclaimed bestselling book, *Other People's Money: The Inside Story of the S & L Mess (Simon & Schuster). His follow-up, Unlimited Wealth* (Crown), an historical and futuristic view of the economy, greatly expanded his worldwide reading audience and prompted a number of rave commentaries, including this one from the *Business Book Review:*

> *This work is so revolutionary that we can only recommend that you read it from cover to cover and in*

the order presented. We also suggest that you set aside time to read it more than once, and that you prepare to highlight and make notes. We predict that you will immediately want to share Wealth's ideas with colleagues and associates.[20]

Today, Pilzer is managing partner of Zane May Interests, a Dallas-based national real estate investment company. Paul has taught as an adjunct professor of finance at New York University since 1979. He is a leading-edge voice in helping people to understand the new principles of distribution, and he writes in *Success* Magazine:

> *Prior to the past few decades, the greatest personal fortunes in American history were built on the bedrock of natural resources and manufacturing. Think of the Astors (fur trading), the Rockefellers (oil), the Carnegies (steel), and the Fords (automobiles).*
>
> *But in the past two decades, the majority of great personal fortunes have been made by people who found better ways of distributing things.*[21]

In the same article, it is stated:

> *As today's billionaire founders of Wal-Mart, Amway and Federal Express have proven, distribution is the wave of the future. The industrial, agricultural and information agers have come and gone leaving distribution as the next path to wealth. Those who choose to participate will prosper.*[22]

As Pilzer has explained on such top-rated programs as CNN's "Larry King Live!" and National Public Radio's "Marketplace," technological change is the driving force behind our economy. We are at the beginning of a period of economic expansion of unprecedented proportions. Clearly, the future belongs to people who tap into the new paradigms of distribution.

---

20. *Business Book Review*, Summer 1991.
21. "The Golden Door to Wealth," *Success*, March 1993, p. 7A.
22. *Ibid.*

THE HOTTEST TREND OF ALL

Thus far we have written about some of the hottest patterns in the world's marketplaces which are laying the foundation for the future of our economy. Of all that we have discussed thus far, there is one that is probably the most exciting of all. It is called network marketing or interactive distribution.

Of all the businesses in the world, none, it seems, is experiencing the unique paradigm-upheaval as the powerful distribution concept of network marketing.

Why is network marketing so crucial to the marketplace? According to *Success* Magazine, "Network marketing is the most powerful way to reach consumers in the 1990s." It offers a chance for you to own a business and to tap into the hottest trends.

Frankly, **retailing** is quickly going the way of the dinosaur. Many experts say that 50% of all retail businesses will be gone by the year 2000. Predicts *Retailing 2000*,[23] a study produced by the accounting firm Price-Waterhouse:

> *Even as architectural blueprints are being drawn up and foundations are poured for newer, bigger and more sophisticated malls throughout the country, the great age of the retail-dominated mall in America faces a fitful demise by the end of the decade.*[24]

How bad is it? Statistics from a top accounting firm drive home a painful retailing point: The U.S. is awash in a sea of empty buildings. A study from Coopers & Lybrand offer these ugly retail-oriented numbers:

- There's enough empty office and retail space to give every U.S. worker another 62 square feet of space— almost the equivalent of an 8-foot-by-8-foot room. For every industrial worker, there's another 52 square feet of empty factory space.

---

23. Chris Burritt, "Study: Half of Retailers Will Be Gone by Year 2000," Cox News Service, June 4, 1993, p. 3.
24. *Ibid.*

- Every night, a million hotel rooms—more than one in three-are vacant.

- There are enough empty retail stores in the U.S. to fill 3,800 average-size shopping malls.[25]

The outlook? More of the same, according to industry analysts! And even if you wanted to get involved in a retail operation, you would need a huge capital investment plus tremendous experience in what you would be doing.

Discount stores should be around for some time to come, but few people can be able to afford the megabuck investment which is required. Can you imagine the hassles with financial downturns, advertising, employee problems, inventory, insurance, federal regulations and so much more?

Warehouse clubs continue to flourish, but the newness of the big-box stores has worn off, and earnings have slid as much as 16%.[26] At the same time, since the number of stores has grown from 15 in 1983 to 577 in 1992, many clubs overlap. Pace Membership Warehouse, for example, faced direct competition from another warehouse club in 89% of its locations, and in 1993 its parent Corporation, K-Mart, finally decided to get out of the warehouse club industry altogether. The warehouse club industry is clearly in a battle for market share. According to Ellen Neubourne, writing in *USA Today*, the grim reality of the 1990s is not a pretty sight: "Since the chains' profit margins are already very thin, competing through price cuts is not an option."[27]

How about **franchises?** These are excellent choices because the best franchise corporations have helped eliminate many of the start-up and ownership worries which are connected with running your own business, but you still have to purchase your franchise. This can run from $20,000 up into the millions. Plus, you still have to deal with many of the employee, red-tape and economic up-and-down struggles associated with retail and discount operations.

25. Desiree French and Bill Montague, "Plenty of Room to Spare," *USA Today*, August 14, 1992, p. 4B.
26. Ellen Neubourne, "Warehouse Clubs Diversify to Survive," *USA Today*, USA Today, p. 4B.
27. *Ibid.*

One of the hottest franchises today is Subway Sandwich Shops with 7,000 franchises worldwide, nearly four times the number the company had in 1987. The franchisee pays $70,000 to get started, not counting such staggering costs as employees, health insurance, leases, equipment and accounting. William Bygrave, professor of entrepreneurship at Babson College, analyzed the Subway Shop investment using Subway's most recent cost and revenue estimates. He figures the typical Subway franchisee would have to work extremely long hours and take no vacation to earn $49,000, **before taxes and excluding disability insurance and retirement savings**. That assumes a good location. With a poor location, Dr. Bygrave says the franchisee stands to lose the entire investment. It is no wonder, according to the *Wall Street Journal*, approximately 40% of the franchise holders give up within three years.

In the midst of these startling, often-gloomy figures, network marketing continues to emerge as the up-and-coming trend.

NETWORK MARKETING

During 1959 and continuing through the 1960s, **Phase One** of this new phenomenon began, primarily in the form of direct sales. The company, with a relatively small number of pioneering distributors and a limited number of well-received products, did $500,000 in sales the first year. By the end of the decade, sales reached over $300 million.

Looking back, we can see now that **Phase Two** began emerging during the 1970s as a new term was added—"multi-level marketing"—which emphasized the long-term aspects of building organizational depth. Distributors began to recognize the additional security through this new business dimension.

During the early 1980s, not only did Amway's retail sales cross the $1-billion mark and we started exporting our marketing method to other countries, we moved into a new phase. With the introduction of numerous corporate products and services (beginning with the Amway/MCI efforts) into the system, **Phase Three** heralded the advent of network marketing—building on the then-new concept of networking, as prefaced in John Naisbett's *Megatrends*. Corporate America and Wall Street began awakening to the power of network marketing and began knocking on Amway's door.

Needless to say, hundreds of network marketing companies emerged on the scene during Amway's **Phase Two** and **Phase Three**, but most went out of business for a variety of reasons, such as under-capitalization, poor management, misrepresentation to consumers and the legal battles that resulted. One weakness of most multi-level and network marketing companies continues to be the tendency to focus on one or two product lines. Amway, on the other hand, continues to set the pace by emerging as not only a top-rated manufacturer and distributor of its own products (approximately 400), but also adding an array of over 5,000 name-brand products and services, with access to over 1,100 manufacturers through the *Personal Shoppers Service Catalog*.

In the late 1980s and early 1990s, Amway began to position itself for a new era of unparalleled hypergrowth and worldwide recognition. We are now entering **Phase Four**—which we now refer to as interactive distribution. We believe Amway has positioned itself as a manufacturing and marketing force to begin to truly compete with such retail and discount giants as Wal-Mart and K-Mart during the next decade. Amway's presence as the leader in the interactive distribution industry continues to be cemented with sales now reaching $4.5 billion and distributorships rising to more than two million. Amway's international expansion already circles the globe, totalling 60 countries and territories.

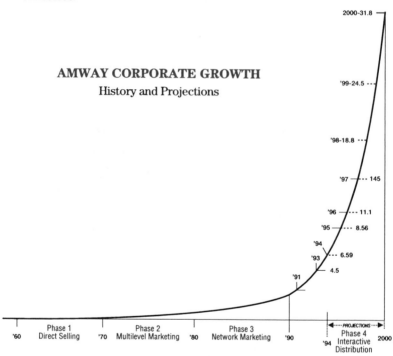

AMWAY CORPORATE GROWTH
History and Projections

Now, through the incredible phenomenon known as network marketing and interactive distribution, you are able to combine the very best aspects of retailing, discounting, warehouse clubs and franchising, and then blend the features with the hottest trends known as IN-HOME SHOPPING, INTERACTIVE MEDIA, SMALLER AND NICHE BUSINESSES and HOME-BASED ENTERPRISES.

Network marketing, distribution and personal business ownership offers immediate income and room at the top for an unlimited number of people. These people come from all walks of life. The high levels of achievement depend solely upon one's own efforts in his or her individual quest for rewards, recognition and income.

In a capsule, the interactive marketing distributor is in business **FOR** himself or herself, but not **BY** himself or herself. The person normally buys products that are already developed and marketable, then he or she has the potential of selling this merchandise to retail customers and sponsoring other distributors while teaching "downline" people to follow the wholesale product use/retail/selling/ sponsoring/teaching pattern. For that person's efforts, he or she receives either a bonus or a series of bonuses from the parent company. Sponsoring, personally and in-depth, is the key factor in making that multi-generation business into a long-term success.

More importantly, as a self-employed businessperson, the network marketing entrepreneur has control of the success of one's own business. He or she has the flexibility, freedom, and opportunity to fail or prosper. Since the person owns his or her own business, that entrepreneur has no boss nor salary, though obviously the person's upline has a vested interest in helping him or her succeed. The distributor needs no employees nor building in which to operate (to start with, at least; and there are Diamonds who still choose to operate out of their homes), so the overhead remains minimal.

The network marketing businessperson ideally has a number of both customer/clients and downline associates, the loss of one usually is not catastrophic, compared to the misfortune of a salaried employee who losses his or her entire paycheck.

The network marketing entrepreneur has an almost-unlimited growth opportunity. Saturation never has and never will be a problem. In fact, a recent *Success* magazine article about Network Marketing was titled, "Unlimited Future: why the market can never be saturated.[28] He or she can enjoy legal tax deductions from operating a home-based business. And, most impor-

---

28. *Success*, September 1993, p. 20.

tantly, it opens many doors to becoming a family operation. Both husband and wife can contribute their talents to building the business, and children can quickly become involved in the day-to-day operations of product flow, paperwork and—at the right time—downline communication as well as other various responsibilities.

With all network marketing systems, unless products move, nobody gets paid, either immediate profit (commissions or percentage mark-ups) or bonus income, which is a major difference between true network marketing and pyramids.

Yet network marketing is certainly not all that unique or mystical. It is merely product movement through a system of multiple generations of distributors and consumers. The unique part of network marketing is that large sums of profit go to the distributors, instead of being divvied up by manufacturer's representatives, the jobbers, the wholesalers, or into retail overhead.

At worst, it is an ingenious system which eliminates the disadvantages found in other types of businesses. At best, it can be an avenue toward greater opportunities for success recognition, lifestyle and friendships.

DIFFERENCES

Specifically, network marketing differs in form from other, more historic methods of product movement. Compare:

Figure 3-1

Manufacturer Reps

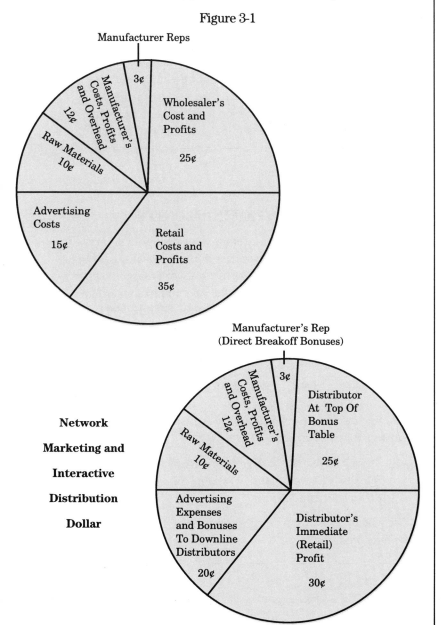

Network

Marketing and

Interactive

Distribution

Dollar

Manufacturer's Rep
(Direct Breakoff Bonuses)

This comparison of the marketing dollar should quickly help the reader to understand why network marketing is the fastest growing method of distribution.

As long as there are goods and services to be exchanged for money, there will continue to be retailers in every community, but the network marketing entrepreneur espouses a simpler method of supplying merchandise to the consumer, with a distribution system which essentially cuts out the middlemen. By getting back to the basic free enterprise system, the network marketing professional can develop a higher percentage of profits and bonus for himself while delivering better quality, more advantageously-priced products and/or services to the consumer.

THE BEST OPPORTUNITY

Network marketing or interactive distribution, no matter which terms are used, has been called "the Wave of the Future." On this point most economists agree: Network marketing is exploding throughout the free world. According to an article entitled *"Seize the Future,"* published in the March 1990 issue of *Success* Magazine, by the year 2000, every other one of 80 million households in America will be involved in some form of network marketing.

Industry analysts, including such leading voices as Richard Poe, Senior Editor of *Success* Magazine, have called network marketing the most powerful way to reach consumers in the years to come. He writes:

> *Experts predict that 'network marketing'... will fuse Americans from coast to coast into one gigantic, pulsating sales amoeba.*[29]

William Plikaitis, a manager for one of the nation's top telephone systems, says:

---

29. Richard Poe, "Network Marketing: The Most Powerful Way to Reach Consumers in the 90s," *Success*, May 1990, p. 74.

With network marketing, you reach people through their families, their neighbors, their co-workers. There's no better way today to get your product right in the consumer's face.[30]

Quoting again from Richard Poe:

Some 12 million (network marketing) devotees now move billions of dollars a year worth of everything from washing machines to life insurance. More and more of these sales zealots are ex-CEOS, attorneys, stockbrokers (and) doctors.[31]

He adds:

Even staid corporate America is catching (network marketing) fever. Industry sources say that The New York Times has been considering selling subscriptions (through this form of distribution). Even AT&T might be taking notice of network marketing after losing approximately 26% of its long-distance market share to MCI and US Sprint—companies that use (network marketing) sales forces.[32]

Network marketing is a concept that has been used, not just in the United States, but in Canada, Australia, Brazil, Europe, Spain, Mexico and in more than 50 other countries throughout the free world. As a result, you can build an international business while riding the crest of today's most futuristic trends.

It is a time-proven concept that allows "everyday" people–regardless of our education, experience, or financial portfolio–to have the potential of becoming successful entrepreneurs.

Today, practically anything can be distributed through the concept of network marketing, and practically everything IS! It is no wonder that network marketing has been called the wave of the future, for it is a paradigm that is virtually exploding throughout the free world.

---

30. *Ibid.*
31. *Ibid.*
32. *Ibid.*

The beauty of this system is that it offers both positive income potential and room at the top for a large number of entrepreneurs–people from all walks of life. As a network marketing businessperson, you have many powerful options:

- control of your success,

- flexibility,

- entrepreneurial options,

    and

- the opportunity for worldwide growth.

As a distribution marketing entrepreneur, you can— through a time-tested and highly-efficient system—tap into an array of thousands of the world's most popular and demanded products and services.

You can not only enjoy wholesale purchases for yourself and a secondary income, but you also can have access to a proven success system as a networking entrepreneur.

You can own your own business—the number one dream of people around the world. Of recent graduates from the prestigious Harvard Business School, for example, a whopping 70% say their goal is to own and manage their own business within the next five to ten years.[33]

Mark McCormack, bestselling author of *What They Don't Teach You at Harvard Business School* and *What They Still Don't Teach You at Harvard Business School*, writes:

A lot of people are convinced that they will never achieve total job satisfaction by working for someone else. Given the choice of becoming chairman of their company OR owning their own small enterprise, they would opt for the latter. Starting a business has become the new Great American Dream.[34]

With Amway, regardless of the country in which you live, you can participate in the entrepreneurial dream. You can join the world of personal business ownership without facing the

---

33. *U. S. News & World Report*, September 25, 1989.
34. Mark McCormack, *What They Don't Teach You ask Harvard Business School* (New York: Bantam Books, 1984), p. 241.

three major blockades: a lack of capital, a lack of knowledge and a lack of time.

What our network marketing system does is create businesses, which grow to be large and successful through the help of our financially-stable corporate sponsor. In fact, even the *Wall Street Journal* has called Amway a sleeping giant, with over $1 billion in assets and over $400 million in cash reserves.

Our network marketing system also provides the finest knowledge program. By overcoming the financial investment required and by providing all the knowledge you will need, you are already seeing that network marketing has eliminated two of the greatest factors which normally holds people back from starting their own business.

The best part is that you can build your own network marketing business as a second-income diversification while continuing your present career or business. When your enterprise develops into a substantial income, as it has for thousands of people, you will have the ultimate luxury of a career choice.

In other words, the future of network marketing can be your ticket to seize the lifestyle and future that you desire. If you desire success and have plenty of creative ambition, your future in network marketing can be whatever you decide to make of it!

THE FUTURE OF NETWORK MARKETING

Corporate America is already discovering network marketing as a successful means to getting its products and services into the far-reaches of the marketplace. In fact, after our corporate sponsor signed a joint venture with MCI, 18,000 companies—from small to very large–approached our sponsor wanting to be part of this incredible network.

After all, consumers have discovered network marketing as a successful source for purchasing products and services, and entrepreneurs everywhere are realizing that network marketing is the low-cost, affordable, practical ticket to economic freedom.

Instead of trying to get people to leave their homes, we have developed a tremendous system for giving men and women exciting discounts as well as conveniences. The greatest advantage, however, is that we can also give visionary people the opportunity to own their own businesses and potentially develop an economically free lifestyle.

What could be more exciting?

The greatest opportunity network marketing offers is by giving people a chance to run a business from their home. What we offer is not a network phone ordering system or network catalog system, but an extensive network marketing system which provides access to more and more products and services (over 6,400 in the U.S.), plus all the joint ventures involved in Amway's marketing plan.

Think of it, by getting involved in network marketing, you can buy your own consumables at wholesale and discounted prices, you can merchandise a little or a lot and you can develop potentially a worldwide network with other business people. Your associates, in turn, can duplicate their own businesses through their home-based enterprises.

It is a phenomenon that is already happening. According to Link Resource surveys, currently over 34 million people or 28% of the total American workforce now earn a part-time income from home run businesses.

This is a trend that will continue, and network marketing is a significant force in the home-based business industry.

The advantage of network marketing is that you can have all the advantages and opportunities of owning your own business. You can do this with little risk of failure. And you can do it while tapping into the fastest growing business concept.

An issue of *Working World* reported:

> *Because of the drastic changes in the marketplace, existing marketing and distributing methods are no longer effective. As more and more companies are forced to reduce their prices to stay competitive, the use of network marketing will accelerate at record levels in the 1990s.*

Just how big is the opportunity? Consider what is happening in the world's leading corporations. In the 1980s, 30% of all Americans, mostly blue-collar workers, lost their jobs. In the 1990s, the layoffs hit white-collar workers–from Citibank to Boeing, McDonnell Douglas, Tenneco, TRW and Xerox. In 1993 alone, Sears laid off 50,000 and even the U.S. Postal Service clipped 30,000.

During the same year, Raytheon, the Patriot missile-making hero of Desert Storm, announced a massive layoff. The number of employees leaving, 674, seems paltry compared to the thousands already mentioned, but the significance of the layoffs rises immeasurably considering the fact that Raytheon is the biggest private employer in Massachusetts.[35]

Also during 1993, IBM offered early retirement to its employees, expecting a maximum of 25,000 to take the buyout. Instead, what they witnessed was a stampede! At least 50,000 men and women, nearly 17% of the company's workforce, grabbed the chance to leave, prompted in part by new CEO Louis Gerstner, who made it clear that any future buyouts would be less generous.[36] But that's not the end of the story: The 50,000 left voluntarily, but insiders are already pointing to reports that thousands of other jobs will be eliminated in the near future.[37]

Currently, 700,000 jobs are being lost every year in the U.S. That's 2,690 jobs lost every day! It is happening everywhere as corporations seek to be "lean and mean." Even formerly-secure jobs in the U.S. military have become dispensable, with more than 600,000 positions slated to be cut by 1998.[38] That number is only the proverbial "tip of the iceberg," since base-closings directly affect thousands of civilian employees; plus, most local economies around these installations depend (sometimes almost exclusively) upon military money for survival.

Often these downsizings and layoffs have less to do with the economy than with governmental restrictions. Consider, for example, how the U.S. Northwest timber industry was flattened when the President ordered a severe cut in tree harvests to pro-

35. Alex Pham, "Pink Slips," *USA Today*, June 30, 1993, p. B1.
36. Leslie Cauley,"50,000 to Take Latest IBM Buyout," *USA Today*, July 2, 1993, p. B1.
37. *Ibid.*
38. Julia Lawlor, "Job Outlook Is Grim for the Military," *USA Today*, May 10, 1993, p. B1.

tect the northern spotted owl. By fall 1994, it's expected that 6,000 jobs will be lost, added to another 20,000 who have already been let go since the spotted owl controversy escalated in 1990.[39] However, as with military base closings, that initial number will directly affect and stagger many local economies that rely on lumber for survival. In fact, Wes Marchbanks of Williamette Industries, a Sweet Home, Oregon-based company which operates mills in 18 states, said:

> *This is devastating to the industry. There will have to be massive plant closures and massive layoffs.*[40]

Who knows how the higher prices for paper, wood-based materials and homes will affect people throughout the nation? Even the most optimistic analyst must admit that thousands of other jobs throughout the U.S. (paper manufacturing, newspapers, publishing and the construction trade—just for starters) will be affected.

However, with corporate executives, computer workers, military personnel, loggers and home builders, as with all other areas of the marketplace, all of the people who have been laid off simply cannot find jobs in their chosen industry because so many other corporations are downsizing. These workers must either start a whole new career or start a new business. Those who still have jobs have not let this situation go unnoticed, for no one knows who will be next.

In fact, an article in the *Wall Street Journal* points to the severity of the job situation:

> *Alumni flood campuses for career counselling in the stagnant job market... Amherst College says use of its career center had doubled in five years; the University of Pennsylvania sees a 25% jump in alumni traffic in the past year...*

> *Each Friday at 8 a.m., UCLA schedules appointments to see its counselors the following week. They are all booked up by 8:10 a.m. A year ago, it took three days to fill all of the time slots. It is "to the point where we're at a loss to manage it," says Walter Brown, who runs the program.*[41]

39. Linda Kanamine, "Clinton Slashes Timber Harvest, Offers Jobs Aid," *USA Today*, July 2-5, 1993, p. A1.
40. *Ibid.*
41. Kelvin G. Salwen, "Labor Letter," *Wall Street Journal*, April 27, 1993, p. A1.

How bad is this situation? In the same *Wall Street Journal* article, Victor Lindquist of Northwestern University (where alumni traffic is up 30% from 1990), says:

> *I keep a box of Kleenex behind my credenza [for] people who come in feeling like their legs have just been cut off.*[42]

This situation does not exist everywhere, of course. Anytime certain parts of the world experience recessionary times, other areas thrive.

Still, lots of these people–from corporate executives to frontline employees and military personnel–are now considering an opportunity such as network marketing because they no longer have job security.

Plus, the sheer demographic changes that are happening during the 1990s are significant. Although network marketing appeals to people of all ages and backgrounds, the prime years for getting into any business, including interactive distribution, according to extensive market research, are between 35 and 55– for obvious reasons. In 1990 there were 63 million people in that age group, according to the U.S. Bureau of Census. By 2000, that number will swell to 81 million. By now you must know where all these figures are leading.

Thus far, we have written about the changes which are coming to the global economy and how people in network marketing are positioned for growth in a worldwide marketplace.

If that is exciting, grab this: Free market economies are expected to expand at an average annual rate approaching 5% during the rest of the century. Don't let that seemingly low statistic fool you. What it means is that the gross national product for many countries will double by about 2004, and double again early in the third decade of the 21st century. That is REAL growth, figured AFTER inflation.

That pattern, if it continues, will be an extraordinary record of sustained growth. And that figure is smaller than the increase expected in some other countries.

---

42. *Ibid.*

What does it mean for you? Quite simply, our distribution system incorporates all the best parts of the hottest trends. We are the BIG opportunity. No matter how you look at the situation, network marketing has incredible advantages. We are now reaching around the globe.

That is nothing new, because most businesses are going in that direction. What makes network marketing so attractive is the fact that you can do business anywhere today with the electronic conveniences available to nearly anyone.

With FAX machines, computers and overnight express services, it no longer matters nearly as much where you are or where your business is located. The phenomenon known as Interactive media is just around the corner. Plus, think about it—English is the official language of the communication age. Most Japanese speak eigo (English) when they travel to Europe or North America, and many Europeans follow suit no matter where they travel.

This trend, this opportunity, is hot right now. It will continue to be, obviously, for one out of every two people in many free market countries are expected to get involved by the end of this decade and for it to continue to flourish throughout the world.

But the opportunity has never been more advantageous than right now. Frankly, this is an opportunity that you will be glad you seized NOW.

Why now?

Let us draw an analogy. If you had been visionary enough to invest $1,650 in Wal-Mart stock, not when they were getting started, but ten years later in 1970, your investment would be worth a million dollars today. That is a fact.[43]

That opportunity, however, will probably never happen that way again. Opportunities are often like that. Now, understand that Wal-Mart is still a good buy. Yearly, Wal-Mart continues to grow by approximately 25%. K-Mart, is even a good buy at 8% annual growth.

But Amway has grown during the fiscal year 1990-91 by 50% from $2 billion to $3.3 billion worth of business, during 1991-92 to 3.9 billion, and during 1992-93 to $4.5 billion.

---

43. *Wal-Mart Annual Report 1993.*

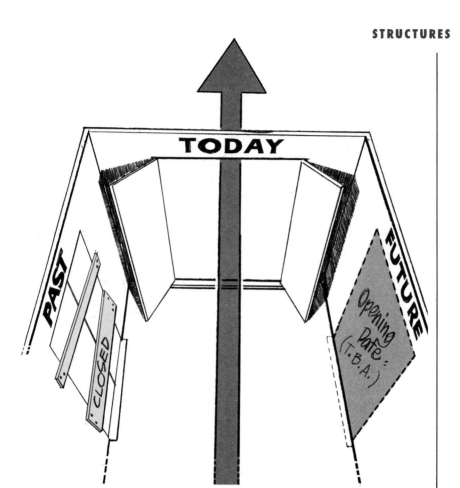

Again, we believe Wal-Mart will continue to be very profitable. In fact, in a special profit-sharing plan, Amway's Direct Distributors own $1.3 million dollars worth of Wal-Mart mutual fund stock. While we are on the subject of stocks, we have a $1.6 million stake in Disney, $1.8 million in AT&T, $1.4 million in Silicon Graphics, $1.4 million in Toys 'R Us and $1.7 in Apple Computer. All together, Amway's Direct Distributors own over $55 million worth of stock in other companies.[44]

What we are spotlighting is that our corporate sponsor has been around for some time. Amway continues to grow steadily and spread worldwide. New products and services are being added every year to an already extensive line-up.

---

44. "Schedule of Investments," *Amway Corporation Stockholders Annual Report,* December 31, 1992, p. 13-15.

Consider the strength of network marketing. Already, it is growing faster than the retail sales industry.

Granted, we are not creating a new market. Instead, we are simply offering people an opportunity to buy commonly-used products and services at wholesale or competitive prices through an alternative distribution and marketing system, as well as offering a much-sought-after opportunity to own their own profitable business.

There are simply too many reasons not to get others involved with network marketing.

Again, the time is NOW!

PYRAMID "PROGRAM" vs. NETWORK MARKETING

- "ROOM AT THE TOP" FOR ONLY ONE

- CROWDING IN MIDDLE LIMITS POTENTIAL

- SINCE THERE IS NO "TOP," THERE'S PLENTY OF ROOM FOR UNLIMITED PROGRESS

PYRAMIDS

"But," people ask, "isn't network marketing just another one of those chain-letter or pyramid-type things?"

At times when the discussion of network marketing arises, the question about pyramids may follow. This method of so-called "sales" or "marketing" has been confused universally with the network marketing business—more in the past than today. However, let's discuss pyramiding for a moment.

Most states have stringent anti-pyramiding statutes, yet there seems to be a never-ending succession of get-rich-quick "business networks" and chain-letter schemes.

Here is a rule of thumb: The illegal ones can generally be described as requiring a fee for the opportunity to bring others into the "program," then an inductee receives a portion of the fee which "downline" associates pay for the same opportunity to bring others in.

The U.S. Federal Trade Commission has released numerous descriptions of illegal pyramid systems, including the following:

Such schemes are characterized by the payment by the participants of money to the company in return for which they (1) have the right to sell a product and (2) have the right to receive, in return for recruiting other participants into the program, rewards which are unrelated to the sale of the product to ultimate users.

As is apparent, the presence of this second element, recruitment with rewards unrelated to product sales, is nothing more than an elaborate chain letter device in which individuals who pay a valuable consideration with the expectation of recouping it to some degree via recruitment, are bound to be disappointed.

One of the major differences, then, is that legitimate organizational and income growth must be based on increased product sales, rather than simple downline expansion. Unfortunately, even some companies who call themselves "network marketers" fall into this unethical category.

Another note of comparison is that such illegal pyramids and questionable schemes are built from the top down-only those who get involved in the beginning can reach the top (in terms of profit and recognition). However, with true network marketing systems, each new distributor starts at "zero," but has an equal opportunity to build his own organization to an even larger scale than his own sponsor.

Some people have lumped together all network marketing systems as being this type of illegal network, but you can rest assured in the fact that the Federal Trade Commission, an arm of the U.S. Federal Government, ruled in 1979 that the Amway Corporation is a legitimate network marketing business, and definitely NOT a pyramid.

According to Jeffrey Babener, an attorney and acclaimed authority on the network marketing industry:

> In essence, Amway received a "stamp of approval" by the Federal Trade Commission. This decision was a landmark case that opened the door for many of today's most successful network marketing companies.[45]

Therefore, anyone who still argues, "Amway is just another pyramid," has nothing more than erroneous personal opinion—certainly not economic logic or factual information.

A FINAL NOTE

One of the most important facets of the ideal network marketing company is that its goal should be a steady, continual growth of both the distributor organization and product sales volume. "Flash in the pan" companies, on the other hand, almost always promote rewards based primarily on either recruitment, or on large initial merchandise or inventory purchasing requirements.

Another test is the concept of maintaining a consistent, growing balance of <u>both</u> retail sales <u>and</u> sponsoring, of training (or duplicating) the new distributors in such a plan, and rewarding those who follow this balanced pattern. The key word is duplication.

Additionally, the Better Business Bureau (BBB), a national network of private agencies in the United States which provide consumer protection information, has published a booklet called *"Tips on Multi-Level Selling Plans"* (Number 239 B 25174), which lists the following protective guidelines concerning network marketing businesses:

---

45. Jeffrey Babener and David Stewart, *The Network Marketer's Guide to Success* (Scottsdale, AZ: The Forum for Network Marketing, 1990), page 21.

(1) The basis for the company's promotion should be the retail sale of the product, not just the unending recruitment of distributors.

(2) The firm should acknowledge that it is not necessarily easy to sell or recruit and train other sales people, but that it requires time, effort, and personal commitment.

(3) Investors should be wary of promises of quick, high potential earnings.

(4) The firms should provide national or regional advertising on a regular schedule along with the introduction and promotion of new products.

(5) Distributors should be assured of a continuous supply of quality products.

(6) The recruitment of additional distributors or sales personnel should be based upon the potential market, population of the specific community, or prior sales competition. Limiting the total number of the entire state population may not be adequate protection for a distributor in any given community within the state.

(7) The company should set standards for advertising local business opportunity meetings and also for all sales recruitment literature.

(8) The company should accept the responsibility of checking the qualifications of potential distributors and remove those who violate company policies or local laws.

(9) No more than a minimal initial inventory should be required to become a distributor or dealer.

(10) A reliable firm should guarantee in writing that any products ordered, but not sold, will be bought back by the company within a reasonable period of time for a certain percentage of the original price.

Few companies meet these strict criteria. Though we are prejudiced, we believe that the Amway Corporation not only stands above the rest but has stood the test of time. In the next chapter, we will explain why you can profit from your relationship with this company.

You can build your own
SUCCESSFUL DISTRIBUTION BUSINESS!

BUILDING BLOCKS:

I truly believe that the future of this nation depends on our youth. If we teach them about free enterprise and how to dream, if we give them the love they need, and if we instill in them a confidence and pride, then we will see a better world in the years ahead.

BIRDIE YAGER
Former Air Force Base
Keypunch Operator
Crown Ambassador
Direct Distributor (USA)

Make it a rule to seek advice from people who know. There's a lot of incorrect thinking that successful people are inaccessible. The plain truth is that they are not. As a rule, it's the more successful people who are the most humble and ready to help. Since they are sincerely interested in their work and success, they are eager to see that the work lives on, and that somebody capable succeeds them when they retire. It's the "would-be-big" people who are most often the most abrupt and hard to get to know.[1]

DAVID J. SCHWARTZ, Ph.D.
Bestselling Author and
Professor (USA)

---

1. David J. Schwartz, Ph.D., *The Magic of Thinking Big* (Englewood Cliffs, NJ: Prentice-Hall, 1959), pp. 112-3.

Some people wonder why they have to face challenges as they build this business. Frankly, challenges are a fact of life— not just in Amway, but in any endeavor.

For almost all of us, at the beginning of our journey, negative motivations are there to spur us on and to make us more effective. When our negatives get too bad, we finally are forced to react positively to change them.

In fact, adversity is an important ingredient to success. It gives you the "I'm-never-going-back" attitude, and that attitude helps you keep going through the tough times.

CARYN AVELSGAARD
Former School Teacher
Diamond Direct Distributor (Australia)

Why is network marketing spreading so quickly throughout the world?

There are many reasons. FREEDOM is one of the biggest! It offers incredible time-leveraging abilities. There is room at the top for an unlimited number of entrepreneurs. It offers positive cashflow very quickly.

But most of all, network marketing is exploding because this system allows the entrepreneur to have control of his or her own success.

TY BOYD
Businessman, TV and
Radio Personality,
Professional Speaker and Author (USA)

What we are is God's gift to us, but what we become is our gift to God.

TOBY HALE
Homemaker
Diamond Direct Distributor (USA)

Nowhere do habit patterns count for as much, and nowhere does the force of habit demonstrate its might more emphatically than in the business world. A businessman's habits are among the most important factors that determine whether he will be a success or a failure.

J. PAUL GETTY (1892-1976)
U.S. Oil, Real Estate and
Airline Magnate
Millionaire by Age 22

We spent ten years in real estate and construction. We worked hard. We were relatively successful, and yet when we walked away from the housing industry, we left with nothing— no personal income or security.

By contrast, during the first decade we were in this business, we built a great income. It allowed me to become a full-time husband and father. We have helped a lot of people change their lives through this business.

And the best part is that anyone can build it—anyone, at least, with a dream and the commitment to back up that dream.

HOWARD ECKMAN
Former Real Estate
Sales Manager
Diamond Direct Distributor (USA)

Genius is only the power of making continuous effort.

CONRAD HILTON (1887-1979)
Founder,
Hilton Hotels (USA)

What we are experiencing today in the Amway phenomenon is the reawakening of that heritage and understanding who we are in regards to the stock of people we come from.

What we offer is very simple: hope, a chance to achieve dreams and the opportunity to grow.

What we ask is also very simple: "What is financial flexibility worth to you and your family?"

BOB BOLIN
Former Professional Baseball
Player with the San Francisco
Giants, Milwaukee Brewers
and Boston Red Sox
Diamond Direct Distributor (USA)

You cannot push anyone up the ladder of success unless he is willing to climb himself.

ANDREW CARNEGIE
(1835-1919)
U.S. Industrialist and
Philanthropist

This business has changed our life in so many ways. We always have something new and exciting to look forward to. We're able now to enjoy a lifestyle what would have been impossible through traditional jobs.

MOLLY HUGHES
Homemaker
Diamond Direct Distributor (USA)

Wisdom comes not from age, but from education, learning and experience.

ANTON CHEKHOV (1860-1904)
Russian Dramatist and
Short-story Writer

People get into this business for a lot of reasons. I was told that if I worked smart and very hard for five years or so, I could eventually have all the time I wanted to spend with my wife and children. That idea really hit me hard. I had always thought that I would have to spend most of the rest of my life working just to afford a decent lifestyle. Naturally, the whole Amway concept seemed too simple. I was skeptical. I kept trying to find a catch. Once I did understand it better, I knew I had to get involved.

RON RUMMEL
Former Architect
Diamond Direct Distributor (USA)

Nothing stays the same. Things either progress or retrogress. We seem to sometimes underestimate the qualities of our fellow citizens. If we pull together, we can effect progress and make this a better world for our children.[2]

PETER UEBERROTH
Founder of First Travel Corporation,
President of the 1984 Los Angeles
Olympic Organizing Committee,
Major League Baseball Commissioner (USA)

2. Peter Ueberroth with Richard Levin and Amy Quinn, *Made in America* (New York: Morrow, 1985), p. 374.

I believe that if you live in any free market economy, you have an obligation to be as productive as possible. Building your own Amway business allows you to do that. As you plug into the proven success system of books, tapes and meetings, you tap into a powerful source of business-building information and personal inspiration.

But no system will work if you don't. That's why you have to make a commitment—a strong commitment. With your belief and this system, you can be unstoppable.

DENNIS DELISLE
Accountant
Second Generation Triple Diamond Direct Distributor (USA)
Past ADA Board President ('92-'93)

Foundations

...Your Network Marketing Challenge

According to Venture Economics, a marketing-research firm, the average entrepreneur needs at least $8,000 to start a home-based business, $50,000 to start the same business in commercial office space and $200,000 to finance a retail business such as a bakery or video store.[1]

With Amway, you have a minimal investment. With a signed application, you can begin to build your own independent business immediately. What you get when you purchase your initial Sales and Product Kit is so much more than a few top-quality products and important literature. You access a proven foundation of integrity and innovation, starting at the top with the company's co-founders.

---

1. Tom Eggleston, "Legal Briefs," *Amagram*, April 1992.

By joining the world of Amway, you have chosen to participate in one of the greatest adventures man has ever known. Let us explain.

YOUR FUTURE WITH AMWAY

Several exciting books have been written which detail the progress of Rich DeVos and Jay Van Andel's brainchild:

The Possible Dream,

The Winner's Circle,

Uncommon Freedom,

Promises To Keep

and

Compassionate Capitalism.*

The most important parts of this adventure are not the manufacturing plants, truck fleets or worldwide media attention. The most exciting element in the sales and marketing plan is people, specifically YOU.

You are the future of both our free enterprise system and this business. Though it is already confirmed by industry analysts to be the most prestigious of all network marketing programs, most observers (inside and outside the "circles") believe that Amway Corporation and its distributors worldwide are just beginning to see the greatest periods of growth in the history of the company AND the industry.

Still, the mention of terms such as "network marketing" (previously known as "multi-level marketing" or MLM) draws the full gamut of emotions. Everybody has an opinion, but sometimes there are few facts to back up those personal ideas.

Even today, with many distributors gaining financial flexibility each year, there are people who still ask about the legality of the Amway Sales and Marketing Plan.

Let's put the plan under a glaring searchlight.

---

*These books are recommended reading and are available through your upline. However, these business support materials are optional and not required. Information is available from your upline.

AMWAY ADVANTAGES

What makes an ideal network distribution company? One of the most important facets of the ideal network marketing business is that its goals should be the steady, continual growth of both the distributor organization AND product sales volume.

"Flash in the pan" companies, by contrast, almost always promote rewards which are based primarily on recruitment or on large initial merchandise and inventory purchase requirements. And why not?

Let's face it—if that company fails, despite the inevitable, glowing projections, the leaders of that enterprise will have enough capital to start another scheme for unsuspecting hopefuls. Of course, the requirement of large initial investments often leads to hundreds and thousands of people who are stuck with garages and basements filled with out-dated merchandise. It has happened to many people who have jumped at the "latest, greatest" network marketing business.

Let us hasten to add that Amway is not like this. We operate under the Amway Code of Ethics and Rules of Conduct which will show anyone why our corporate sponsor, the Amway Corporation, is held in such high esteem by economic experts, consumer advisors, as well as political and social leaders!

In fact, other network marketing companies openly admit that the Amway Corporation is the premier standard for this growing industry. This is due, directly, to Amway's long-term commitment to fairness, excellence, achievement, entrepreneurial freedom, environmental awareness and overall marketplace share. Amway has been the trail-blazing pioneers for other companies who now seek to follow.

Unfortunately, many involved in these networking imitators have been "burned." Too often, inconsistent company policies have resulted in mediocre product quality, inadequate distribution, poor payment processing and eventually bankruptcy.

Such tendencies are not true, of course, with all these networking businesses, but the fact remains that most of these systems have passed into oblivion.

As mentioned previously, we are *slightly* prejudiced, experiencing firsthand the high level of Amway's integrity for three decades. We believe there are many superb reasons why the Amway Sales and Marketing Plan is truly the "Cadillac" of all network marketing and interactive distribution companies. Here are a few reasons:[3]

FACILITIES: Amway's phenomenal growth from a small converted gas station back in 1959 to today's modern, beautifully landscaped facilities located throughout the world reflects the long-term, consistent success of Amway Corporation.

In Michigan alone, Amway now occupies 81 buildings covering over 3,500,000 sq. ft. of office, manufacturing, research, distribution and other support facilities for more than 5,000 employees. In addition, the new Personal Shoppers Catalog Distribution Center is a 630,000 sq. ft. high-tech facility. Tens of thousands of both distributors and visitors tour Amway's mile-long complex each year.

With a growing number of corporate acquisitions, the company's internationally-owned and leased building space is in excess of 7,500,000 sq. ft., and the worldwide staff totals in excess of 10,000. The expansion continues with plants in Korea and China.

---

3. Information is gleaned from Amway literature, including "The Miracle Mile," *Amagram*, August 1992, pp. 36-41; *Hoover's Handbook of American Business*, 1992; and Amway's Public Relations, Communications, Distributor Relations and International Communications departments.

That doesn't even include such widespread facilities as the farm in California (where NUTRILITE food supplements are grown organically), to the acerola cherry orchards in Puerto Rico and Mexico, to the elegant Amway Grand Plaza Hotel, the luxurious Peter Island resort and a growing list of other related Amway-owned localities.

RESEARCH: Amway invested heavily in the future when it built a $11.5 million Research and Development Center in 1981. Nearly 400 R & D scientists in 40 state-of-the-art laboratories work to perfect the ever-expanding, 400-plus Amway-manufactured product line. As a result, more than 40 patents have been issued for Amway products, and 37 more are pending.

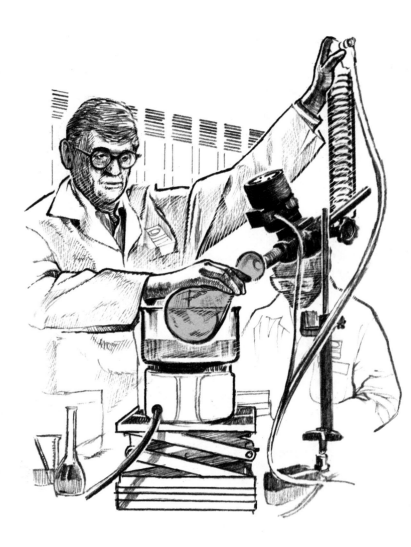

MANUFACTURING: Amway's modern, sophisticated facilities reflect a commitment to quality. Taking into account the company's 100% satisfaction guarantee, product return rates annually average a fraction of one percent! That number is remarkable considering the enormous variety and quantity of products. For example, Amway mixes up to 450,000 pounds of liquid products alone in an 8-hour shift.

DISTRIBUTION: Using a network of Regional Distribution Centers (RDCs) and catalog warehouses, an extensive rail, truck and shipping system efficiently transports more than 350 million pounds of distributor-bound products to 60 countries and territories each year.

ADVERTISING: Amway uses powerful images to carry the message about the corporation, its products and the network marketing opportunity through such major consumer and trade magazines as *Sports Illustrated, Fortune, Time, Ebony, Money, Life* and *Newsweek.*

WORLDWIDE RECOGNITION: Amway enjoys a number of positive spotlights which draw attention to the company's dedication to excellence and achievement. In addition to well-publicized involvement with the Easter Seals Campaign (Amway is one of a select group of companies that belong to the Easter Seals Million Dollar Club year after year, now with contributions totalling over $10 million) and sponsorship of Iditarod dogsled teams, Amway has received even greater attention from these three heralded programs:

- In 1987, the corporation first began sponsoring Scott Brayton's entry in the PPG Indy Car World Series competition—a move that has drawn international recognition. Says Scott Brayton (Ruby Direct Distributor):

*An auto racing sponsorship has been a great vehicle
in promoting Amway car care products. It's also made
an increase in awareness of other product lines and
services, such as our fashion catalogs and the Amway
Auto Network.*[4]

• During 1993, Amway and the National Basketball
Association made a two-part announcement: Amway's
Nutrilite products became "Official Vitamins and Food
Supplements of the NBA" and Amway/Nutrilite was
named sponsor for the NBA's "Defensive Player of the
Year" Award. NBA Commissioner David Stern said:

*Amway has built an impressive worldwide
presence—just as the sport of basketball has taken the*

4. "Amway and Auto Racing: Two Similar Businesses," Amway Press Release.

*world by storm—and we look forward to working
together here in the U.S. and around the globe.*[5]

• The United States participation in Taejon Expo '93 is
unique. For the first time in the history of U.S. participation in world's fairs, the U.S. Pavilion is being entirely organized, managed and funded by the private sector—led by the Amway Corporation. As an international corporation with markets in Korea and throughout the Pacific Rim, Amway saw a need for the U.S. to
be among the 113 countries participating in this major
international exposition. Since federal budget cuts
prevented U.S. governmental agencies from participation, Amway took the lead with financial support and
the formation of a consortium of businesses to sponsor a U.S. Pavilion. This group of corporate sponsors
now includes AT&T, A.E.A International Business

5. "Amway Corp. Teams with NBA as a Worldwide Sponsor," Amway Press Release, June 11, 1993.

Consultants, American International Group, CIGNA Insurance Company, the Coca-Cola Company, DuPont, General Electric, Kodak, Lockheed, Motorola Electronics & Communications, Nike, Northwest Airlines, Price Waterhouse, the Shilla Hotel and the State of Michigan.[6]

What do all these breakthroughs in worldwide recognition mean to you? As an Amway distributor, you can enjoy unparalleled benefits from these well-publicized programs. Not only do these sponsorships spotlight Amway's products and services, but they give you tremendous levels of credibility as you show the plan to prospective distributors.

COMMUNICATIONS: Co-founders Rich DeVos and Jay Van Andel recognized the importance of communication with distributors from the beginning, so the very first piece of equipment they purchased was a printing press. Amway's printing department is one of Michigan's largest commercial print shops. It uses more than one million pounds of paper every month—more than 3,000,000 copies of magazines and newsletters, along with exclusive product and business opportunity literature and motivational audiovisuals. These materials keep distributors and customers informed about people, products and places.

ENVIRONMENTAL COMMITMENT: Amway's Environmental Mission Statement points to a clear-cut dedication:

> *Amway Corporation believes that the proper use and management of the world's limited resources and the environment is the responsibility of industry and individuals alike. As a leading manufacturer of consumer goods with a direct sales network of more than two million independent distributors worldwide, Amway recognizes its responsibility and role in both fostering and promoting sound environmental stewardship.*

To act on this mission, Amway created a corporate Environmental Task Force (comprised of executives representing manufacturing, research & development, marketing, public relations, communications and other areas) to set and formulate corporate environmental policies and to coordinate activities

---

6. "United States Participation in Taejon Expo `93," USA Taejon Expo `93 Press Release.

that fulfill those well-thought-out and planned strategies. Amway has assumed an active role in environmental stewardship through such sponsorships as ICEWALK: THE INTERNATIONAL NORTH POLE EXPEDITION (a world-class exploration of the Arctic) and ICEWALK INTERNATIONAL STUDENT EXPEDITION (a study conducted by 22 youths from 15 countries), GLOBAL RELEAF (an American Forestry seedling project), THE AMWAY/EVEREST EXPEDITION 1992 (a 10-man climb), the AMWAY/EBONY ENVIRONMENTAL SCHOLARSHIP FUND (administered by the United Negro College Fund to needy students who are majoring in one of the environmental sciences) and ECOLOGICALLY-FRIENDLY ADVERTISING (spotlighting support for conservation and wildlife). In addition, Amway has been a standard-bearer in environmental action through:

- Biodegradability—the first product marketed by Amway was L.O.C. (Liquid Organic Cleaner), which has always contained only biodegradable surfactants and no phosphates. Today, Amway continues that tradition.

- Product Concentration—since the nation's landfills are quickly running out of room, product concentration becomes increasingly important. Concentrated products require less packaging for the same number of uses, which, in turn, means less solid waste from packaging materials. Many Amway products produce from 50% to 75% less solid waste than similar products available in the marketplace.

- Aerosol Reformulation—in the 1970s, Amway led the way in responding to research that linked CFCs (clorofluorocarbons) with damage to the protective ozone layer in the stratosphere by aggressively reformulating its aerosol products to eliminate the use of CFCs in all Amway aerosol products.

- No Animal Testing—Amway eliminated all animal testing as of June 1989, using ecologically-friendly "in vitro" techniques instead.

- Polystyrene Substitute—polystyrene packing "peanuts" are clean and chemically inert, but they take up space in our landfills. Amway found a manufacturer who makes a cornstarch version of packing materials that dissolves quickly and thoroughly in water.

• Recycling—Amway opened its new recycling center in January 1992—a $750,000 effort to save resources and protect our environment. Already, this center is used to recycle paper products and office waste, with plans currently underway to recycle waste plastic and steel. Presently, Amway generates 24 tons of solid waste each working day (6,500 tons annually), and the company's goal is to recycle 90% of that waste. Amway was one of the first companies in the world to adopt the Society of Plastics Industries voluntary coding system to assist recyclers in sorting plastic containers by resin composition.

• Source Reduction—Amway has been conducting a waste-minimization study to find ways to reduce the generation of waste at the source, by reducing the number of defective bottles that have to be removed from the production line.

• Catalog Products—The Amway Personal Shoppers Catalog features tissue, napkins and other recycled paper products; light bulbs that conserve energy; recycling aids; and greeting cards that create an end-use for recycled products and encourage environmental awareness through source reduction, recycling and conservation.

As a result of this comprehensive commitment, Amway has received a long list of awards, including the 1992 UNESCO TRANSPOLAR Medal (from the United Nations Education, Scientific and Cultural Organization) and the 1991 National Wildlife Federation Conservation Achievement Award. One of the highest honors to date has been the 1989 United Nations Environment Programme Achievement Award (only the second corporation to receive this accolade).[7]

MEETINGS: Each year, more than 100 corporate and organizational seminars, meetings and rallies bring together product, sales and marketing specialists to help you build your business.

Diamond-produced functions[8] (from local to regional seminars and rallies to Spring extravaganzas, Go-Diamond Direct

---

7. Alan Eggleston, "Green for Life," *Amagram*, April 1992, p. 38-41; "Facts About Amway and the Environment," Amway Press Release, April 4, 1993.
8. These functions are strongly recommended; however, they are optional and not required. Information is available from your Upline.

Distributor Leadership Conferences, Family Reunion summer conferences, leadership retreats and Dream Nights to Free Enterprise Celebrations) give you and your distributors an added, exciting insight into training, motivation and the growing number of success stories.

In addition, qualifying distributors are invited by the Amway Corporation to attend exclusive, corporate-sponsored leadership seminars in a variety of locations- from Michigan to Maui, and from Switzerland to Thailand—throughout the world.

LEADERSHIP: It has been said that any organization rises and falls with its leaders. Amway's co-founders, Rich DeVos and Jay Van Andel, are prime examples.

Not only are they closest friends, but they serve as joint CEOs and much-heralded leaders for the worldwide, four and a half-billion-dollar-a-year corporation.

They are individually featured in the top ten percent of the famed *Forbes* 400 richest people in America and are listed as sixty-first and sixty-fifth in Fortune Magazine's "World's Richest People." Their company is listed consistently among the country's largest privately-owned businesses (30th in the 1992

Forbes 400 Largest Private Companies in the U.S., up from 46th in 1991 and 78th in 1990), above hundreds of such well-known firms as Hallmark Cards, Thrifty Drug Stores and Domino's Pizza.[9]

In addition to being featured in such well-known publications as *Reader's Digest* and *Saturday Evening Post*, both have

---

9. "The Forbes 400," *Forbes*, October 18, 1993, p. 123; "The 400 Largest Private Companies in the U.S.," *Forbes*, December 7, 1992, p. 178; "The Billionaires," *Fortune*, June 28, 1993, p. 54.

Richard M. DeVos

received such prestigious honors as the George Washington Honor Medal from the Freedoms Foundation, the "Golden Plate" Award from the American Academy of Achievement, the Religious Heritage Business and Professional "Leader of the Year" Award.

Besides the long list of distinguished positions both have held, Jay Van Andel has served as Chairman of the Board for the United States Chamber of Commerce, and Rich DeVos was appointed Chairperson of the National Congressional Leadership Council.

Jay Van Andel.

Both Rich and Jay are leaders in their church, and they
actively support a wide range of civic, political and cultural
interests—from Christian films to international symphony tours.
Recent projects have included the Helen DeVos Women's and
Chidren's Center, a state-of-the-art women's and pediatric addition to the Butterworth Hospital and the Van Andel Museum
Center, a new facility for the Grand Rapid public museum,
named in honor of Jay and Betty Van Andel and their families,
not only for their personal financial support, but also for their
leadership efforts in helping to raise funds for the facility.

Dick DeVos

A historic day occurred on December 21, 1992, when Dick DeVos succeeded his father as Amway's president. First joining the company in 1974, Dick subsequently held positions in several Amway departments, including R&D, manufacturing and distribution, marketing and finance. From 1984 to 1989, he was vice president of international operations, responsible for all aspects of Amway's overseas business. During this period of time, he opened eight new markets and Amway's international sales exceeded U.S. sales for the first time. Then in 1989, Dick founded the Windquest Group, a multi-company management firm in Grand Rapids, Michigan. He continues to serve as president of the Orlando Magic, the NBA team owned by the DeVos family.[10] His wife, Betsy, now serves as president of the Windquest group.

---

10. Amway Public Relations Department.

Tom Eggleston

Tom Eggleston, Chief Operating Officer and Executive Vice President of Worldwide Direct Sales, joined the Amway Corporation in May 1991. A Phi Beta Kappa, varsity basketball player, Rhodes Scholar finalist and Senior Fellow at Dartmouth College, Tom received his law degree and the Raven Award for outstanding service from the University of Virginia. After a distinguished ten-year career with a law firm, he moved into the corporate world, serving as Vice President, General Counsel and Secretary of Ransburg Corporation and General Manager of Worldwide Automotive Finishing Operations at Illinois Tool

Works. In addition to many civic and charitable responsibilities, he has served for a decade on the Gospel Films Board of Directors as chief legal counsel.

Amway's Policy Board includes the Co-founders and their children: Dick DeVos (as previously mentioned, now serving as Amway's President), Dan DeVos (Vice President of the Pacific), Cheri DeVos VanderWeide (Director of Special Projects), Doug DeVos (Vice President of North American Sales), Nan Van Andel (Vice President of Catalog and Communications), Steve Van Andel (Vice President of the Americas), Barb Van Andel-Gaby (Vice President of Amway Properties) and Dave Van Andel (Vice President of Manufacturing and Operations).

Both first and second generations of the DeVos and Van Andel families work officially as a corporate body responsible for all aspects of the Amway Corporation worldwide.[11]

In addition to the executives and Policy Board, you also have a unique foundation—the Amway Distributor's Association Council. The A.D.A. Council meets with Amway Corporation personnel in a cooperative effort to help determine business policies and overall direction of this business. The group of distributors achieve a broad representation throughout North America (U.S. and Canada) by an election of 30 distributors at the Diamond level and above, fifteen members elected by Direct Distributors and above, and fifteen council members nominated from a slate submitted by Amway Corporation, with a minimum of two members representing Canada. This distinguished group of men and women whose backgrounds cut across lines of sponsorship, pin levels and geography is dedicated to improving every facet of the Amway business. The fact that Amway Corporation has made this type of commitment to bring all proposed new policies or proposed policy changes to this legal body for discussion, evaluation, recommendation and approval is an additional factor why Amway has pioneered the way and remains a trendsetter in the network marketing business.[12] (This body remains the only one of its kind in the industry and was formed in 1959, even before Amway Corporation was formed. The A.D.A was known then as the American Way Association.)

---

11. "Amway Forms Policy Board Comprised of Co-Founders and Second Generation Family Members," Amway Press Release, August 20, 1992; "A Family Affair," *Amagram*, March 1993, p. 3.
12. "A.D.A Council Welcome New Members," *Amagram*, February 1993, p. 42.

Dexter & Birdie Yager

YOUR UPLINE
CROWN AMBASSADOR DIRECT
DISTRIBUTORS

As part of your leadership foundations, Dexter and Birdie Yager have been featured on such television shows as *60 Minutes*, *PM Magazine* and various Christian programs. They have been profiled in many leading newspapers and magazines, including *USA Today*, *Christian Life*, *Forbes* and *Success*.

Active in Amway since 1964, the Yagers have reached the pinnacle of Amway's recognition ladder. A Crown Ambassador Direct Distributor has sponsored 20 groups, each of which qualify at the 25% Performance Bonus level for at least six months of the fiscal year.

Jerry Boggus, who has used the Yager system to build a far-reaching Diamondship, says:

The Yagers are known throughout the business world for their achievements. Not only have they written about their beliefs on success and positive attitudes in several bestselling books, but Dexter and Birdie show their dedication to their faith, country, family and achievement in everything they do. It's no wonder, then, why Dexter received the "Networking Man of the Year" Award bestowed by the Amway Distributors Association in 1991. Since he is the only one who has ever received this award, it's quite a distinction. It's also very deserved. Likewise he has been the first to receive the industry-wide "MLM Lifetime Achievement Award."

Greater than all of the worldly acclaim and achievements, they cherish the relationships with people in their organization, from the encounters with hundreds of thousands of distributors through worldwide meetings, to the thousands of extended distributor leaders with whom they meet on a regular basis, to the close, personal friendships with hundreds of distributors they consider most precious.

YOUR PLACE ON THE TEAM

Business experts around the world are realizing the tremendous advantages of viable network marketing companies.

As mentioned previously, home shopping is already responsible for $175.6 billion worth of business a year—27% of all retail sales in America. With the advent of interactive shopping, this method of distribution will continue to explode, and distribution marketing will continue to play an important role.

Estimators insist that such systems will collectively continue accelerating by 20% or more each year. One can only imagine how many billions of dollars worth of business will be done through network marketing into the Twenty-first Century, but it is already BIG business by anyone's standards.

More importantly, a large portion of that amount will be merchandised through Amway's network of distributors—people such as you.

No wonder Richard Jaccoma, a writer in *Dealerscope Merchandizing*, the marketing magazine for consumer electronics and major appliance retailing, wrote:

> *Imagine a retailing operation whose salespeople are so enthusiastic they actually pay a small fee for the privilege of starting to work for it, attend stadium-size pep rallies in support of it and organize local recruiting meetings for potential new salespeople to explain the wonders of it.*
>
> *Next, imagine that this retailing operation's sales force, along with all the potential new salespeople this force contacts, are also primary customers for its goods and services.*
>
> *Now, imagine that, in the midst of a recession, this operation has become a vast international company whose sales have been growing at the rate of almost $1 billion annually for the past three years: from $2.2 billion in fiscal 1989-90 to $3.1 billion in fiscal 1990-91 to $3.9 billion in fiscal 1991-92 to $4.5 billion in fiscal 1992-93.*
>
> *And finally, to invest this operation with the menace of a nightmare, imagine that it began with a core line of a few home cleaning products—concentrated soaps and such—but has expanded its offerings to include cosmetics, vitamins, food staples, clothing, charge cards, phone services, real estate sales and, yes, products in every significant category of consumer electronics, major and minor appliances, computer and home office equipment that traditional dealers sell—and some that they don't.*
>
> *But once this nightmare is planted firmly in your mind, don't bother pinching yourself to try to wake up, because it isn't a dream. It's real, its name is Amway, and it is growing in your market.*[13]

---

13. Richard Jaccoma, "The Amway Menace," *Dealerscope Merchandizing*, October 1992, p. 1.

By deciding to develop your own Amway business, you have the opportunity to be part of the largest, most profitable network marketing team in history. The benefits are far-reaching.

For one thing, you do not have to re-invent the proverbial wheel. As mentioned previously, so many other network marketing companies have developed their organizations around one product line, then they look for another product to pass down their network for increased profitability.

Neither you nor we must do that, since Amway has its own qualified staff of researchers, scientists and developers to acquire new product lines.

In addition, Amway stands behind each piece of merchandise with their incredible 100% full-satisfaction-or-your-money-back guarantee. By joining ranks with your co-distributors, you place yourself, so to speak, under a very competent, highly esteemed and ever-expanding umbrella. You become a member of a dynamic team!

Plus, in addition to the sales and marketing plan, you have joined a time-proven success system within this organization. A glance through the *Profiles of Success** will illustrate this fact.

No other mutual-benefit marketing group can match our organization in terms of reputation or success-building records. You have many, many people to whom you can look and say, "They made it in Amway, and so can I."

---

*This book is strongly recommended; however, these business support materials are optional and not required. Information is available from your Upline.

A FINAL NOTE

J. Paul Getty once wrote, "There are six requirements that must be included in your plan for success." He then listed the following:

(1) You must be in business for yourself.

(2) You must offer a product that is in demand.

(3) You must guarantee the product absolutely.

(4) You must give better service than the competition.

(5) You must reward those who do the work.

(6) You must build your success upon the success of others.

If any network marketing company has fulfilled Getty's guidelines through the years, it has been the Amway Corporation. As your corporate sponsor, they have pledged to offer an increasingly wide range of professional support services to help you build your business.

By properly utilizing those services, you have the exciting potential to become an independent, highly successful businessperson. Others have—you can, too.

Unlike nearly every other level of society, you will have no boss standing over you to push, discipline or browbeat you. In network marketing, however, you will have experienced teachers and advisors leading and guiding you. You are the boss. It is all up to you. That is the bittersweet, scary, uncomfortable, invisible reality of owning your own business—with the added bonus of a proven, workable, do-able system. In simple terms, you have no boss, except yourself. What you do have is a growing number of friends and encouragers.

But there is more good news. As your own employer, you control your own promotions and paychecks. Perhaps that is frightening to some, but there are millions (even billions) of people in more controlled countries who would gladly give almost anything for such an opportunity. One look at the incredible growth of our business in once-communistic countries proves this.

How you fare during the coming weeks, months and years will depend upon how closely you follow and duplicate the blueprint (success pattern) and how well you habitually develop all the basics.

You can do it!

**You are working with the greatest
mutual-benefit marketing system as you
BUILD YOUR OWN INTERACTIVE
DISTRIBUTION BUSINESS!**

BUILDING BLOCKS:

Although it seemed to many people that Don—a chemical engineer—and I had very fulfilling jobs, we got involved with network marketing because we saw it as a way to eventually have freedom to work whatever hours we wanted to. But as we built the business, we found so many other benefits. We quickly fell in love with our newfound friends. We eventually developed the kind of income that helped us to become financial secure and debt-free. Best of all, this business has allowed us to be full-time parents to our daughter Kristen.

GRETCHEN SEAGREN
Former Flight Attendant
Executive Diamond Direct Distributor
(USA)

Some see private enterprise as the predatory target to be shot, others as a cow to be milked, but few are those who see it as a sturdy horse pulling the wagon.[1]

WINSTON CHURCHILL (1874-1965)
Prime Minister of Britain

---

1. Quoted from the Foreword of Peter Ueberroth's *Made in America* (New York: Morrow, 1985).

There's one main thing that counts in this business: building the self-esteem of the people who work with you. In a very real and special way, nothing else matters quite as much, because what your associates feel about themselves is what they give to other people. If your team members don't feel good about themselves, they will face an uphill battle in being able to sponsor others or reaching their goals.

But when they can see themselves growing and improving—with your encouragement—the momentum can be nothing short of spectacular!

JIM PAULLIN
Former Financial Planner
Diamond Direct Distributor (USA)

If the Amway story were a tale only of corporate success and the piling up of many dollars, it would fit comfortably among many other such stories in American business history. Other men than Jay Van Andel and Richard DeVos have made fortunes from modest beginnings. Brand names other than Amway have jumped from an entrepreneur's brain into the national vocabulary in just as short a time. Modern life has no shortage of business success stories, but Amway is a bigger story than any of them.

Amway is a big story because it touches people in a way that Wal-mart Stores and Domino's Pizza and Apple Computer do not.

When you talk about Amway, you're talking millions of people. You're talking about a story of American life that plays on the wide screen. This is a story about which people care so deeply that they stand in big convention halls by the thousands and sing and hold hands and sometimes cry.

CHARLES PAUL CONN
President, Lee College
Bestselling Author of
The Possible Dream,
Promises to Keep and *Man in Black*
(The Johnny Cash Story) (USA)

If it is a good thing to feed a man, it is infinitely better to teach him to feed himself. Dexter believes in this concept, and he is teaching hundreds of thousands of people. They, in turn, will teach millions. Dexter Yager is sharing his dream!

SUE LYNN SETZER
Former Elementary
School Teacher
Triple Diamond
Direct Distributor (USA)

The strength of any network marketing organization lies in the people who make up the network. Amway's distributors' collective ingenuity, courage and faith in free enterprise represent the true spirit of entrepreneurship and the quest for personal freedom.

LORNE GREENE
(1915-1987)
Canadian-born Star of
TV's *Bonanza*

Dex and Birdie's success pattern has been the prime ingredient in our growth. Their love and understanding have helped us to build that stronger marriage and family life that we all strive for.

We have grown as individuals who are excited about our future together and our opportunity to offer the same future to many others.

JERRY HARTEIS
Former School Teacher
Diamond Direct Distributor (USA)

Success is based on imagination plus ambition and the will to work.

THOMAS EDISON (1847-1931)
U.S. Inventor

There are many things in life which matter: beliefs, dreams, family, purpose, friendships, peace and goals. The Amway business is one of the few things I have ever seen that helps you fulfill and touch all the things that really matter.

ROY BULMER
Former Policeman
Diamond Direct
Distributor (Canada)

The journey of a thousand miles begins with a single step.

ANCIENT CHINESE PROVERB

I've heard Amway called a great business concept. Others refer to the company as simply a manufacturer. But we know that Amway is so much more. This business represents hope. It is a way to achieve your dreams. And because of the hope and dreams, to us it has become a lifestyle.

TERRI GULICK
Former Clothing
Store Manager
Executive Diamond
Direct Distributor (USA)

One of the primary natural laws of success is to pick out the key people who can help you become successful in reaching the goals you have set, and then associate with these people. First of all, these people have the power to help you get ahead by giving you instruction, suggestions and opportunities.

Second, constant association with successful people enables you to observe the way they conduct themselves and to absorb some of their attitudes and outlooks. Soon you begin to mentally envision yourself on that level.

Third, outsiders who see you for the first time tend to evaluate your worth and stature by the quality of your associates.[2]

LOWELL LUNDSTROM
Chancellor, Trinity College
Author, Broadcaster
and Minister (USA)

*This is a **people** business. The reason our marketing and distribution system has grown so dramatically is because we are taught to think in terms of what people can become, not what they are now.*

This business helps you look at people in such a different light—you get involved and fall in love with them. You become best friends. Most of all, you see such positive things happen among the people with whom you get involved. That is priceless!

FRANK MAZZEO
Former Dentist
Diamond Direct Distributor (USA)

---

2. Lowell Lundstrom, *How to Enjoy Supernatural Prosperity* (Irvine, CA: Harvest House Publishers, 1979), p. 23.

We all have the same amount of time each day. The difference between people is determined by what they do with the amount of time at their disposal. Don't be like the airline pilot flying over the Pacific Ocean who reported to his passengers, "We're lost, but we're making great time!" Remember that the future arrives an hour at a time. Gain control of your time, and you will gain control of your life.[3]

JOHN L. MASON
Author
Founder and President of
Insight International (USA)

The commitment to build this business seems to come in installments, not all at one time. You listen to a tape and make a commitment. Then you hear someone at a rally and make more of a commitment. Then you go to a major function and your level of commitment grows to an even higher level.

Here's the amazing part: Once you make a deep, heartfelt commitment, the way to do it will become clear. Dexter Yager says, "When your dream is big enough, the facts don't count." It's true, and it really works.

You see, a focused commitment to your dream will help make you more creative and will push you to a higher level of performance than you ever thought possible!

TOMMY HARPER
Former High School Teacher
Diamond Direct Distributor (USA)

---

3. John L. Mason, *An Enemy Called Average* (Tulsa, OK: Harrison House, Inc., 1990), p. 24.

When I began as a plebe at West Point, "Duty, Honor, Country" was just a motto I'd heard. By the time I left, those values had become my fixed stars. It was a tremendous liberation.

The Army, with its emphasis on rank and medals and efficiency reports, is the easiest institution in the world to get consumed with ambition. Some officers spend all their time currying favor and worrying about the next promotion—a miserable way to live. But West Point saved me from that by instilling the ideal of service above self—to do my duty for my country even if it brought no gain at all. It gave me far more than a military career—it gave me a calling.[4]

GENERAL (ret.) H. NORMAN
SCHWARZKOPF
U.S. Commander during Desert Storm

The benefits from building this business are so far above anything we imagined in the beginning. We have now bought our farm. We've got a beautiful training facility for our thoroughbred horses. We have a private training track that's nearly five furlongs. The stables are completely equipped, even down to the exercise treadmills. All those things are fine, but the finest benefits from building this business are the relationships we have developed. Briony and I are closer than ever. Our kids are such great achievers. And the people in this business are the best in the world.

BILL SMART
Former Dairy Farmer
Thoroughbred Horse
Breeder and Trainer
Diamond Direct
Distributor (Australia)

---

4. H. Norman Schwarzkopf with Peter Petre, *It Doesn't Take a Hero* (New York: Bantam, 1992), p. 73.

I love sharing this business. I truly enjoy seeing that light in people's faces when they realize there IS hope after all. For, you see, hope—when it is translated into dreams and goals— can change almost everything about your life. It can even change your view of life. We've seen it happen so many times, but it never gets old. That's why I'm more excited about this business now more than ever.

Here's the thing I often tell people who are getting into the business: "If you don't know where you're going, any road will get you there."

Frankly, people don't plan to fail; instead, they simply fail to plan.

Define your dreams and set realistic goals. There is no other opportunity I know of that can help you get where you want to go very quickly.

JERRY BOGGUS
Former Army Captain
Diamond Direct Distributor (USA)
ADA Board Member

Dreambuilding
...Your Goal-setting Action Plan

Building a shimmering glass-and-metal skyscraper requires much more than joining a few beams together and hiring an interior decorator. In fact, the largest, most important amounts of expense and mental output take place in the architectural offices and muddy foundation trenches.

Just as the space shuttle Atlantis burns up nearly all of its half-million gallons of fuel just to lift its 74-ton cargo the first few inches off the launch pad, so the skyscraper construction must seem painfully slow and unrewarding before the gigantic framework finally begins to take form.

We have seen many new Amway distributors become discouraged when their initial efforts go somewhat unheralded and seem unfruitful.

When that skyscraper construction begins, it seems to take forever before it finally starts rising from the ground. No one

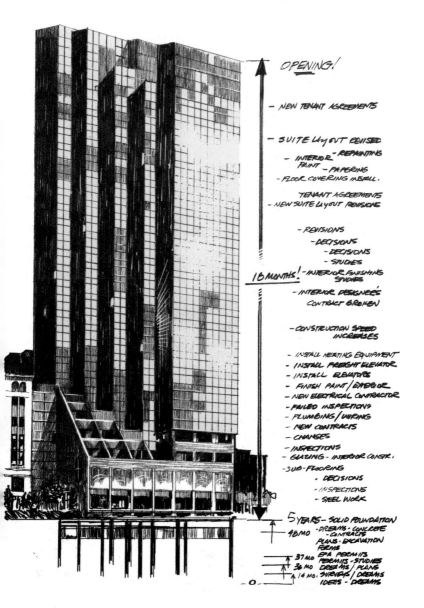

considers *that* process ridiculous or unreasonable. The architects, contractors and project managers realize that the necessary foundational work must be done well before the seemingly quick, above-ground construction starts. A blueprint and timetable are always nearby at the construction site for easy reference.

Why then does a distributor wonder what happened when he or she rushes headlong into unforeseen problems? Even after he or she has initial rewards, what happens when that person encounters apparently monumental obstacles on the road to success?

Without the proper **vision** (concepts and desire), **dreams** (the artist's rendition of the finished skyscraper) and goals (blueprints)—all broken down into a workable **action plan** (daily and weekly steps)—the construction contractor might become quite confused and discouraged.

Likewise, without the proper **vision** (your WHY? or overriding desire for building the business), **dreams** (bills paid, private

education for children, luxurious automobiles, vacation homes and exotic getaways), **goals** (1000 PV, 1500 PV, 2500 PV, 4000 PV, Silver Producer, Gold Producer, Six-month qualifying Direct, Ruby, Pearl, Emerald, Diamond, Executive Diamond and beyond) and **action plan** (daily and weekly success steps), the distributor cannot properly build his or her own business.

VISION

Before we set out on any journey or dream-building expedition, we ought to know something about where we want to go, how we are going to get there and when we expect to arrive. After all, one of life's greatest mysteries is why some people succeed while others don't. There are a number of qualities possessed by achievers, but perhaps the most prominent is the desire, the drive to achieve. Desire is directly related to **vision.**

The necessary ingredient in any formula for success is **vision**—your underlying, driving, desire-filled concept of what you value most in life.

Solomon, one of history's wisest men, said:

*Where there is no **vision**, the people perish* (Proverbs 29:18).

Granted, as you build toward your dreams, you will get tired. You will grow weary. You will need to stop and recharge. When those times come, you will need inspiration. Beyond inspiration, you will need great vision.

Many people are severely handicapped by short-sightedness. When someone has his or her eyes focused too closely on the present, the future tends to be blotted out of vision. Therefore, short-sightedness is often caused by being more interested in the immediate than we should be. That does more damage to a person's potential than anything else.

For starters, take a few moments and write out a short vision statement. In a few sentences, explain what you want to do with the remainder of your life—especially in relation to building your own distribution business.

MY VISION STATEMENT

Before we leave this section on creating a vision of your future, let us agree on a two things:

money cannot make you happy,
and
things will not bring fulfillment into your life.

Tim Foley is an Amway Triple Diamond who was an All-American football player at Purdue University and All-Pro with the World Champion Miami Dolphins. He says:

> *If you have a poor self-image, a Mercedes is not the solution. If you are selfish and friendless, a new boat is not what is missing in your life. On the other side of the coin, you are not necessarily a more caring individual just because you cannot pay your bills. A lack of time or money doesn't make you a better person. It is a matter of establishing priorities in your life. If the acquisition of "things" is the most important activity in your life, you will never be at peace. But, on the other hand, if you develop your God-given talents, live a productive life, perform a vital service, have your priorities in order, contribute to the prosperity—both physical and spiritual—of those with whom you come in contact and those in need, you will be at peace while you enjoy the result of your efforts. That is networking!*

You will only be moved to action by the prospect of results. That is what you must decide. What will move you? What do you want? How will it benefit you? These are all questions that you must answer as you put together your own vision statement.

DREAMS

Let's move one step closer to achieving the things that you value.

What are your dreams? If you could double your monthly income, what would you do with it? What do you want?

Use the following checklist to select your dreams:

___Debt-free financial flexibility

___New home

___Swimming pool

___Vacation to _____

___Fun cruise

___Dental care

___Sewing machine

___More time to enjoy sports

___Motorhome

___Private medical care

___New clothes

___Microwave

___Mountain bikes for the family

___Shopping trip

___Sauna

___Van

___Landscaping for yard or garden

___Paying off credit cards

___New refrigerator

___Live-in domestic help

___New furniture

___Investments in _____

___Motorcycle

___Outdoor deck and barbecue area

___Airplane

___A fur coat

___Skiing trip

___Adopt a child

___Diamonds

___Tickets to the Superbowl

___New car

___Education of children

___Support of ministry or missionary

___Flying lessons

___Pets

___Jewelry

___Jet ski

___Savings account

___Stereo

___Physical fitness equipment

___Care of parents

___Gifts for family and friends

___Insurance

___A horse

___Piano or musical equipment

___Antiques

___Vacation home

___Sailboat

___Donation to church, synagogue, school or charity

___Entertainment center

___Trip around the world

___Yacht

___New curtains

___Scuba diving equipment

___Learn a foreign language

___Home addition

___Publish book of poems

___Learning a craft

___Entertain graciously and comfortably

___Church building program

___Scholarships

___Houseboat

What other dreams can you add?

_____

_____

_____

_____

_____

_____

_____

_____

_____

_____

_____

Now it is important to be specific with what you want:

• What home do you desire?

_____

_____

_____

_____

• Where would you like to live (country, state, city, sub-division)?

_____

_____

_____

_____

• What long-term debts, bills and credit cards would you like to pay off?

_____

_____

_____

_____

- What educational opportunities would you like to provide for your children, including college?

_____

_____

_____

_____

- What would your financial portfolio contain, including savings accounts, stocks, bonds, securities, investments and other holdings?

_____

_____

_____

_____

- What kind of automobile do you aspire to drive?

_____

_____

_____

_____

and

- What kind of charitable contributions would you like to make?

_____

_____

_____

_____

Just saying, "I want to live in a gorgeous home someday," or "I would like to have a big boat in the future" doesn't mean a thing. You must define the exact reason that will motivate you to work toward the income you really want or a lifestyle of which you have always dreamed.

You must have a clear, concise image of exactly why you need more income. Especially for those immediate goals (since you learn first with the smaller ones to define those which are larger), it is important to visualize your dreams and aspirations.

Write them down. Consult your upline to acquire "Goal Setting: Your Gateway to Freedom" pamphlet (TL-302).* Consider what you want to purchase when you reach each new level. How much will that dream cost you? How soon do you want to get it? Write the information down!

If one of your dreams is to buy a new car when you reach Direct, then get out your pen and paper. Ask yourself:

• What make and model do I want?

_____

_____

_____

_____

• What color?

_____

_____

_____

_____

• Do I want velour or leather seats?

_____

_____

_____

_____

If you want a new car, go to the dealership. Sit on the plush upholstery. Smell the new-car aroma. Turn on the stereo. Drive the model that you want. Go back and build your dream again and again each and every week until you think about owning it so much until that dream becomes a burning desire (a "burn").

Let your mind wander. Can you imagine the satisfaction of achievement as you drive that shiny car into your own driveway? Better yet, how would it feel for you to drive to work in your dream car for the very last time before enjoying your "retirement"/freedom party?

---

* These items are strongly recommended and available through your Upline. However, business support materials are optional and not required.

Your dreams really can come true! Define them. Do whatever it takes to attain them.

GOALS

How often have you heard people say:

"I just never set goals."

or

"I don't believe in goals... that way, I am never disappointed if I don't reach them."

Such statements, while popular, are pure rubbish. Everyone sets goals every day to:

- Turn off the alarm,
- Get out of bed,
- Eat breakfast,
- Go to work,
- Pay bills,
- Watch a TV program,
- Run two miles

or

- Do anything!

We have just become so accustomed to setting and reaching those everyday goals that we don't even recognize what we are doing.

What if we *didn't* set those goals? We wouldn't get up, we would starve, we would lose our jobs and they would turn off our utilities. Right?

The same principle applies to your daily, weekly, monthly, yearly and lifetime goals. You are setting *something* as a goal, even if it is only to exist, but unless you learn to determine the proper way to set goals, you will never reach your best destinations. You see, if you don't know where you are going, any road will get you there.

Your vision empowers your dreams, and your dreams fuel your goals. Fulfillment of those dreams comes through realistic goal-setting on these three levels:

LONG-RANGE GOALS: If you want to construct a building, you first conceptualize the entire structure. You don't focus on a brick or a pane of glass.

Recently, in our hometown of Charlotte, North Carolina, we witnessed the construction of a new bank building. We actually heard people complaining during the initial months because it seemed as if nothing was being done. It took nearly the entire first year to reach ground level. Why? Obviously, someone with an eye on the blueprints and engineering specifications knew that it would require an inordinate amount of foundation work to make it safe to stand on the sixtieth floor one day.

Frankly, for workers on the bank building, it was a year spent in the mud among ugly metal and concrete mazes.

Similarly, the success-oriented distributor must think BIG (Diamondship, financial flexibility, a thousand distributors in your network, early retirement, more freedom with your time and money), rather than dwelling on one specific challenge, or temporary struggles such as rejection or hurt feelings.

You must keep your eyes on the blueprints and artists' renderings, not on the mud.

MEDIUM-RANGE GOALS: The contractor must consider the steps from foundation mortar to high-rise glamor. He or she needs to set a day-by-day timetable. Even though that person may be equally concerned with foundations and the final decorating touches, he or she knows that the first-floor framework must be completed before the second-floor construction can begin.

Likewise, the networker cannot get so concerned with going Diamond that he or she forgets the goals and necessary action between signing the application and receiving that gem-encrusted pin.

SHORT-RANGE GOALS: Even the most prestigious builder of skyscrapers must still handle dirt-moving and mortar-pouring details.

Short-range goals are extremely important for anyone. Unfortunately, many people ignore this category. Even those who do take the time for such details often set their short-range goals too high, so elevated that they become unreachable. It is as if they try to complete the third floor before the first floor's framing is completely finished; as a result, everything collapses.

Build your business step by step. Follow the system. Listen to your upline.

The fulfillment of your vision, dreams and goals is a gradual process and needs to be worked out on a day-by-day basis. The establishment of immediate goals provides the stairway which eventually spans the distance between attainment of medium- and long-range goals.

But what happens when you reach the short-range goals? It should be the mere beginning of a new adventure. Just before reaching those short-range goals, transform those medium-range aspirations into more short-range ones. Change your long-range goals into medium-range ones. Then develop new long-range goals. This continues your momentum.

Correspondingly, those dreams which go along with each goal help to reward your efforts, but they must also be realistic. Planning to buy a Rolls-Royce when you reach 1000 PV hardly seems realistic, but neither would owning a second-hand Chevrolet seem to be a fitting dream when reaching Diamond.

Be realistic, but once you have reached one goal, decide to set your sights on something bigger and better. Dreams are the radiant force which fuels you to do more and become more.

When your plan is well-defined, properly-pursued goals and dreams direct your life toward positive achievement. No one can set these for you, since they are a personal matter. Each must set his or her own goals and build toward them day by day, week by week, month by month and year by year.

As with any construction project, the foundation, as with your plan, must be strong and well-thought-out in order to allow for future planning, additions and alterations.

Success is the progressive realization of a worthwhile dream or goal. The goals you set, then, are extremely important.

Take a few moments to jot down your long-range, medium-range and short-range goals.

MY LONG-RANGE GOALS
(WRITTEN FIRST IN TERMS OF DECADES,
THEN DIVIDED INTO YEARS)

_____

_____

_____

_____

_____

_____

_____

_____

_____

_____

_____

_____

_____

_____

_____

_____

_____

_____

_____

_____

_____

_____

_____

_____

_____

_____

MY MID-RANGE GOALS
(WRITTEN FIRST IN TERMS OF YEARS,
THEN DIVIDED INTO MONTHS)

MY MID-RANGE GOALS
(WRITTEN FIRST IN TERMS OF YEARS,
THEN DIVIDED INTO MONTHS)

_____
_____
_____
_____
_____
_____
_____
_____
_____
_____
_____
_____
_____
_____
_____
_____
_____
_____
_____
_____
_____
_____
_____
_____
_____
_____
_____
_____
_____
_____
_____

ACTION PLAN

As mentioned previously, your vision statement becomes the basis for your dream list. Your dreams form the foundation for the goals you set. Those goals, then, become the bedrock for your action plan.

A strong action plan—most importantly your daily, weekly and monthly steps, but also including your yearly schedule— when carefully written and consistently followed, can lead eventually to the attainment of your ideals. All else—your vision, dreams and goals—will be lost unless you add the fourth element, **action!**

Take a few moments to put together an action plan to help you reach some of your primary dreams and goals (you can begin by using the "Plan to Make Direct" Chart in the *Schedule Book Pocket Calendar* (TL-14) and goal-setting pamphlet (TL-302); then sit down with your Direct for counselling.*

MY ACTION PLAN
(continued on next page)

_____
_____
_____
_____
_____
_____
_____
_____
_____
_____
_____
_____
_____
_____
_____

* These items are strongly recommended and available through your Upline. However, business support materials are optional and not required.

MY ACTION PLAN

HABITS

With a clear-cut **vision,** defined **dreams,** tightly-held **goals** and an **action** plan—fused together by hard work—achievement becomes easier. Someone has said:

"Inch by inch, success is a cinch!"

Success, once determined, becomes closely tied to the habits you develop.

It seems unbelievable that the majority of people spend their lives wanting to be successful, and yet never set clear-cut daily, weekly, monthly and yearly goals. Worse yet, they never DO something about their vision or dreams. Why? The hardest part is where the proverbial rubber meets the road—daily habits.

The saddest part is that anybody—yes, anybody—can succeed in network marketing. It does not matter where people are right now or where they have been, they can succeed and build a large, profitable business if they only develop the right kind of patterns and habits.

Let us share this long quote about those habits:

I will push you onward or I'll drag you down to failure. I'm at your command.

Half the tasks that you do, you might just as well turn over to me, and I'll do them quickly and correctly.

I am easily managed. You must merely be firm with me. Show me exactly how you want something done and after a few lessons, I will do it automatically.

I am the sermon of all great people, and a lash of all failures, as well. Those who are great, I have made great; and those who are failures, I've made failures.

I'm not a machine, but I work with all the precision of a machine, plus the intelligence of a person.

You may run me for profit or run me for ruin—it makes no difference to me.

Take me, train me and be firm with me, and I'll lay your work at your feet. But be easy with me, and I will destroy you.

Who am I? Habit is my name!

Develop the right habits now to help you reach your goals. So many default through negligence or procrastination, and thereby they choose to fail. They start dying the moment they stop dreaming BIG dreams.

What are some of the habits you need to delete or improve?

CHANGES I NEED TO MAKE WITH MY HABITS

_____
_____
_____
_____
_____
_____
_____
_____
_____
_____
_____
_____
_____
_____
_____
_____
_____
_____
_____
_____
_____
_____
_____
_____
_____
_____
_____
_____

BELIEF

It has been said that the most difficult part of succeeding is believing that you can succeed. If you don't believe you can do something, that lack of belief will cause you to sabotage your efforts.

Action never occurs until you believe you can do something. Belief comes primarily by both outward and inward empowerment.

What do we mean?

Outward motivation, in this business, is the reason why we have worked so hard to build the system of books, tapes and meetings. Your leadership is committed to providing the best belief-building tools in the world. It is up to you to take advantage of the wealth of information which is available to you.

Inner belief, often fueled by outward motivators, relates to your ability to focus on positive things. Sometimes this occurs when you put new information to use, thinking beneficial thoughts, praying for guidance or speaking good affirmations to yourself. Sometimes this happens when you reprocess seemingly bad things into good things, reminding yourself that "all things work together for those who are called to God's purpose."

Belief, while certainly spiritual in nature, is still tied directly to your choices.

What do you choose to believe about your business? About your upline? About yourself? About your downline people?

YOUR BELIEFS

What do you choose to believe in? List some of the most important statements you believe about God, life, your family, your work, your business and your self.

_____

_____

_____

_____

_____

_____

_____

_____

_____

_____

_____

_____

_____

_____

_____

_____

_____

_____

_____

_____

_____

_____

_____

_____

_____

_____

_____

_____

_____

_____

_____

_____

_____

_____

_____

_____

_____

_____

Unbelief, generally, is not a problem of the intellect but of the will. In other words, what you choose to believe is what you become.

Therefore, your choices about what you believe can be the catalyst to every phase of your success—from your vision to your dreams, and from your goals to your habits.

A FINAL NOTE

Unfortunately, most people are willing to sacrifice the future on the altar of the immediate. That universal tendency must be overcome by putting together your vision statement, dreams, goals, action plan and habits.

Previously, you have written your ideas in each of these areas. Now it is up to you to work your business.

Do everything needed to reach your goals so you can eventually achieve your dreams. Practice delayed gratification. Avoid activity traps. Major on the majors. Develop good time-management habits (more about this in Chapter Fourteen).

YOU CAN DO THIS BUSINESS! You can wade through your fears, doubts, lack of knowledge, rejection and discouragement. When the clouds of doom begin to overshadow your vision, you must begin thinking of the advantages you will obtain by not allowing yourself to become discouraged. You can think of how happy and proud your spouse and children are of you as you achieve even the smallest goals. You can imagine the way your heart will beat when the spotlight spills over you and you are introduced onstage as a new Direct Distributor, Pearl, Emerald, Diamond or Executive Diamond! You can consider the great regard in which you will be held by others as they realize what you have done in becoming a beacon for others to follow.

Success is only fulfilled through living a life of accomplishment and achievement. Doing the things that most people refuse to do may initially seem uncomfortable, but the results will be very, very rewarding.

Napoleon, the great French commander, always won the battles in his mind before he ever entered the field of combat. He often said:

> *I see only the objective. The obstacle must give way!*

You can become a great objective-seeker. With victory visualized, the struggle then means little.

What does this mean as you build your business? Whether you have been a distributor for hours, weeks or months, visualize your dreams over and over. Don't be discouraged by momentary setbacks. Refer to your goals. Stick to the success pattern and principles presented throughout this book. Listen to those leaders in your upline and follow their guidance.

Remember that building any skyscraper requires time-consuming foundation work. Recall how the space shuttle *Atlantis* expends most of its energy just to rise the first inches off *terra firma* (launch pad).

For you, making the initial steps may seem gargantuan, but gradually, as you follow the same guidelines which have led hundreds toward Diamondship and beyond, you can begin to set higher goals, reach greater aspirations and accomplish successes you never previously considered possible.

Most importantly, *don't let anybody steal your dreams.*

Develop your own vision.
Define your dreams.
Set your goals.
Work out your action plan.
Develop the right habits.
Then just do it!
Build your own
SUCCESSFUL DISTRIBUTION BUSINESS

BUILDING BLOCKS:

A lot of people ask me, "What's a race car driver doing in the Amway business?" Well, my wife Judy and I have been Amway distributors since 1976. We love and use the products and we like what Amway stands for—private enterprise and freedom.

Amway is a great business. One thing's for sure: There's a lot more security in Amway than there is in driving a race car for a living!

BOBBY ALLISON
Legendary NASCAR Driver
Amway Distributor (USA)

Entrepreneurs traditionally have been the most adventure-some, courageous and successful people in all the world. We have been the pace-setters, the fast-trackers, the dream seekers— the standard for the rest of the world, to strive to be the best.

CHERRY MEADOWS
Former School Teacher
and Broadcaster
Double Diamond
Direct Distributor (USA)

The heights by great men reached and kept were not attained by sudden flight.

But they, while their companions slept, were toiling upward in the night.

HENRY WADSWORTH
LONGFELLOW (1807-1882)
U.S. Poet

One of the greatest joys we've received is from showing the business to others who had stopped dreaming. It has become a never-ending thrill to see the spark of belief as they see that there is a way to reach their goals.

JODY DUTT
Former Manufacturing Worker
Second Generation Crown
Direct Distributor (USA)

All personal achievement starts in the mind of the individual. Your personal achievement starts in your mind. The first step is to know exactly what your problem, goal or desire is. If you're not clear about this, then write it down, and rewrite it until the words express precisely what you are after.

Every disadvantage has an equivalent advantage—if you'll take the trouble to find it. Learn to do that and you'll kick the stuffing out of adversity every time!

W. CLEMENT STONE
Founder of Success Magazine
and Author of *The Success
System That Never Fails* (USA)

Here is a fact to which there are no exceptions: We must labor for all we have, and nothing is worth possessing or offering to others which costs us nothing.

HANK GILEWICZ
Former IBM Staff Engineer
Diamond Direct Distributor (USA)

Whatever you see on the screen of life was first seen in your mind. If you don't like what you see, change the reel of film, change your attitude, change your thoughts. Change your thoughts and you change your world.

WALLY "FAMOUS" AMOS
Cookie Entrepreneur,
Motivational Speaker
and Bestselling Author (USA)

The best part of this business is that you may achieve incredible things—no matter what your background is. But no matter what you do, you can keep dreaming bigger dreams. We have been building this business for awhile, but we feel as if we are just getting started.

GEORGE HALSEY
Former Policeman and
Insurance Adjuster
Triple Diamond
Direct Distributor (USA)

Sometimes we're so concerned about giving our children what we never had growing up, we neglect to give them what we did have growing up.[1]

DR. JAMES DOBSON
"Focus on the Family"
Broadcaster
Speaker and Bestselling
Author (USA)

Poverty and wealth is all inside you. The poorest person is not the man or woman who has no money, but he or she who no longer has a dream. Achieving your dreams, reaching your goals and building this business—all depend upon your decisions. Staying poor, likewise, is a decision. So much depends upon your choices.

PEGGY BOGGUS
Homemaker
Diamond Direct
Distributor (USA)

One of the most important results you can bring into the world is the you that you really want to be. What happens to the blank canvas is in the hands of the artist. What you really want to be is for the most part in your hands.

ROBERT FRITZ
Philosopher (USA)

1. Dr. James Dobson, "Points to Ponder," *Reader's Digest,* July 1993, p. 150.

The secret to building this business is the size of your dream. In fact, we reached Double Diamond because our dream was that big, but then we plateaued for awhile. Getting new dreams got us going again. For us, those newfound dreams were to help more people achieve the economic and emotional freedom we had developed. Once we got started again, we were already on our way to Triple and our organization was spreading quickly throughout the United States, Europe and Asia.

KAY SHAW
Former School Teacher
Triple Diamond Direct
Distributor (USA)

You never conquer the mountain. You only conquer yourself.[2]

JIM WHITTAKER
First American to climb
Mount Everest

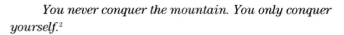

Everyone falls in love with results, but few people have the determination to fall in love with the effort. That, to me, is the real difference between those who succeed and those who don't. You have to fall in love with the effort. It has to come first. The results will follow.

DEWEY TOBIAS
Former Pharmaceutical
Representative
Diamond Direct Distributor (USA)

---

2. Quoted from James M. Kouzes and Barry Z. Posner, *The Leadership Challenge* (San Francisco: Jossey-Bass Publishers, 1987).

Michael J. Arlen, a wonderful writer, said to me once that the greatest act of love is to pay attention. That's so true. I think the one lesson I have learned is that there is no substitute for paying attention. [3]

DIANE SAWYER
Broadcaster

In the upholstery business, it took five years to show any profit. So when we started this business, we didn't expect to make lots of money overnight. However, so many people don't see that.

We've found that too many men and women simply don't give themselves enough time to build a large, profitable organization. They want it right now, and when it takes time, they sometimes get discouraged.

*This business is fueled by your dreams and goals, and it often takes some time to develop the **real** reason why you want to build it.*

*For us, our **real** reason was that our life was out of control. We wanted to make better use of our time and money.*

AL LeBLANC
Former Upholstery
Business Owner
Diamond Direct Distributor (USA)

If you haven't any charity in your heart, you have the worst kind of heart trouble. [4]

BOB HOPE
Comedian and Actor

---

3. Quoted from Craig M. Hoffman in *Working Woman Weekends*, June 1989, p. 14.
4. Bob Hope, "Quotable Quotes," *Reader's Digest*, July 1991, p. 1.

One of the great things about building this business is that you only succeed by helping other people succeed. Your only limitation in this business is the size of your dream and how much you are willing to help other people reach their dreams.

As a banker I talked with many business owners and would-be entrepreneurs. The one common denominator of any successful business, from my experience, is a sound business plan. Strategies and contingencies must be in place.

This business is certainly no different. Once you understand how well-thought-out Amway's structure is, you can concentrate on using these strong foundations to build your own profitable organization.

JACK REID
Former Bank Asst. Vice President
Diamond Direct Distributor (USA)
ADA Board Officer

The Geometric Progression of Distribution

...Your Marketing Strategy

Network marketing succeeds when distributors share the "plan" with several people, then teach those people to share with others.

Most people who are new to the Amway Sales and Marketing Plan* look at the circles and get excited about making money, dreaming again and possibly becoming free from the "rut" system.

That is great, but we quickly tell men and women, "It's the DREAM that you need to share."

It is true. It is the dream which motivates potentially-successful distributors to action.

---

* Refer to the Amway Sales and Marketing Brochure (SA-4400), included in the Amway Sales Kit, for further details.

But when that first-night euphoria wears off, we often see negative clouds begin to form inside the new person's mind. This is not unusual, since humans naturally lean toward the negative. You can almost see the unspoken words forming:

> *I like everything about the plan, BUT there's just two questions: How in the world am I going to use or market enough products to become successful? And how can I possibly sponsor enough people to ever reach Direct?*

DUPLICATION

Sometimes people who have been in the business awhile draw the circles casually, and we forget that sponsoring 75, 100 or 150 people, for the new distributor, looks somewhat like gathering together a vast army. On face value, these figures were once scary even to the most seasoned network marketing veteran.

But the secret of our multi-dimension business rests in the PHENOMENON OF GEOMETRIC PROGRESSION. Let us explain. We teach the 100 PV circles in the plan. Ideally, by the fourth generation deep, one who follows the pattern will be 11,800 PV and already starting to reap the financial rewards and recognition of a Gold Producer.

But 118 new people? It seems as if it would take forever. Who even knows 118 success-oriented men and women? That can be a very frightening thought.

But remember the amazing way in which the circles multiply. Just sticking by the board, let's say that you first find three, then six, then nine people to come into the business with you. *Everybody* knows up to nine men and women, or can find them over a period of time.

And when you can sponsor those nine, even if all are a little less motivated than you, each can sponsor four. Plus, if those four people are less than half as determined as their sponsors, they can help two couples or individuals see the vision.

It is as simple as using or merchandizing 100 PV or more worth of products, then you qualify as a Silver Producer!

Mathematically, it looks like this:

1 (YOU) X 100 PV = 100 PV

X   9 PERSONALLY-SPONSORED DISTRIBUTORS

---

9 2ND LEVEL DISTRIBUTORS + 1 (YOU)

= 10 x 100 PV = 1,000 PV

X   4

---

36 3RD LEVEL DISTRIBUTORS + 9 2ND LEVEL DISTRIBUTORS

+ 1 (YOU) = 46 x 100 PV = 4,600 PV

X   2

---

72 4th LEVEL DISTRIBUTORS + 36 + 9 + 1

= 118 X 100 PV = 11,800 PV

The system works well if you work it. It is certainly possible, since thousands of people just like you have achieved their financial goals and dreams with those figures.

Naturally, everyone is not going to put together a model organization exactly the same as the circles on a board. Some will sponsor less, some more.

However, before we leave this section, let us give another illustration which shows how exciting the geometric progression can be.

We talk about duplication a lot, and though veteran distributors draw the circles on the board to let everyone know that *anyone* can work this business, such tapering off in numbers is not *true* duplication. Far from it! That would wrongly assume that each new generation is less motivated than the previous one.

If you sponsor nine or more, then with pure duplication, each of those people will more likely sponsor at least nine (and probably more!), and so on.

1 (YOU) X 100 PV = 100 PV

X   9 PERSONALLY-SPONSORED DISTRIBUTORS

---

9 2ND LEVEL DISTRIBUTORS + 1 (YOU)

= 10 x 100 PV = 1,000 PV

X   9

---

81 3RD LEVEL DISTRIBUTORS + 9 2ND LEVEL DISTRIBUTORS

+ 1 (YOU) = 91 x 100 PV = 9,100 PV (which makes you a SILVER PRODUCER!)

X   9

---

729 4th LEVEL DISTRIBUTORS + 81 + 9 + 1

= 820 X 100 PV = 82,000 PV (you not only went SILVER PRODUCER and RUBY, but also went PEARL and into qualification for DIRECT, EMERALD, DIAMOND and E.D.C., since on an average, each of your nine personals did over 9,000 PV a month, thereby also qualifying them for both SILVER PRODUCER and into qualification for DIRECT!)

To get you to see the amazing principle at work with pure duplication, let me take the mathematic possibilities to one more generation.

729 X 9

6.561 5TH LEVEL + 729 + 81 + 9 + 1 = 7,381 X 100 PV

> = 738,100 PV!!! (In our mathematical model, not only would you be in qualification for E.D.C., but each of your personally-sponsored distributors would also be in qualification for the same pin, and your 81 second generation distributors would be averaging over 9000 PV each, thereby making them SILVER PRODUCERS!)

Now, let us bring you back to earth by saying, in reality, that you may have to sponsor 20 or more distributors to find nine who will become motivated enough to also sponsor nine (or even four, as with the circles we draw), who can each then go sponsor four (or two, as with our circles), but the figures— either with the nine personally-sponsored distributors or with the pure duplication numbers—are staggering!

DEPTH

We teach working in **depth,** so you will be helping your nine or more people (or whatever number initially join you in business) to sponsor others and build their own organizations.

Still, to think that you have to accumulate and work personally with a vast army of "recruits" is false. All you need is at least nine active distributors, and all they each need are four. All those third generation associates need are two.

Suddenly you could be cashing those Profit Sharing checks!

FIRST:

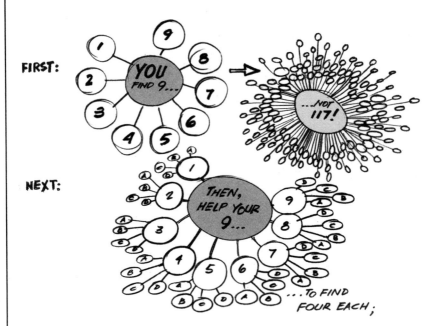

NEXT:

...TO FIND
FOUR EACH;

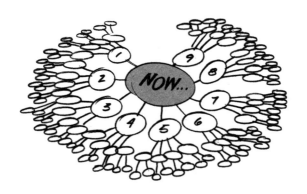

*...HELP THE FOUR
...EACH SPONSOR TWO!*

As you teach this success pattern and plug those personally-sponsored distributors into the motivational books, self-development cassettes and exciting meeting/rally system*, soon they will stand on their own more and more. As this happens, while continuing to work with them on a slightly more limited basis, you can go on to helping others, both personally and in depth. In fact, the fastest growing leaders generally work in threes (at least three personals and at least three in depth), and those can be at different levels in the business, as you will eventually be working with several groups of threes—all at varying growth stages. Just remember, you will have to sponsor five-to-ten wide in order to find your initial three "hot" ones, then do the same for your three, and so on.

The power is in the "one." What really matters is that *next* phone call, that *next* meeting, that *next* personally-sponsored associate and that *next* "warm" contact.

The next "one" is crucial, not the many, many calls and meetings and associates and contacts that will be required on your way to Diamondship. It is the next one that is vitally important.

Anybody can do just one, then one more, then one more. Remember the wise counsel: "How do you eat an elephant? One bite at a time!"

Likewise, "How do you build your business?" One phone call, one meeting, one associate and one contact at a time. And by plugging into our success support system (books, tapes, and other business support materials, open meetings and rallies),* you can literally watch that network of distributors (personally-sponsored and in depth), as they grow in numbers and business knowledge.

Who knows? It is entirely possible that your organization will eventually reach around the globe!

---

* These items are strongly recommended and available through your upline. However, business support materials are optional and not required.

A FINAL NOTE

Just remember that whether your business grows like the circles, or if it explodes more in line with pure duplication, the phenomenal power is in geometric multiplication. Best yet, the progression comes one step at a time.

You don't have to be a miracle worker to make this business work. You just have to be a believer and a doer. You also don't have to be extraordinarily smart or be dripping with business acumen (although they will probably call you a genius after you reach Diamond and Executive Diamond)!

Anybody can do this. Anyone who can sponsor nine people can also teach his or her downline associates to duplicate this sponsoring pattern. Anyone can use and sell 100 PV of products, then teach his or her downline distributors to do the same.

You have a tremendous opportunity for success with the geometric progression of distribution—especially in Amway, the "Cadillac" of them all. You can do it.

**You can find nine individuals
or couples who want to become successful
and who will do whatever it takes
to make their dreams come true
through INTERACTIVE DISTRIBUTION!**

BUILDING BLOCKS:

A lot of people talk about personal business ownership and entrepreneurship. Owning your business, by definition, explains why you want to be an entrepreneur. A successful entrepreneur wants to be judged on the merits of his or her own work. Owning your referral-based business allows you to do this--probably better than any other opportunity available today.

TOM AVELSGAARD
Former School Teacher
Diamond Direct Distributor
(Australia)

Even if we do not like the shape and content of the merging trends, they at least give information that allows us to anticipate certain consequences. Of course, explosive trends can cause great turbulence; but most trends take time to gather momentum, and we can use that time to reduce their negative impacts on us and optimize the opportunities they hold for us.[1]

JOEL BARKER
Former Advertising
Executive and Teacher
Bestselling Author,
Futurist and Speaker (USA)

1. Joel Arthur Barker, *Future Edge* (New York: William Morrow, 1992), p. 204.

This is a simple business. There's so much logic to the plan. Owning your own Amway business is the fastest, smartest way to financial flexibility and exciting income. Because of this opportunity, success does not just have to be an impossible dream. It's there for those who go for it!

TREVOR CHATHAM
Former Veterinarian
Executive Diamond
Direct Distributor (Australia)

When you are confident in your ability to achieve what you want in life, you will also be free of fear. You will not be tied to your present job or to any given set of circumstances. You will be ready to adapt to change whenever necessary or desirable, and you will be free to respond to any situation in the most appropriate, productive way.

If you have the commitment to change, grow and leave behind the frustrations, the limitations and the security of an old way of life, the rewards will be greater than you now imagine possible.[2]

MICHAEL FRIES and
C. HOLLAND TAYLOR
Authors (USA)

Thankfully, we learned fairly early in the business to listen to upline counsel. We tried to duplicate what we were taught. If there is any secret to our success, it is the fact that we became students of this success building system.

SHERRI BRYAN
Former Legal Secretary
Diamond Direct Distributor (USA)

2. Michael Fries and C. Holland Taylor with Diane Frank, *The Pro$perity Handbook: A Guide to Personal & Financial Success* (Oakland, CA: Communications Research, 1984), pp. 417-8.

Far better is it to dare mighty things, to win glorious triumphs, even though checkered by failure, than to rank with those poor spirits who neither enjoy much nor suffer much, because they live in the gray twilight that knows not victory nor defeat.

THEODORE ROOSEVELT
(1858-1919)
Twenty-sixth President of the
United States

It's exciting to be able to share what we've found in this business with others. Some people get jealous of others' successes, but we never have because we have realized that we all have the same plan. Besides that, the further we go, the more we see that we're really just getting started.

PAUL STEVENS
Award-Winning Motion Picture
and Television Producer
Diamond Direct Distributor
(USA)

There's an old expression, 'Seeing is believing.' But it's more accurate to say that 'believing is seeing.' That is, you tend to see what you believe you're going to see. You bring to a situation what you expect you're going to experience.

CARL SORENSEN, PH.D.
Professor, Stanford
University (USA)

I was always looking for something better. I liked playing football (soccer), but one's career eventually has to end, and I didn't want to wait until I was older to start thinking about my future. When the Amway business came along, we were ready.

One of the great principles of the success system is that you can be around successful people through the books, tapes, meetings and upline support.

Being around other winners and having it rub off on you—that's what really makes the difference. If you want to be a success in life, you have to get around successful people. This is a pretty simple principle when you get down to it. All I know is that the rewards we enjoy today are directly related to getting around successful people.

DAVE BRADLEY
Former Professional
Soccer Player
and Insurance Salesperson
Diamond Direct Distributor (New Zealand)

My affiliation with Amway covers more than 30 years as a United States Congressman, Vice President, President, and now as a private citizen. The thousands of Amway distributors are dramatic proof that the spirit of free enterprise is and will continue to be a vibrant force of good around the world.

GERALD R. FORD
Thirty-eighth President
of the United States

Initially, Gretchen and I didn't see the Amway opportunity as a way to quit our jobs, but it sure made life more secure as our income from this business reached the point that we could decide whether we wanted to continue working in our professions or not. Finally, it simply made more sense for us to leave our jobs behind.

The main thing is that this business gave us an option— something few people ever get!

DON SEAGREN
Former Chemical Engineer
Executive Diamond Direct
Distributor (USA)

I've had a special friendship with Rich DeVos and Jay Van Andel for over 30 years. I have closely observed their business dealings and their personal lives. I've watched their families grow up and there is no one I know that has more integrity than these two men.

Twenty years ago I met Dexter Yager, and another special friendship began. Dexter's relationship to me has always displayed the same integrity and vision of Rich and Jay.

These three men are strong community leaders and through their humanitarian efforts have championed charitable causes. Through our ministry they have literally helped hundreds of thousands of Junior and Senior High school students throughout the world. Because of their efforts these students have expanded their understanding and vision of the potential that each one has within them.

BILLY ZEOLI
President, Gospel Films

We love the Amway business because it helps people build on their dreams. There is plenty of opportunity for everybody, and no matter what a person's goals may be, this business offers the vehicle for reaching them.

JANE PAWLAK
Former Dairy Cattle Rancher
Diamond Direct Distributor (USA)

Even if you're on the right track, you'll get run over if you just sit there.

WILL ROGERS (1879-1935)
U.S. Cowboy Entertainer and
Rope-twirling Satirist

My advice to anyone who wants to build his or her Amway business is pretty simple—become a student, keep things simple and be teachable. Beyond that, listen to the people who have gone before you. Do those things and you can go as far as you want.

PHIL SKEHAN
Former Dairy Farmer
Diamond Direct
Distributor (Australia)

A glimpse is not a vision. But to a man on a mountain road by night, a glimpse of the next three feet of road may matter more than a vision of the horizon.

C. S. LEWIS (1898-1963)
British Scholar and Writer;
Author of *Mere Christianity*
and the *Narnia* series

Owning your own Amway business is the fastest, smartest way to financial flexibility. Success does not just have to be an impossible dream. It's there for those who understand the power of personal business ownership and network marketing and are willing to work hard within the proven system for success.

That's the key—working within the system, becoming a student of the business and pursuing the answers.

It all comes down to your commitment!

VINCE BERLAND
Rancher and Greyhound Kennel Owner
Diamond Direct Distributor (USA)

CHAPTER SEVEN

Building Blocks

...Your Marketplace Advantages

If all we had to deal with were numbers and geometric progressions, this business *would* be so simple that it would be trite. Not only *could* everybody do it, but everybody *would* do it.

Not so. We are not dealing with mere circles, marks on a board and products. This business is so much more! To succeed in this business, we must deal with people. REAL people!

Men and women do not follow form. They change without any apparent reason. Some may react negatively to your positive strategies or may fail sometimes to see the most simple business principles.

And you really have no way of knowing exactly what people will do. For example, we have been in meetings drawing the circles and observed that the Jones couple are having trouble sitting down because they are so-o-o-o excited.

Joe Jones exclaims: "We can do this thing! We're gonna go Diamond!"

"Where do we sign up?" Jane adds. "We've already written down 93 people on our prospect list while you were talking. Let's go for it!"

And over in the corner Sally Smith has just elbowed her husband, sleeping Sam. He looks up and sheepishly mumbles, "Did I hear you say that this was Amway?"

Naturally, you look at Joe and Jane with dollar signs in your eyes, lavishing them with first night literature and a promise to make that follow-up call the next day. You know that they will be walking across stage as new Diamonds in record time.

But as for Sam and Sally Smith, you don't perceive them getting in, let alone doing anything with the business; and so— even though you hand them the same literature and say that you will call—you sigh a silent "Next?" as they walk out the door.

But people are funny. Mr. and Mrs. Joe Jones may call you up the next day and whine, "Well, we talked it over with a neighbor and decided not to... !" The Smiths may be the ones who listen to the cassettes, look over the literature, just "happen" to see an Amway advertisement in a magazine or otherwise admit they have a "need" and something "clicks" to make them decide to build their business to Direct, Diamond and beyond.

That is just an example, but it is not so farfetched. Nearly everyone who has been active in this business very long can tell you stories that would make the ones about the Joneses and the Smiths seem quite ordinary. People are like that.

So how do you build this business?

It comes by following a proven pattern, one that has helped many others build successful, profitable and freedom-oriented businesses.

It happens when you place one building block upon the next, following an architect's blueprint. Like any building contractor, you will come upon situations over which you have little control. You will face always-changing circumstances. But you must adhere to a proven plan if you want to succeed.

As mentioned in previous chapters, no one can lift an entire wall in place by himself or herself, but just as a building can be formed as you place brick upon brick, likewise your business can be built as you work geometrically, teaching others to follow the pattern.

There are many such building blocks. The following are some of the most important principles you will need to build your own business. Everyone who has succeeded in this business has traced each of these blueprint lines with his or her life.

GET STARTED

It has been said that there are only two ways to fail in this referral-based marketing business:

(1) Not get in,

     or

(2) Quit.

That may be a quaint oversimplification, but there is much truth to it. One thing is for certain—you will never be able to cash one single bonus check unless you get started.

How do you begin?

READ THE LITERATURE AND BOOK, THEN LISTEN TO THE TAPES.* Most likely, you were loaned a First Night Pack. Teach your distributors to do the same. Provide first night materials as a service to help your prospect make a decision about the sales and marketing plan. Do them a favor. Have them listen to the people who are successful in the business as you help them decide, not those critics who "tried and failed" or the "experts" who love to put down the Amway Corporation, your line of sponsorship or your ability to build your own business.

Why books and tapes?

Bill Childers, one of the fastest growing Executive Diamonds in this business says:

Books and tapes are the glue to this business.

---

*These items are strongly recommended and available through your upline. However, business support materials are optional and not required.

What comes first, growth or books and tapes? There is no doubt in my mind that the tapes and books have to come first.

What will keep you consistent in building your organization? Books and tapes!

We don't know of anyone who has succeeded and helped countless others to do the same in this business without lots of positive input. You can learn from their example.

GET BACK WITH YOUR POTENTIAL SPONSOR. Ideally, you should see the "circles" a second time as you cement your decision. Count the costs, as you understand them. Ask your sponsor and other upline leaders lots of questions. Ask yourself, "Am I willing to work as hard for myself as I am for my boss?" Or, "Will I start putting aside a few hours a week for my own business and freedom?" (Please understand, we never advocate a person leaving his or her current job until the profits from the business are double one's salary. If a couple makes $40-80,000 at their jobs and attain a network business income level of $50,000,

perhaps it is time for one of them to "retire." Even then we suggest that you counsel upline with your Emerald and Diamond before making the move.)

Remember that your dreams and desires are vital to your success. Without a dream, even in the beginning, you are like a ship without a sail. Make sure that you know what you want from this business? Your dreams are the reason why you take the next steps.

GET AN AMWAY BUSINESS KIT. Okay, you have decided to build your own business. If you haven't done so already, the next step will be to purchase a kit. However, merely signing the application and opening that First Phase box of your kit hardly signals the impending showers of revenue, recognition and rewards.

Success doesn't come in any of the four phases of your kit, because these boxes lack the most important ingredient: **PEOPLE.**

To get those people, you must first create an atmosphere for success. Self-discipline is the basic foundation for building this people-based business, so you must get serious about your decision.

In **Phase 1** of your 4-phase Amway Business Kit (AD-2000), you receive a package of starter products, business materials and audio-visuals.

Phase 2 arrives two to three weeks after Amway receives your application or is notified through telephone sponsoring. The mission of **Phase 2** is to expand the new distributor's product knowledge beyond the products in **Phase 1**.

Arriving two weeks after the previous mailing, **Phase 3** acquaints the new distributor with Amway's training and support materials, with the primary emphasis on product information.

The final package, **Phase 4**, arrives about two weeks after the third. Besides a cover letter from the Amway Policy Board, the new distributor receives a Questionnaire and return envelope. The survey asks a few questions that will help Amway continually improve the Business Kit as well as the Amway business opportunity.

MAKE COMMITMENTS. In addition to your business kit, you should order ten additional products. (Why not use your own products, rather than those bought in a store?)

Then obtain several positive-thinking, self-help books and business-basics cassettes to help you get a quicker knowledge of the most important essentials.*

Before you can excite anyone else about this fabulous opportunity, you must be enthused about it yourself.

---

*These items are strongly recommended and available through your upline. However, business support materials are optional and not required.

FACT: You can search the world for a business like Amway, and yet you cannot find one to match what you have within your grasp now. And when you make a solid commitment to your business, you will one day attain the level of success you desire.

That sort of dedication comes through believing in your business, your goals and yourself. Once that believability factor rises to the proper level, nothing can stop you.

That commitment should lead you toward purchasing a cassette tape player, a marker board (the 2' by 3' size) and easel, as well as several AD PACKS (advertising packs), FIRST NIGHT PACKS, additional books and cassettes* and PRO PACKS (product advertising packs).

All of these are what we describe as "tools of the trade." Just as a carpenter needs a hammer and nails, and as a mechanic cannot work effectively without a box full of screw-drivers and wrenches, so you also need precise tools to produce the proper results. You need business support and training mate-rials—lots of positive, informational, motivational, inspirational and educational input—to succeed. Otherwise, without the proper tools, how are you going to build your own business?

You must also make a commitment to be consistent. This is very important, right from the beginning. You don't build a showcase home by slinging a few boards together and tapping

---

*These items are strongly recommended and available through your upline. However, business support materials are optional and not required.

once in awhile with a rusty hammer. We believe that when you decide to do something, it's best to go ahead and DO IT!

If you are going to poke around, go ahead, but be honest with your sponsor by letting him or her know the percentage of time you will devote to building your business. This allows him or her to budget time for other parts of the organization accordingly.

Time is your most valuable asset (more about this in Chapter Fourteen). Don't waste your hours and days. It is absolutely necessary that you schedule your time. Get *The Schedule Book Pocket Calendar** or the *Your Pattern for Success (Franklin Planner Insert)** and begin writing down the upcoming meetings and activities. Decide how much time you are willing to devote to your business and how fast you want to grow. Plan your work, then work your plan!

Remember, you either create your own environment and control your time, or someone else will.

TAKE ACTION

In talking about getting started, it is apparent that the initial stages of this business involve choices about how you will build your own business.

Let us offer several rock-solid action steps which you must do to succeed.

MAKE A PROSPECT LIST. We'll deal with this in Chapter Eight, but it is certainly worth mentioning here. Get started immediately. Your upline can help with this important project.

LISTEN TO A TAPE A DAY FOR THE FIRST MONTH IN THE BUSINESS. Start benefitting immediately from the wealth of information available to you. Start with tapes from your upline's starter tape sets.*

SIGN UP FOR THE STANDING ORDER TAPE and ASK ABOUT the GO-GETTERS TAPE. Why ride to work with your local deejay's banter when you can spend that time with the most successful men and women in the world of mutual-benefit marketing?

---

*These items are strongly recommended and available through your upline. However, business support materials are optional and not required.

READ DREAM-BUILDING BOOKS. Start with *Don't Let Anybody Steal Your Dream*, *The Magic of Thinking Big* and *Compassionate Capitalism.*

READ THE EIGHT-STEP PATTERN. Go through this powerful information, found in your calendar, every day.

GO TO MEETINGS. Ask your upline about the next seminar and rally. Be there with your downline.

SET BUSINESS GOALS. We suggest that during your first 30 days, you set at least four goals for yourself:

(1) Sponsor five new distributors and begin to work depth on your way to QUICKSILVER.

(2) Qualify as a GO-GETTER by showing the plan at least 15 times per month.

(3) Set a goal to bring ten people to the next seminar.

(4) Do your own 100 points. How? Buy from yourself and merchandise a little or a lot.

ACT THE PART. At first, you may want to emulate people who are building this business successfully. Some might even refer to this as acting, in terms of being an actor, but in reality this is a natural process in your development of a successful, enthusiastic image! At first, admittedly, this image must be developed on faith.

William Shakespeare wrote:

All the world's a stage and all the men and women merely players: they have their exits and their entrances; and one man in his time plays many parts.

Everyone is an actor, but the majority of people dress, think and perform as though they believe they cannot amount to much during their lifetime.

If you want to succeed, you must first envision yourself as successful, then you must practice becoming that person.

Says Dexter:

When I was only 25 years old, I started building my Amway business. There was one major problem: I stuttered. This had been an excruciating, lifelong problem for me.

But I also realized that if I was ever going to be successful in this business, I was going to have to change.

Sure, I was embarrassed and fearful. Sometimes I couldn't complete sentences or express what I really wanted to say. But was I going to let fear and a speech impediment control my future? Absolutely not!

So I began creating mental images of the person I wanted to become. I saw myself successful and speaking with confidence.

Then, in every situation, I tried to act and speak as if I were already an achieving, confident person. As my accomplishments grew, the confidence became REAL, and my increased self-esteem freed me.

Admittedly, my life didn't change overnight, but during the next few years, I grew into the image which I kept pictured in my mind.

Stuttering may not be your problem. Perhaps you are shy or a result of "poverty thinking." You may be "hung up" on limited status symbols or trying to overcome an inferiority complex. Regardless, you know the nature of your personal obstacles, but do you also know what your incredible potential is and how to tap into it while achieving more?

POSITION YOURSELF POSITIVELY

Webster's Third New International Dictionary defines positioning as:

...a spot, situation or condition that conveys some advantage.

Positioning is the strategy designed to enable you to present yourself, your products and your services in the best possible light. With every action centered on creating and maintaining a positive image in the prospect's eyes, a positioned person can obtain a tremendous competitive advantage.

Positioning is persuading a prospect to reach a decision by meeting his or her needs. It is comprised of need fulfillment, solution finding, teaching and helping. Positioning is creating all the right perceptions. It is doing all the things it takes to get others involved in your business—NOW!

Positioning is a combination of many elements:

Listening
Dressing for success
Being an expert on competitive information
Planning
Professional demeanor (posture)
Understanding character types
Integrity
Knowing the sales and marketing plan
Knowing your products and services
Continuing distributor education in your business
Persistence
Goal setting
Maximizing the environment
Organization
Time management
Understanding body language
Self-discipline
Mentorship
Credibility
Single-mindedness of purpose
Using the Yager 8-step pattern properly

There are two issues which can position you well as you start building your business:

• Differentiation

Differentiation is a major key to positioning. You must differentiate yourself, your business and your product from others.

If there is no competition, or if you have a brand new product or service, you can sell based on **features**. You have a niche—a captive market. Basically, you can therefore charge anything you can get for the product or service, and you can make a lot of money (General Motors of the 1960s, IBM of the 1970s, Apple of the 1980s and MicroSoft of the 1990s are prime examples).

But as with the IBM PC computer or Apple Power Book clones, most ideas, products or services are quickly adapted into the mainstream of the marketplace. Your niche product becomes a not-so-special commodity. When that happens, you face stiffer competition. You must therefore begin to emphasize **benefits**.

Differentiation helps you move your product and services back toward competing on unique features, rather than price alone.

If you are able to create a superior perception, then Amway's products and services will be distinguished from the others. That is what you are trying to do through differentiation—to set your product, your company and yourself apart from the crowd.

• Marginal Advantage

One of the best elements of positioning is also one of life's greatest "secrets." You see, you can be a phenomenal success by building only a relatively small advantage in the marketplace.

What do we mean?

You have heard of "winning by a nose." It happens all the time. In 1985 the Kentucky Derby was won by a quarter of an inch and the winning horse sold for $1,000,000. The loser only brought $10,000.

The World Series has often been won by one run in the seventh game.

The Superbowl Championship has been decided several times by less than a touchdown.

recorded
photo finish

The Master's Golf Tournament check has gone to the one-stroke winner in a sudden-death ending.

In 1989, Orel Hershiser shattered baseball salary records by inking a three-year contract worth $7,900,000. On his way to a world championship the previous year, the Los Angeles Dodgers' pitcher kept a portable computer in the dugout which gave marginal advantage information about the batters to whom he would pitch. His intense dedication, superb talent and attention to details helped him win 26 games during the season, and 17 of the games he pitched—including both of his world series outings—were decided by one or two runs.

"Winning by a nose," or the marginal advantage phenomenon occurs outside sports, as well.

In 1960, John F. Kennedy defeated Richard M. Nixon by only 113,000 votes, one-half vote per precinct. Political analysts since then point to the crucial television debate when JFK'S tousled hair and warmth edged Nixon's five o'clock shadow and cold demeanor. Kennedy's people had simply done *a slightly better job of preparation.*

a "slightly better" job of preparation

In any competitive arena, which naturally includes sales and marketing, attention to detail—that marginal advantage—makes all the difference in the world.

Marginal advantage is the center fielder's extra two steps to the left. It is a business manager's last review of a proposal. It is a hotel chain's extra determination to provide "one more" service, such as two Godiva chocolates on the pillow of a turned-down bed.

As a network distribution professional, your professional success will undoubtedly depend on being a percent or two better than the rest, yet that marginal advantage doesn't always come easy.

It requires extra effort. When you are slightly better than others, you can use that marginal advantage masterfully.

Remember, the secret for every top network marketing success lies in the fact that he or she has developed a habit of doing things which mediocre businesspeople don't like to do.

Positioning, simply put, calls for a whole new way of thinking and acting.

ACTION STEPS

If you want to put together all the building blocks we have mentioned in this chapter, try as many of these exercises as possible for the next 30 days:

(1) Set a goal to overcome your insecurities and inadequacies.

(2) Whenever possible, rehearse difficult situations before they happen.

(3) Strive to look your best. A businessperson's clothing influences any viewer's judgement of the wearer.

These prejudices immediately establish or destroy credibility for you. Credibility, you must remember, is one of the most important qualities in any business relationship.

(4) Talk constructively and positively to yourself. Focus on uplifting, constructive adjectives and adverbs. Everything you say to yourself either builds up or tears down your subconscious self-image.

(5) Observe others who appear to be sure of themselves. Accept yourself as you are, but continually seek to upgrade your own standards, lifestyle and behavior patterns by associating with winners within your line of sponsorship.

(6) Concentrate on direct eye contact when you listen and respond. It is one of the most valuable, nonverbal indicators of your growing self-confidence.

(7) Smile a lot! It lets people know that you are both confident and sincere.

(8) Expect success from your earnest efforts to overcome personal shortcomings.

(9) Keep an ongoing list of the personal improvements you have accomplished, are achieving and plan to attain.

Remember—triumphs, especially over our entrenched habits and fears, don't come easily. Still, we can only become what we expect of ourselves. We cannot over-emphasize the power of your thoughts and your words. Reality starts in the mind, then actions must take place to make the thoughts real.

As W. Clement Stone once said:

> *When there is nothing to lose by trying and a great deal to gain if successful, by all means, TRY!*

A FINAL NOTE

Everything depends upon your willingness to change. You alone can position yourself and your enterprise wisely.

You can build on your successes in this business by following the pattern. It's as simple as this to build your own PROFITABLE DISTRIBUTION BUSINESS!

BUILDING BLOCKS:

Positioning starts with a product. A piece of merchandise, a service, a company, an institution, or even a person. Perhaps yourself.

*But positioning is not what you do to a product. Positioning is what you do to the mind of the prospect. That is, you position the product [or the **concept**] in the mind of the prospect.*[1]

AL RIES AND JACK TROUT
Bestselling Authors
and Consultants (USA)

You can only have two things in life, reasons or results. Reasons don't count—except as a motivation for obtaining results. For us, our reason was time. What I saw in the Amway business was an opportunity to make a lot of money without having to work such incredible hours for the rest of my adult life. When I truly understood my reason, building the business became a simple matter of following the proven system. That's when the results happened. The main point is that we didn't sit around thinking about our reasons for building this business. We soon started pointing toward the results. That change made all the difference in the world.

BERT GULICK
Former Restaurant Manager
Executive Diamond
Direct Distributor (USA)

---

1. Al Ries and Jack Trout, *Positioning: The Battle for Your Mind* (New York: Warner Books, 1986, p. 2.

Don't go after money. Go after success. If you have the success, they'll throw the money at you.

ED McMAHON
TV Personality and
Author (USA)

It takes faith to build your Amway business. When you first get started, there are so many things you have to do purely because you have faith in the success system.

Well, I've heard it said that faith is believing what you don't see, and the reward of your faith is eventually seeing what you believe. It takes faith to listen to your upline. It takes faith to keep showing the plan, even when you don't see as many results as you would like.

The great thing about this business is that we have so many heroes who have blazed the trail before us. All we have to do is follow them and our faith will be rewarded.

JIMMY DUNN
International Church
Administrator
Diamond Direct
Distributor (USA)

I think most of us are looking for a calling, not a job. Most of us, like the assembly line worker, have jobs that are too small for our spirit. Jobs are not big enough for people.

NORA WATSON
Bestselling Author (USA)

Hoping and wishing often become excuses for doing absolutely nothing. What the world needs more of are people of action. People who make a difference in life are those who DO things, not those who merely TALK about them.

JIM KINSLER
Former Coach and
High School Teacher
Diamond Direct
Distributor (USA)

The way I see it, if you want the rainbow, you gotta put up with the rain.

DOLLY PARTON
Singer, songwriter
and businesswoman (USA)

Some things about this business are non-negotiable. You have to be committed to your goals. You have to put together a clear-cut action plan. You must refuse to listen to your fears. Refusing to negotiate on these things is the only way to achieve any level of success.

DONNA STEWART
Former Pre-school Teacher
Crown Direct Distributor (USA)

For a long time it seemed to me that life was about to begin—real life. But there was always some obstacle in the way, something to be got through first, some unfinished business, time still to be served, a debt to be paid. Then life would begin. At last it dawned on me that these obstacles were my life.

ALFRED D'SOUZA
Philosopher

Today is such a time of opportunity. With layoffs, business closings, the economic ups-and-downs and people with little security, more and more men and women are looking for something that provides excellent income potential with little capital risk.

The time has never been better for this distribution and marketing business. That's why we are more excited about sharing the Amway opportunity than ever before!

JERREL SHAW
Former Director of USDA
Farm Programs Division
Triple Diamond Direct
Distributor (USA)

The greatest rewards come only from the greatest commitment.[2]

ARLENE BLUM
Mountain Climber
Leader of the American
Women's Himalayan Expedition

To succeed at this business, you've got to keep your mind focused on your dreams and goals. You have to sustain the discipline to keep pushing forward—no matter what the circumstances look like.

Allow the unbelievable momentum of this system to sustain you. This momentum will make your climb toward success a steady climb to the top!

JIM SHIRER
Former School Teacher
Diamond Direct
Distributor (USA)

---

2. Quoted in James M. Kouzes and Barry Z. Posner, *The Leadership Challenge* (San Francisco: Jossey-Bass Publishers, 1987).

When we moved our business (The Better Life Institute) from California to Michigan and began to work with Amway and all of you, we came here strictly for business. But in the process we received a blessing in disguise, and that blessing is Amway. It's you and your leaders and it's who all of you are and became and stand up for. I've experienced it firsthand and I am a better person for it.

PAT ZIFFERBLATT
President, Better Life Institute

You can make it a family affair with this business because you are building it together. I realize that being in business as a couple and involving your children is rather revolutionary to some people, but you don't know how wonderful it is until you have experienced it.

That's why we are always looking for people with whom we can share this business. That's how much we believe in what it can do in anyone's life and how it can help couples and families grow together.

HELEN MCKENNA
Former Teacher
Diamond Direct
Distributor (Australia)

Do the best you can in every task, no matter how unimportant it may seem at the time. No one learns more about a problem than the person at the bottom.[3]

SANDRA DAY O'CONNOR
U.S. Supreme Court Justice

---

3. Sandra Day O'Connor, "Quotable Quotes," *Reader's Digest*, April 1993, p. 17.

When MJ & I got started in this business, we had so many hurdles to get over. I had such low self esteem, a lack of confidence and a fear of failure. But my fear of living my life broke won out over the other fears. That's what motivated me to get started and to do the things that I didn't like doing.

Granted, I stumbled around for awhile, but my dislike of poverty eventually led my wife and I to this level of success. Once we plugged into the system, things started happening.

SCOTT MICHAEL
Former Food Processing Plant Manager
Diamond Direct Distributor (USA)

Action Steps

...Your Guidelines for Getting Started

As we have pointed toward the way you get started, it is apparent that the initial stages of this business involve **your choices** about how you will build your own business. Many of these choices revolve around contacting and inviting.

Let us offer several rock-solid action steps which you must do to succeed.

MAKE A PROSPECT LIST. Start things right by writing out a long list of people who might be interested in making more money and owning a business. Such a file, even from the beginning, is worth its weight in gold. It is your key to getting started. Use the "Who Do You Know?" worksheet (TL-242).*

---

*These items are strongly recommended and available through your Upline. However, business support materials are optional and not required.

Until you are willing to make a list and then move into a starting position (setting up appointments and showing the marketing plan), you really are only a card-carrying member of the club, so to speak, but you aren't really a distributor. Only when you make your list and start to show the plan (STP) are you truly beginning to build your Amway business.

The most frequent mistake made by people who are starting to build their mutual-benefit marketing business is taking this step for granted. Don't make that error! You have probably already thought of a few people who would be great in this business. Now is the time to sit down and compile a list of everyone you know. Dedicate a few hours of your time to this vital step.

Listen to the tape, "Making a List" (DBR 377).* As mentioned previously, making the list and beginning to show the plan to people is how you work the Amway business. Also, as described in Chapter Six, for you to become successful in this business, you need to find at least nine personally-sponsored distributors who want to create more cashflow, diversify their income, produce more time for themselves and develop a greater level of security.

Ask yourself, "If I could pick the first 20 people that want these things, and if they may get in the business anyway—with me or without me—who would those people be?" Write those names on your list. Then add more.

As you make your list, follow several guidelines. Write your list down. Don't pre-judge anyone. Don't separate a "chicken" list ("Maybe I'll show them the plan AFTER I am really successful."). Diligently keep a list of your results. Most importantly, keep your list current by adding and subtracting people.

---

*These items are strongly recommended and available through your Upline. However, business support materials are optional and not required.

212

Your immediate prospects can include:

family,
relatives,
friends,
associates,
your accountant,
apartment landlord,
someone in the armed forces,
bank cashiers,
builders,
those with whom you carpool,
dentists,
doctors,
dry cleaners,
those with whom you fish,
golf buddies,
the grocer,
those at your health club,
your insurance agent,
the lawn keeper,
a lawyer,
your mechanic,
mail person,
minister,
music teacher,
PTA members,
Rotary Club members,
salespeople,
seamstresses,
secretaries,
schoolmates,
teachers,
truck drivers,
the veterinarian,
waiters and waitresses,
        and
work associates.

Continually add to your list by asking yourself:

Who needs to make more money?

Who would like to travel more?

Who wants to be his or her own boss?

Whose lifestyle would drop dramatically if he or she could no longer continue in a chosen profession?

Who is concerned about retirement?

Who needs more financial security?

Who is not able to keep up with inflation?

Who would like to save money?

Who wants more recognition for achievements?

Who has a boss who is giving him or her a hard time?

Who is a responsibility taker?

As you get involved with network marketing, you will probably be pleasantly surprised to find that so many people are searching for solutions that their present jobs and financial situations cannot answer.

Refer back to Chapter Three for some of the industries that are being hit hard by corporate reengineering and down-sizing. Few companies have been untouched. Hundreds of thousands of men and women are looking for an answer to the layoff blues.

You can be part of that solution through the opportunities you will share with those with whom you come in contact.

Get out your address book, your Christmas card list, your school yearbooks and list the names of previous job colleagues. Refer to the additional literature for help in developing your prospect list.

One of the most tragic mistakes made by many new people in the business is to pre-judge people—failing to list people whom they consider to be too busy or too successful to want a business such as ours.

Nothing could be farther from the truth. Take our word: If you want something important done quickly, find a busy person to do it.

It has been said that 20% of the world's population does 80% of the work, and that the remaining 80% does the other 20% of the work. So as you make your prospect list, look for people who are "hungry" for success. They can be broke or rich and still be searching for more in life.

Try to think of people who want to help others succeed.

Again, don't pre-judge. Many distributors have done that, only to see a friend or relative go across the stage as a new Direct but sponsored by someone else!

Get busy filling out your prospect list. Your sponsor will help you add to this group later, but you should start with at least 50 names. Done right, those names may turn to gold.

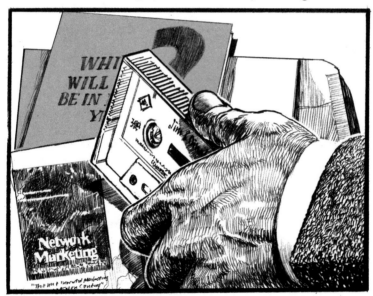

PROSPECTING TAPES: You may wish to use one of the specialized prospecting audio or video tapes and litera-ture to help make this contact. (These are commonly known as Ad Packs.)*

---

*These items are strongly recommended and available through your Upline. However, business support materials are optional and not required.

You have a wealth of interesting and informative cassettes, videos and brochures available to interest men and women in your new business. These are precise, razor-sharp tools to deal specifically with businesspeople, young adults, golden agers, single parents, farmers and so many more. In addition, there are general tapes which can be used for anyone—from a businessperson to a housewife or student.

You can use tapes to intrigue the prospect with the concept of network marketing. You can also loan tapes to follow-up initial conversations.

We will cover how to use tapes to your full advantage in Chapter Nine.

The main point is to GET STARTED! Do something now. Don't put off making your prospect list. Many of the people whom you write down during the first days and weeks may become the lifeblood of your business.

PROSPECTING IS THE KEY

A big stone lay for centuries under shallow Meadow Creek near our home of Charlotte, North Carolina. Then a farmer's young son, Conrad Reed, saw the boot-sized lump and decided to take it home. It was surprisingly heavy, so his father, John Reed, took it to a silversmith in nearby Concord.

The craftsman might have known silver, but he didn't recognize anything valuable about this rock. Disappointed, Reed took it back home and used it for a doorstop for three years. Something about the rock, however, kept intriguing him, so in 1802, he carried it to a jeweler over in Fayetteville. The man looked at it, grunted and scrutinized a bit more, then he offered to buy the pretty rock for $3.50.

Later, Reed heard that he had been hoodwinked by the jeweler. In the end, he demanded and received $3000.

Why?

The rock proved to be a 17-pound gold nugget! It's still one of the largest ever found east of the Rockies. In fact, within a short while, that lump set off the first American gold rush.

What does this story have to do with you?

Our truth is very pointed: You have many "gold-nugget" friends and acquaintances in your life—ones that probably look like lumps and cold stones right now, and many that you still haven't uncovered.

Here are a few facts of life: You cannot make much long-term money in network marketing unless you generate a large volume of business, but you usually cannot generate much volume unless you show this business to a lot of people. You probably won't share this business with too many people unless you first do enough prospecting.

In a nutshell, the foundation of this business is sharing this business with others. You must come face to face with lots of qualified prospects for the entire process to begin.

Every person I have known who has become successful in network marketing has also become a master at prospecting. Let us say without any reservation, your eventual success in building your network marketing business will be determined entirely on your ability to prospect. The larger your selection of prospects, and the more you know about them, the better your chances are for success.

Above all, keep a positive attitude about prospecting. Make it enjoyable. Remember, it is the lifeblood of your business. Good prospecting means good business. The more you prospect, the more successful you will become.

Never forget that prospecting is a business of numbers. If 20 telephone calls and getting out 20 prospecting tapes result in eight appointments; if those eight appointments result in three new business associates, the secret to getting nine new people is simply to make 60 telephone calls and getting out 60 prospecting tapes.

Since getting a number of appointments to show the plan depends upon getting a greater number of turndowns, you also must learn to live with rejection (not of you, but the opportunity). Just as a grain of sand cuts up the inside of an oyster, so failure, rejection and anxiety can cut up our insides. But the oyster has a God-given ability to convert that irritating grain of sand into a pearl. It takes time, of course, but the result is always worth the effort. The great thing, in this business, is that your "pearl" can eventually turn into a "diamond." That is exciting.

THE PROCESS

Gain from your prospecting mistakes. Practice harder. Become tougher, more aware and develop a keen insight into what works for you. Counsel upline.

Certainly you will improve your percentages as you learn better ways to prospect.

Take nothing for granted. Do more checking, more prodding, more observing and you will end up with more prospects than you can handle. That's a problem you would like to have, right?

Begin to expand your network of acquaintances by taking a sincere interest in the people whom you meet every day. Even if they never become prospects for your mutual-benefit networking business, this habit of showing genuine interest in others will make your life more interesting. Compliment people who serve you in stores or restaurants. Take a sincere interest in new people you meet. Ask questions such as:

What are your interests?

How long have you been doing what you are doing?

What do you like best about your work?

Do you see yourself doing your job for a long time?

More specifically, especially for those who find it difficult to think about things to discuss in a conversation, remember the word **FORM**.

> **F**amily
> **O**ccupation
> **R**ecreation
> **M**oney and **M**essage

Ask a number of prospecting questions about a person's **F**amily ("How many children do you have?"), **O**ccupation

("What do you do for a living?") and **R**ecreation ("What do you do when you just want to relax?"). People generally love to talk about the things that they value most.

Money questions are simple:

Do you ever look for ways to diversify your income?

What ways have you found?

How would your life change if you had all the money you wanted?

Then move to **M**essage questions:

Have you ever considered having a business of your own?

Why?

What benefits are you looking for in a business of your own?

Don't follow these ideas by rote. Be flexible. Primarily use the FORM questions as a guideline.

You see, prospecting can be an enjoyable experience. Don't look at people simply as prospects. Take an interest in them. Who knows? Even if they don't get involved in the business immediately, you may still find a friend.

A FINAL NOTE

Above all, add to your prospect list every day. Francis Bacon, the Seventeenth Century English philosopher and statesman, once wrote:

A wise man will make more opportunities than he finds.

You can make your own opportunities by becoming a good list-maker and master prospector.

As you take action you will get results. Remember to develop the basics. And as you find people and teach them those basics, you will then BUILD A SUCCESSFUL NETWORK MARKETING BUSINESS.

BUILDING BLOCKS:

Success is not measured by what a man accomplishes, but by the opposition he has encountered, and the courage with which he has maintained the struggle against overwhelming odds.

CHARLES A. LINDBERGH
(1902-1974)
U.S. Aviation Pioneer

Happiness is found in doing, not merely in possessing. This business has taught Tami and me so much, but one of the more important things is that when you have a purpose, life has true meaning.

You see, without goals and dreams, you merely mark time. That truth is what runs this business, not just the desire for financial flexibility.

MARK CRAWFORD
Former Oilfield Instrument
Mechanic
Diamond Direct
Distributor (Canada)

The purpose of life, after all, is to live it, to taste the experience to the utmost, to reach out eagerly and without fear for newer and richer experience.

ELEANOR ROOSEVELT (1884-1962)
Speaker, Author
and First Lady (USA)

People seem to be able to sense whether you are truly interested in them or not. If they believe that you are genuinely concerned about their dreams and goals, they will be more willing to put in the time and energy which is needed to build their Amway business. We can look back and trace our success to this one fact: We cared about the people who became associated with us in this business. That's the difference. That's also the secret to everything that we've accomplished.

BUNNY WILLIAMS
Homemaker and
Former Bookkeeper
Crown Ambassador
Direct Distributor (USA)

To be always intending to live a new life, but never to find time to set about it; this is as if a man should put off eating and drinking and sleeping from one day and night to another, till he is starved and destroyed.

JOHN TILLOTSON
U.S. Philosopher

The kind of cash flow that can come in from the network marketing business can revolutionize at least 90% of the people whom you know—even people who love what they do and are making good money at it.

RUTH STORMS
Homemaker and
Former Television Host
Diamond Direct
Distributor (USA)

I couldn't wait for success, so I went ahead without it![1]

JONATHAN WINTERS
Comedian and Actor

When you bring this business down to its basics, you begin to realize that it is a very simple process of getting the plan in front of enough people. When you are able to do that, the percentages are pretty high that they will get involved in the business with you. But you must be able to get them to sit down and see the plan. That's why you must become skilled at prospecting. It takes work. It means overcoming your fears. But when you learn good prospecting skills, you are on your way to success.

MERRITT WIESE
Rancher
Diamond Direct
Distributor (USA)

---

1. Jonathan Winters, "Quotable Quotes," *Reader's Digest,* April 1991, p. 33.

People need more than something to do. They need something to live for.

FRANKLIN DELANO
ROOSEVELT (1882-1945)
Thirty-second U.S. President

Something happens inside as you build this business—it strengthens you and makes you appreciate everything else in life so much more. It begins happening when you make the decision to develop relationships and to love people. I believe that everyone has the ability to do those two things, but it all comes down to making the decision to truly care about people around you.

GLENN SHOFFLER
Former School Teacher
and Coach
Diamond Direct
Distributor (USA)

I do not think there is any other quality so essential to success of any kind as the quality of perseverance. It overcomes almost everything, even nature.

JOHN D. ROCKEFELLER (1839-1937)
U.S. Industrialist,
Financier and Philanthropist
Founder and President of
  Standard Oil Company

Since most of the successful people in Amway are married couples, building the business as a single was different, but in no way did that discourage me.

I never cease to be amazed at the people who seem surprised to learn that I built my business to Diamond as a single. Granted, there were times when it would have been easier to have the support of a spouse, but I decided when I got into this business that I was going to build a strong organization—no matter what it took.

After all, all is takes is ONE person who is a big dreamer, a believer in people and an encourager!

GERRY BETTERMAN
Former Investment Banker
Diamond Direct Distributor (USA)

New opinions are always suspected, and usually opposed, without any other reason but because they are not already common.[1]

JOHN LOCKE (1632-1704)
English Philosopher
and Essayist

There are so many benefits to building this business, as opposed to any other opportunity I've ever seen. You can't begin to place a dollar value on the personal growth, the positive impact on your children, the wonderful friendships and the awesome influence you can have on the lives of hundreds of people.

This opportunity came to us as we prayed for a break. Now it has placed us in a wonderful lifestyle!

ALLEN NEUENSCHWANDER
Former Certified Public Accountant
and Certified Financial Planner
Diamond Direct Distributor (USA)

---

1. John Locke, *Understanding* (1690).

*There are a lot of things that make this business work.
One part is consistent, daily effort—prospecting, contacting,
inviting, showing the plan and following through. Perhaps just
as important as those daily efforts, though, is realizing every
day that you are a part of an unbeatable system.*

*When you truly understand how good this system is, your
belief will soar. And with this proven system, daily efforts and
lots of belief, nothing can hold you back.*

DON WILSON
Former Coach and Teacher
Executive Diamond Direct Distributor (USA)
Past ADA Board Officer

*P*rofessional Strides
...Your Contacting and Inviting Skills

As you start building your organization, you must remember that before you can sponsor anyone, you need to get them to see the "circles." Your approach, then, when you contact and invite prospects, is not necessarily to talk about Amway at first. Instead, your basic objective is to get people from each of these groups to look at this business opportunity:

- Friends

- Relatives

- Acquaintances

- Third parties

You will learn to contact people from each of these categories through a variety of methods—from using prospecting tapes (AD PACKS) to telephone approaches and face-to-face meetings.

CONTACTING

We suggest some of the following phrases for contacting:

- *I've started my own business...*

- *We're in the process of expanding...*

- *We're working with mutual-benefit marketing/distribution to provide an advantage for both manufacturers and consumers; plus, there's something in it for entrepreneurs...*

- *I really can't promise you anything, but...*

- *I don't know if you're in a position right now to look at anything, but we had some professionals put together some information on what we're doing...*

- *I'm working with a group of top-flight people to put together some income advantages for paying the higher costs of education and even retiring a lot sooner than they could otherwise...*

- *Like I said, I can't promise you anything, but what I had in mind was letting you go through the material and if it looks good we'll get together for a few minutes and go through the details in the next couple of days.*

- *What is it? A professional distribution business.*

- *What's the name? My own company. (Give it a name)*

- *Who is it? A group of independent businesspeople.*

- *What is it? Well, it would be like trying to explain a McDonald's franchise over the phone.*

- *What's your address?*

That is all. You should never try to explain anything more over the telephone or in person. Say:

I'll go over the details when we get together, Wendell. Mainly, I'd like you to take a look at this and see what interests you most about it.

Or,

I'd love to tell you more, Vivian, but I've only got a few minutes. Trying to explain anything this important over the telephone would be like trying to style your hair through the mail! Is that fair enough?

When talking with a prospect, you shouldn't **push** the Amway name, the products, the fact that selling is involved initially, or anything that might carry a stigma ("part-time" or "a mom and pop business").

Why?

Are we ashamed of Amway, the products or the concept of network marketing? No, of course not! But we would not want anyone to approach us over the telephone about a national hamburger franchise business (up to a cool million-dollar investment, by the way!) or even with a "deal" on an automobile. That approach turns most people off, especially with the increasingly impersonal telemarketing efforts which have blanketed our nation during the past few years.

Every wise businessperson understands that he or she needs as many facts as possible, as well as a detailed explanation of any business venture—*in person*—before making an intelligent decision about becoming involved.

Therefore, you should avoid telling any details to prospects until you can explain *everything*.

Contacting and inviting is incredibly important, but it is important to remember that all you want to do is set a business appointment.

Your sponsor will conduct a meeting in your home (more about this in Chapter Ten) or will do some one-on-ones with you. He or she will present the entire sales and marketing plan in a clear, honest and exciting way.

But your sponsor probably does not know everyone on your prospect list. Therefore, it is up to you to contact and invite them to your meetings. However, your sponsor will sit down with you or your new distributors and help them make several phone calls to show you the right way to contact and invite.

APPROACHES

There are a number of ways to contact and invite people in order to successfully get them to a meeting (their place, your home, an upline's house, or an "open" opportunity meeting). In all cases, your purpose in making the approach is to first get them to go through the AD PACK, not to explain the business. Later you can set an appointment.

As such, you will want to learn how to use these most-common ways to contact and invite, and by doing so you will get the AD Packs into more hands and avoid spending so much of your valuable time with people who aren't looking:

THE TELEPHONE APPROACH: This approach is used with most aspects of the business, so it is good to develop the phone as an excelling tool to contact and invite.

In fact, Alexander Graham Bell's invention is one of the most strategic tools available to anyone who is involved in mutual-benefit distribution.

One of the best advantages of the telephone is that it allows you to control the time spent talking.

Here are a few guidelines for using the telephone to contact and invite:

(1) Keep it short.

Be in a rush. Try to spend no more than one or two minutes on the telephone.

(2) Use a format, especially as you learn telephone skills.

Here is one that works:

• Establish rapport.

- Clear a night or two by asking if the person has a specific evening free.

- Find a need and qualify.

- Create value.

- Confirm the appointment.

- Say goodbye.

(3) Consider using a flexible script, especially at first.

"Ugh!" you say. "Nobody likes canned pitches."

Think about the last television show or movie you watched. Did you stop and say, "Oh, that's not real—aren't they following a format or using a memorized script?"

No, of course not. Most likely you were too wrapped up in the plot to think about a script.

Why? Professional actors using well-written scripts are more "real" than the real people they portray. These well-paid craftspeople are able to take typewritten words and bring them to life.

The beauty of using a script, especially over the telephone, is that you don't have to think about what you're going to say. Instead, you can concentrate on how you are delivering your words and on what is being said by the prospect.

Now, there is no rule that says you must stay exactly with the format. Use words that are warm and comfortable for you. Just don't stray too far.

The FLOW CHART on the following page gives the possibilities for effective telephone approaches and scripts:

FLOW CHART

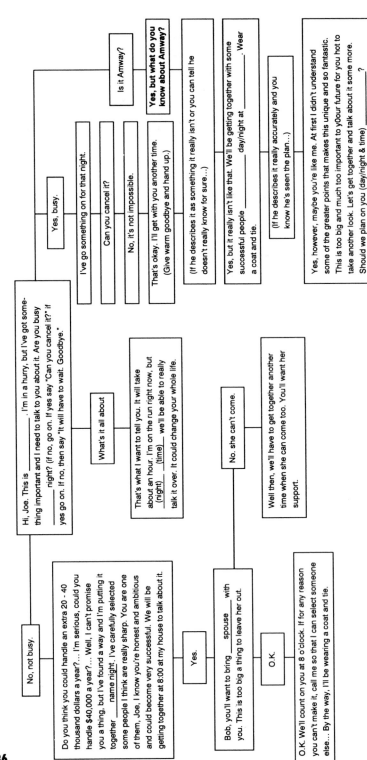

Hi, Joe. This is _____. I'm in a hurry, but I've got something important and I need to talk to you about it. Are you busy _____ night? (if no, go on. If yes say "Can you cancel it?" if yes go on. If no, then say "it will have to wait. Goodbye."

No, not busy.

Yes, busy.

Do you think you could handle an extra 20 - 40 thousand dollars a year?... I'm serious, could you handle $40,000 a year?... Well, I can't promise you a thing, but I've found a way and I'm putting it together _____ name night. I've carefully selected some people I think are really sharp. You are one of them, Joe, I know you're honest and ambitious and could become very successful. We will be getting together at 8:00 at my house to talk about it.

I've go something on for that night.

Can you cancel it?

No, it's not impossible.

That's okay. I'll get with you another time. (Give warm goodbye and hand up.)

What's it all about

That's what I want to tell you. It will take about an hour. I'm on the run right now, but _____ (night) _____ (time) we'll be getting together and we'll be able to really talk it over. It could change your whole life.

Yes.

Bob, you'll want to bring _____ spouse _____ with you. This is too big a thing to leave her out.

No, she can't come.

Well then, we'll have to get together another time when she can come too. You'll want her support.

O.K.

O.K. We'll count on you at 8 o'clock. If for any reason you can't make it, call me so that I can select someone else.... By the way, I'll be wearing a coat and tie.

Is it Amway?

Yes, but what do you know about Amway?

(If he describes it as something it really isn't or you can tell he doesn't really know for sure...)

Yes, but it really isn't like that. We'll be getting together with some successful people _____. Wear a coat and tie. _____ day/night at _____.

(If he describes it really accurately and you know he's seen the plan...)

Yes, however, maybe you're like me. At first I didn't understand some of the greater points that makes this unique and so fantastic. This is too big and much too important to y0our future for you hot to take another look. Let's get together and talk about it some more. Should we plan on you (day/night & time) _____ ?

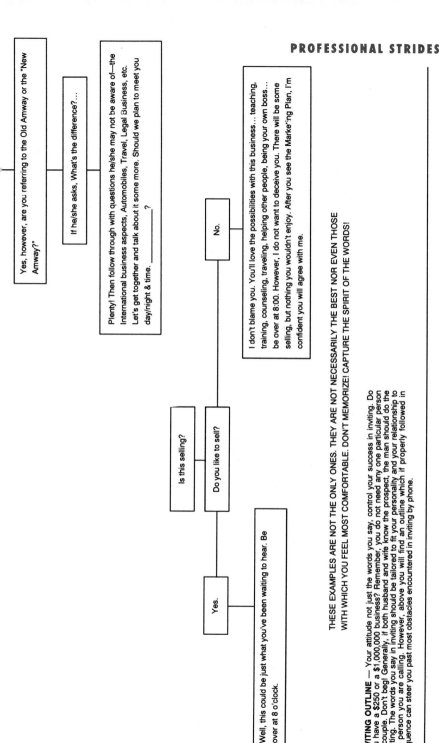

Yes, however, are you referring to the Old Amway or the "New Amway?"

If he/she asks, What's the difference?...

Plenty! Then follow through with questions he/she may not be aware of—the International business aspects, Automobiles, Travel, Legal Business, etc. Let's get together and talk about it some more. Should we plan to meet you day/night & time. _____?

No.

I don't blame you. You'll love the possibilities with this business... teaching, training, counseling, traveling, helping other people, being your own boss... be over at 8:00. However, I do not want to deceive you. There will be some selling, but nothing you wouldn't enjoy. After you see the Marke'ing Plan, I'm confident you will agree with me.

Is this selling?

Do you like to sell?

Yes.

Well, this could be just what you've been waiting to hear. Be over at 8 o'clock.

THESE EXAMPLES ARE NOT THE ONLY ONES. THEY ARE NOT NECESSARILY THE BEST NOR EVEN THOSE WITH WHICH YOU FEEL MOST COMFORTABLE. DON'T MEMORIZE! CAPTURE THE SPIRIT OF THE WORDS!

INVITING OUTLINE — Your attitude not just the words you say, control your success in inviting. Do you have a $250 or a $1,000,000 business? Remember, you do not need any one particular person or couple. Don't beg! Generally, if both husband and wife know the prospect, the man should do the inviting. The words you say in inviting should be tailored to fit your personality and your relationship to the person you are calling. However, above all, you will find an outline which if properly followed in sequence can steer you past most obstacles encountered in inviting by phone.

237

TELEPHONE SCRIPT

Using the FLOW CHART, take a few moments, preferably with the guidance of your upline, to write out a script that feels comfortable to you.

_____
_____
_____
_____
_____
_____
_____
_____
_____
_____
_____

This script may change as you get more familiar with the telephone approach. Revise it often, but always seek the advice of your upline.

One final point about scripting: Write it like you talk, not as you write. Use contractions and smaller words. Don't do anything to sound stilted or phony.

As you are working on your script, make sure you have a good response to the "What is it?" and "Is it...?" questions. Preparation is the key. Don't be afraid of questions, since they mean that your prospect is curious.

(4) Practice, practice, practice!

Use the script and contacting phrases we have already shared—practicing them word-for-word.

You probably learned to drive in the parking lot or on dusty backroads. Likewise, spend time practicing in safe situations—a "dead" telephone is great—before you actually start contacting and inviting.

Every minute you practice, you up your odds at becoming a master prospector.

(5) Seek to arouse curiosity.

Use phrases which we have already mentioned, such as "interactive distribution," "referral-based marketing" or "mutual-benefit marketing."

There is certainly nothing wrong with mentioning "Amway" (notice the next principle), but you may make a mistake by volunteering that information over the telephone (unless you are asked).

Over the years we have found that people have developed some gross misconceptions about the word "Amway," such as:

• They think it's door-to-door selling.

• They think we just market soap.

• They think it is some sort of pyramid scheme where you take advantage of friends or family.

- They know someone who stayed in the business for two weeks and quit because they weren't rich yet!

- Their friends or parents were in Phase One, Two or Three Amway, and they didn't appreciate it.

- They were in the business before and didn't have the upline assistance or training system working for them, and—as a result—it didn't work and they quit.

- They were in the business before with an organization that concentrated solely on selling.

- They joined one of the many network marketing clones that described itself as "just like Amway, only better," but it ended up being a front-loading rip-off and now their garage is filled with boxes of unsalable merchandise.

- They knew someone in Amway but did something that caused a loss of respect.

There are many reasons why people might misunderstand it when you start out a conversation using the word "Amway." Don't walk into that trap.

And as mentioned earlier, be brief. Don't explain everything you know over the telephone.

(6) Don't get people to see the circles under any false pretense.

This doesn't discount our suggestion that you not volunteer the fact that you have an Amway business.

There is no need for deception. Just let people know, in a few minutes, that you are inviting them to hear about an exciting opportunity to make more money. This is the main reason we suggest using AD PACKS.

If the person asks if you are talking about Amway, never lie. One point to remember, however, is that getting the "Is this Amway?" question, while never fatal, probably points to a lack of preparation or confidence. Seek guidance with your upline if the "Amway" question comes up repeatedly.

(7) Use the phrase, "I can't promise you anything." During a short telephone conversation, this statement takes the excuses away from the prospect.

(8) Answer a question with a question.

The purpose of the telephone call is not to give a lot of information. It is only to set up an appointment to drop off an AD PACK or to set up a meeting.

(9) Become a good listener.

Listening is critical to your prospecting and overall success. It is a skill that constantly needs refreshing.

(10) Develop your telephone voice.

This sounds obvious, but very few people ever do anything to position themselves powerfully over Alexander Graham Bell's brainchild.

In reality, over the telephone, our voice is the primary thing we have going for us, isn't it? So, how do we begin to improve our telephone voice?

- Speak loudly enough over the phone that you can be heard (Nothing is worse than straining to hear what someone is saying…), but not too loud (…except having to hold the receiver six inches from your head to protect your ear drums!).

- Work on pronunciation and diction.

- Use vocal variety in terms of speed and volume (in other words, don't use a monotone).

- Become an actor, of sorts, by using your voice to paint pictures in the prospect's mind.

(11) Be enthusiastic.

The last four letters of enthus**IASM** can stand for **I Am Sold Myself**?

Enthusiasm is a sign of belief that your prospects can detect easily. They can tell if you really believe what you are talking about. If you sound like a monotone recording or like someone who is not really involved, you will lose your prospect's interest. Be lively!

(12) Be prepared.

It's not just a Boy Scout motto. As a prospector, you can thrive on total preparation, both on the telephone and in person. Know when you can drop off a tape or set up a meeting. Don't wait until you get a "yes" to start looking for open dates.

(13) Smile before you dial.

As with enthusiasm, your warmth and helpful attitude come through loud and clear over the phone.

(14) Move around if you can.

Whether you use a handset or headset, this principle will help.

Some people who are successful at using the telephone like to stand up while they are on the phone, believing that it helps them stay "up" for the conversation, rather than becoming sluggish.

(15) Consider using a mirror while you talk.

Some of the best prospectors use this method. This gives you an opportunity to "see" what you sound like on the other end of the telephone.

(16) When you speak to prospects, remember that they are busy.

Your first job is to break their preoccupation with other things. Do it with questions.

(17) Be jealous of your own time.

During telephone prospecting, you will be able to find 1001 other things to do. Set a definite time for telephoning, and stick to it—no matter what.

One final note for telephone prospecting: Don't pressure people to come to a meeting. You have a terrific business opportunity to share, not a disease you are trying to give away! Don't beg people to take a look at your plan. In everything you do, especially over the telephone, position yourself as a thoroughly professional business-person.

THE BEST-FRIEND/CONSULTING APPROACH: This form of contacting and inviting can probably be used only during the early phase of your business.

It takes place when you call a close associate or see a friend. You explain:

> *Loyd, are you going to be home for a few minutes? Yes? Great! I've got some information and I'm going to swing by. I won't be able to stay. I'll see you in a few minutes. Goodbye.*

You can also say:

> *I'm excited about a new business venture. Since you are successful at what you are doing, I'd like you to look at this opportunity and tell me what you like best.*

When the prospect questions you, say:

> *I'm just getting started, and I don't really know enough to explain it clearly. So, can I set up an appoint-ment to let one of my associates explain the details.*

When you arrive at the prospect's house, keep the car running, don't go inside the house, be in a hurry and say:

> *I need you to listen to this tape tonight. I'm moving on this business real fast. I'll get back to you tomorrow night for a half-hour or so.*

If the prospect asks you what this is all about, just answer:

> *It's all in the information. I've got to run. Goodbye.*

You can also use the BEST FRIEND/CONSULTING APPROACH when you first start drawing the circles for your-self. With a friend, say:

You are under no obligation, Curt, but I'm just starting to learn some important parts of my new business venture, and I would like to share them with you to get your positive feedback.

Whichever approach you use, you are giving a compliment to your friend or relative. Few true friends, even if they know what your "new business" is, can turn you down under those circumstances.

Most importantly, **you are arousing curiosity so you can explain the sales and marketing plan to them.**

THE PROFESSIONAL CURIOSITY APPROACH: This method can take many different forms, but the primary purpose is to whet a person's interest enough to come see the circles being drawn, without giving away too much information that would cause prejudice against your plan.

As mentioned earlier, we are of the opinion that the professional approach, in whatever form you use, is the best. We are also sure that you could carry a sign around in the middle of your town proclaiming: "AMWAY MEETING TONIGHT... ASK ME FOR DETAILS" and eventually get people to your meeting. The question is this: Which method works best?

After all these years in the business, we still teach what we consider to be the best way to contact and invite by using curiosity.

Get the small talk out of the way, then say something like this:

> *Listen, Don, I can't promise anything, but I am involved in an exciting business venture, and I feel that you are the kind of sharp person I am looking for to make some serious money. Now, I don't have time to get into all the details right now, but I would like to sit down with you and to show you what I'm doing. Check your calendar and see if you are available for Thursday evening around eight. Karen will be with me, so will Trish be available?*

Or,

> *Jim, this is Vernon. I'm putting together a business project. It looks like there can be a good deal of money to be made, and I thought I'd let you in on it. Of course, I can't promise you anything, but how soon can we get together? I think it's also very important that our wives are informed on what we are doing. I'll have Lou with me. Will Monica be able to make it, too?*

If the answer to "Will your wife be able to make it?" is no, say:

> *That's no problem. I believe it's important for Monica to hear what we will discuss, so she can help in your decision. Let's choose, say, Saturday evening. Is that better? Yes? Great!*

If there are any questions, say:

> *I'm not really qualified at this point to answer any questions, but the people I'm getting involved with have agreed to allow me to have a couple of people here to get their opinion of the concept.*

> *So just come take a look and tell me what interests you. If it turns out to be as good as it looks, I don't want*

you asking me later why I didn't call you about it. So you and Monica, come on over for coffee at 8 p.m, Thursday night.

If a prospect asks, "Can't you tell me more?" say:

Look, Brenda, I know you are a busy person, and I would never waste your time. I'm not really qualified to explain anything yet. Just come and take a look and tell me what interests you.

If the person doesn't make a firm commitment, say:

I really respect your opinion, but my friend who is already involved in this mutual-benefit concept told me that he only wanted to talk to people whose opinions I respect. I thought of you first, but I have to know if you are going to be there. If you're not, I have someone else to call.

If a prospect waffles or says, "I'll try to get there," you might say:

*Well, Mabel, my Grandpa used to say that when someone says they're going to **try** to do something, there's a strong chance that it's not likely to happen. This particular get-together is important, so I need to know for sure if you are coming. If you're not, I have someone else to call.*

Plus, I know you're a woman of your word, so if you say you'll be there, you'll be there.

If the person is management or executive level, or if you know he or she has an interest in international business, you can say:

You know, Harold, I've been looking at ways to generate more income and security. From my conversations with you and Mary, I think you're looking for the same thing.

I have been introduced to something that has been extremely successful in Japan, Europe and around the world. Some people I know are expanding the same concept here in our country. I'm not really qualified to answer any questions, but I would really like to have you meet with my friend about this. I'd like your opinion on this.

Plus, it would be great to see you again and talk about some of the ideas we've talked about in the past.

Again, don't be deceptive. Let the person understand that you are inviting him or her to a business meeting. If you are asked questions, counter with your own questions (refer again to the telephone FLOW CHART approach).*

Under no circumstances, as you approach people, should you immediately get involved in a detailed explanation of the Amway Sales and Marketing Plan or the finer points of network marketing or worldwide distribution systems.

Many people have a hard enough time understanding the business after they see the circles drawn, so giving out fragments of the business, either in person or over the telephone, will only cause them either to be prejudiced or to be confused.

We believe the best procedure or technique is to simply hand the prospect an AD PACK. Generally, under these circumstances, you won't find yourself in uneasy situations.

---

*When expressly asked, "Is it Amway?" you should never deceive him or her in any way; rather answer with the following as an example only: "Yes, but which are you referring to, the Phases One, Two or Three Amway or the Phase Four Amway?" Then continue with the appropriate approach.

There are many variations on the above approach techniques, such as the one in which you mail an AD PACK to the prospect:

> *You know, Mark, I am looking for a couple of key people who are interested in making some serious money. I can't promise you anything, and I'm moving on it real fast.*
>
> *I'll mail you and Sheila some information and if it sounds like something you would be interested in, then we'll get back with you in the next few days. I'd like to sit down with you sometime and explain my business, then perhaps you could recommend several friends or associates to me.*

PROSPECTING CASSETTES: We have already mentioned the AD PACKS. One of the real assets to this business has been the introduction of such InterNet tapes as:

"In Search of Financial Freedom"

"Your Financial Options"

"Economic Choices for Today"

"Choosing the Best Network Marketing Business"

"Networking: the Marketing Concept for the 90s"

"How Will You Survive Financially in the 90s?"

"Personal Business Ownership"

"Time and Money"

"Why You Should Be Your Own Boss"

"Seize the Future"

"Business Paradigms"

Also, consider using one of the professional testimonial tapes which are available. "Professionals at Cancun," "Professionals at Hilton Head" and "Professionals at Lake of the Ozarks" are three of the best.

A great tape to use is "Economic Paradigms and the Power of Distribution" by best-selling author and economist Paul Zane Pilzer, (cassette or video) or "Exercising Your Options," (video).

We even have one entitled "Why Amway?" for friends and relatives.

Many of these cassettes or videos also have a glossy brochure which complements the tape for you to hand out.

You can choose specialized prospecting tapes which focus on single parents, young adults, golden agers, farm families and more.

When using the cassettes, be brief and to the point. Let the cassette do its work.

If, for example, you call first to ask about dropping off a tape, say:

Hi, Dave. I'm part of a business with some other successful people. I think you might be interested. I've grabbed a cassette and a piece of literature, and I'd like to drop it off. I won't have time to come in because I'm in a hurry.

Are you going to be around for the next half hour? Great! See you in a few minutes. Goodbye.

As mentioned before, when you arrive at the home, leave your car running, run up to the house and knock.

I'm really excited about this business concept. Can you listen to this cassette and look over this brochure? I'd like you to let me know what questions you have.

Is there a chance you can listen to it tonight? It's important because I need to get it back as soon as possible!

Great, Dave! I'll call you tomorrow when you get off work. What time do you get home?

During the phone call or when dropping off the tape, a prospect may ask, "What's this all about?"

Simply answer:

Look, Glenda, I'm really pressed for time. I've got to be somewhere in a few minutes. The tape will answer

*a lot of your questions, so why don't I call you after
you listen to the cassette?*

When you call back after the person has listened to the
tape, say:

> *Richard, I know you've gone through the informa-
> tion. I'm pressed for time, and I can't promise any-
> thing, but I'd like to swing by about eight tonight to
> explain more of the details.*

> *It'll take 30 to 45 minutes to give you an overview,
> and I'll probably bring my wife with me, so why don't
> you have Lorene sit in with us. It's that important!*

> *See you about eight. Goodbye.*

(Hang up before cheering!)

Or, if you want to invite the person to an open meeting
after he or she listens to a prospecting cassette, you may use
this approach:

It's exciting, Daniel, and I'm sure you want to know more about it. Are you free tomorrow night at eight? Great!

Why don't you and Lora swing by my house (or another meeting place), because it so happens that an associate of ours who is very successful will be covering more details on how it all works, and I'd like for you to ride with us.

Or you can say:

I've learned more about the program we've discussed. The more I learn, the more excited I get. I need my materials back, but I also need to set up an appointment for you to see the program.

If he or she agrees, set up an appointment.

If he or she says, "I need more time," or "I haven't looked at the stuff yet," say:

Michael, I know you're a man of your word. If I leave it one more night, will you take the time to listen to it?

Then wait for a response. If the person says, "Well, I'm just not interested," say:

It's okay, Mike. At some point you may be interested, but for right now I need to get my materials back for another person who is interested. Let's stay in touch.

If the prospect simply isn't interested, don't try to argue or convince the person that he or she is wrong. Why burn bridges?

Above all, when you are prospecting, contacting and inviting, don't be a **SAP!** In other words, don't talk about **S**elling **A**nd **P**roducts *at first*, due to the fact that many prospects may have negative feelings about sales. If they prejudge and close their minds to the full potential, everyone loses. Again, this is the reason we recommend that you simply use the AD PACKS. Follow the process that works so well throughout the world.

A FINAL NOTE

The main point to remember is that you must always keep looking for dream-directed, success-oriented people with whom you can share your business.

So what if a few men and women turn you down? Not everybody is looking!

Trust us—there are many, many more people in your community who are praying to find a way to make additional income. At present there are at least 25% who are working second jobs just to make ends meet.

Remember, by the year 2000, it is estimated that one out of every two people in the U.S. alone will be involved in network marketing. That might seem high, but with so many advancements and credibility-builders on the horizon, people all around you will get committed to building an Amway business whether you sponsor them or allow someone else to do it.

Finding a few men and women who are willing to build this business is worth the effort, even though it may mean that you must screen through those who don't want it.

Billy Florence, an extraordinary Diamond, shares:

If someone says, "Well, I need to know more about this right now before I can commit to coming to your house," you need to build up your positive image more or you are simply talking to the wrong person.

The same thing goes if you face an inordinate amount of problems when you ask about dropping off or mailing tapes.

If someone has to check something out thoroughly over the telephone, even before they listen to a prospecting tape or read a piece of literature, then I would rather go work with somebody else.

Here's why: I have found that this kind of person will drag his or her feet on everything. Probably the worse thing to happen would be for this person to get in the business with you.

And that is really what prospecting and contacting is all about. It is a chance for you to qualify people. That's what you are doing. When you think of it that way, your entire attitude toward this process should change.

Posture yourself positively and professionally. Stay in control of each situation.

If you really believe that you have the greatest opportunity available, then the least you can do is to let your friends, family, acquaintances and other success-oriented people know about it. They can judge the circles for themselves. If your belief level is not yet high enough, then you need to listen to more tapes, read more books and attend more meetings.*

You can learn to make the right contacts. We believe in you. Your upline believes in you. Just don't get "cold feet" over a few simple rejections.

You can do it.

You can have fun meeting people as you BUILD YOUR OWN SUCCESSFUL REFERRAL MARKETING BUSINESS!

---

* These are strongly recommended and available through your Upline. However, business support materials are optional and not required.

BUILDING BLOCKS:

Keeping so many people motivated to do the best job possible involves a lot of different programs and approaches we've developed at Wal-Mart over the years, but none of them would work at all without one simple thing that puts it all together: appreciation. All of us like praise. So what we try to practice in our company is to look for things to praise. Look for things that are going right. We want to let our folks know when they are doing something outstanding, and let them know they are important to us.[1]

SAM WALTON (1920-1992)
Founder of Wal-Mart Stores
and Sam's Clubs (USA)

This business has brought so many wonderful things to us. Time has proven the staying power of this business, and we're more excited than ever because the future holds so much in store for people who get involved and make the commitment necessary to reach their goals.

CHARLOTTE COURTNEY
Former Dairy Farm Owner
Executive Diamond
Direct Distributor (USA)

---

1. Sam Walton with John Huey, *Made in America: My Story* (New York: Doubleday, 1992), p. 140.

The tragedy of mankind is not this or that calamity, but the waste of man's potential for greatness.

WILLIAM ELLERY
CHANNING (1780-1842)
Nineteenth Century
Boston Clergyman (USA)

Success in this business largely centers on getting out of your comfort zones. Sure, it is uncomfortable for most people to prospect, contact and invite. Your mind will bring up lots of things to do instead. But when you force yourself to get out of your comfortable ruts, you begin to find a new strength and power inside you. By facing your fears, you face yourself. By facing yourself, you begin to realize that you can do whatever it takes to carve out a successful lifestyle for yourself and your loved ones.

DWIGHT SMITH
Former Corporate Manager
Diamond Direct Distributor (USA)

No matter what it is called—personal agenda, purpose, legacy, dream, goal, or vision—the intent is the same. Leaders must be forward-looking and have a clear sense of the direction that they want their organizations to take. [2]

JAMES M. KOUZES AND
BARRY Z. POSNER
Bestselling Authors (USA)

2. James M. Kouzes and Barry Z. Posner, *The Leadership Challenge* (San Francisco: Jossey-Bass Publishers, 1987).

People are as happy as they decide to be. If one wants to be happy, he or she must think happy and act happy. If a person wants to be successful, he or she must think success and act successful.

The way we think determines the way we are viewed by others, so people's responses to us essentially come from ourselves.

LINDA HARTEIS
Former Secretary
Double Diamond Direct Distributor
(USA)

Success is not measured by the heights one attains, but by the obstacles one overcomes in their attainment.

BOOKER T. WASHINGTON
(1856-1915)
U.S. Inventor and Educator

I probably didn't appear to be an ideal prospect to any Amway distributors who knew me. I had spent many years in education. Sue Lynn and I survived, but there was always something simmering just below the surface. We wanted more from life.

When I saw the plan, I was very interested. I was tired of the politics in the educational system. I wanted something that would reward me for my time and effort, rather than paying me a predetermined salary which was based on a set of administrative guidelines.

I am proof positive that you should never prejudge a prospect, and this business has changed everything for Sue Lynn, me and our family.

RICK SETZER
Former High School Teacher
Triple Diamond Direct
Distributor (USA)
Former ADA Board Officer

*The most persuasive person in the world is the man who
has a fanatical belief in an idea, a product, or a service. The one
common denominator of all great men in history is that they
believed in what they were doing. If we could choose but one
lantern to guide our footsteps over the perilous quicksands of the
future, it should be the guiding light of dedication.*[3]

CAVETT ROBERT
Speaker, Bestselling Author,
Former Lawyer
and Founder of the National
Speakers Association (USA)

*Nobody said this business would be easy. It wasn't easy
for this eighteen-wheeler driver from Texas. It wasn't easy for
Beatrix either, since her background was in computers, not
business. We had to change, especially me. We had to decide that
changing was less painful than staying the way we were—
broke! Once we made that decision, we got rid of the notion that
things were supposed to be easy. We knew we were on an uphill
climb—at least for awhile.*

*Here's the thing: This system, though nobody promises
that it will be easy, is simple. It's simple enough that anyone
can plug into the system.*

*The secret to this business is to forget about making it
easy. Accept the changes. They are part of the package. Instead,
concentrate on the simple things, the duplicatable pattern.*

Do the simple things and eventually it becomes easier.

LEN GRIFFIN
Former Truck Driver
Diamond Direct
Distributor (USA)

---

3. Cavett Robert, "How to Attract Success," *Og Mandino's University of Success* (New York: Bantam
Books, 1982), p. 298.

Do your homework and know your facts, but remember it's passion that persuades.[4]

H. JACKSON BROWN, JR.
Bestselling Author

Your dreams can come true with this business, but only if you learn to work together as a team. You can build this business for awhile by yourself, perhaps, but you need other people to put together an organization that is both deep and wide.

Focus on building relationships. Learn to develop lasting relationships. Keep this priority in view, and the rewards will follow.

AMY GRANT
Former Personnel Manager
Double Diamond
Direct Distributor (USA)

Discovery consists of looking at the same thing as everyone else and thinking something different.[5]

ALBERT SZENT-GYORGYI
Nobel Prize Winning
Physician (USA)

4. H. Jackson Brown, Jr., *Life's Little Instruction Book*, Volume II (Nashville, TN: Rutledge Hill Press, 1993).
5. Quoted from Roger von Oech, Ph.D., *A Whack on the Side of the Head* (New York: Warner, 1983).

We never imagined, even in our wildest dreams, what was available at Diamond. And we are just beginning!

Our story is a simple message—just get started and never quit. Whatever you do, base your decisions on information you receive from winners and doers, not whiners and doomsdayers. Listen to the people who are making this business work.

Follow the system, and you can make it happen for you, too!

JOHN MINAUDO
Former U.S. Navy Officer
Diamond Direct
Distributor (USA)

A man may perform astonishing feats and comprehend a vast amount of knowledge, and yet have no understanding of himself. But suffering directs a man to look within. If it succeeds, then there, within him, is the beginning of his learning.

SOREN KIERKEGAARD (1813-55)
Danish Philosopher and Author

I was excited about the potential of this business from the very beginning, knowing that our dairy would never give us the lifestyle we wanted. We certainly didn't want to be at the same place—financially, emotionally and career-wise—ten years down the road.

JAMES BEAUCHAMP
Former Dairy Farmer
Diamond Direct Distributor (Australia)

From the very first time you see the plan—to each meeting that you hold and every new pin level that you reach—you should realize that each experience is another opportunity to grow.

So what if you make mistakes? Everyone does. So what if you don't draw the circles perfect every time? No one does. It's your excitement about the opportunity and the way you build dreams that will cause others to get involved in the business with you.

DON STORMS
Former Recording Artist and Broadcast Executive
Construction Business Owner
Diamond Direct Distributor (USA)
ADA Board Member

Construction
...Your First Meetings

You have learned how to prospect. You have also learned how to contact and invite properly. Now, how about that first meeting?

That initial get-together is extremely important for you and your business. Its significance places even more value on the approaches you are learning to make.

Concerning that first meeting, it is crucial to remember why those people you invite would consider giving up an evening in front of the television to drive over and listen about your business opportunity.

Why would they come?

Obviously, there are few people who—honestly—would not like to make more money. However, most people feel that they are overtaxed, underpaid, overrun by inflation and insecure about a down-scaled lifestyle in the future.

Nearly everyone, when candid, knows about the economic problems we face as we look toward the 21st century. But it is up to you, or you and your sponsor, to offer hope to them.

Therefore, *the attitude you carry into that meeting, especially the first one, has an added dimension of importance.*

FIRST MEETING

Ideally, your sponsor will give you suggestions for contacting and inviting, and he or she will show the plan for you at first, but it is up to you to get the people into the living room.

Here are seven recommendations for setting up your first get-together:

(1) Pick two or three definite nights for your first meetings, based upon your schedule and your sponsor's time-table.

(2) Invite *twice as many people* as you think will come. It is not unusual that some invitees will have last-minute conflicts or changes.

(3) Make the meeting room comfortable, but keep the room in its natural form. Put out less chairs than you will actually need. Keep extra chairs out of sight and bring them in only as the seats fill up.

(4) Place the marker board opposite from the room's entrance; therefore, any late arrivals will disrupt the meeting to a lesser degree.

(5) Do not have children or pets in the meeting room. If anyone shows up with either, your sponsor's spouse, your spouse or you should promptly and tactfully take the potential distraction into another area of the house and plan on babysitting while the meeting takes place.

(6) Men should wear a dress shirt, tie and coat, and pay particular attention to shining your shoes. Women should wear a dress or skirt and blouse. This is a business meeting, and proper dress is crucial, even if only your next-door neighbors are coming.

(7) Plan to serve refreshments after the meeting or when your sponsor designates, and always keep everything

simple (Active 8® Drink, SNACK SENSE™ treats, SUN-LIGHT™ Tea, NINE TO FIVE™ Coffee and other Amway products). Don't serve alcoholic beverages.

(8) Greet people at the door in a friendly way.

(9) Give your sponsor a 3 X 5 or 4 X 6 card with the names and occupations of the people in attendance.

(10) Take the phone off the hook during the entire meeting or turn on the answering machine so the phone doesn't ring.

(11) If only one couple shows up for the meeting, act as if they were the only ones important enough to be there. Be excited about them, and forget the no-shows.

Above all, keep things simple! The Amway business works so well because it is easily understood by people who are truly looking for something more in life.

By the way, plan on definitely having the meeting, no matter who says they can come or not. Your sponsor has set aside time, so cancelling the meeting is not an option. Make sure that you have as many people as you can. Make good use of your sponsor's time.

Just be realistic. Things happen that we can't control. Sometimes people really do have a good excuse for missing the meeting. That's why you need to invite twice as many people as you expect.

Also, don't be disappointed—no matter what. If the "unthinkable" happens—nobody shows up—it's not fatal. People who are Diamonds have reached that level primarily because they have gone through more no-shows than others.

Relax and have fun. Remember that your first meeting, as important as it is, is not your last chance. It is merely your first step. Do your part in making it successful.

CONDUCTING THE MEETING

Begin on time. Don't wait for latecomers (10-15 minutes is okay for social conversation). If someone is late or doesn't show up, don't mention it to those who are there. The ones who came are the ONLY ones who are important to you during the evening. They should feel as if they were the only men and women who were invited.

10–15 Minutes

On a related note, don't set up chairs until people arrive (bring out more chairs only when you need them). Don't set up the board until the meeting starts (some people may have a negative response). Also, take the phone off the hook before the meeting starts, (turn off the ringer or turn on the answering machine), and don't put it back on the hook until after the meeting is over. (Who needs the distraction?)

As each person arrives, tell your upline (or the person who will show the plan) a little about each guest. It is very helpful for your upline to know something about each person's background.

The host of the meeting (which is YOU if the get-together is in your home), should introduce the speaker (generally your sponsor or upline Direct). Use a few short phrases, such as the following (which you can read from a card if you are unsure of yourself):

My wife (or husband) and I are just getting started in a fantastic business. We are very excited because a good friend and business associate, Bill Jones, has offered to come and explain the opportunity to you, and he knows what he is talking about! We're going to build this business, and we would love to have you join us. Now, let's welcome Bill Jones?

Take notes and record the meeting. Be alert and smile a lot.

After two or three presentations, you will want to start presenting the plan yourself. Mainly, however, you want to do this to let people know that you are excited and committed to your new business.

You and your spouse should be the most interested people in the room. Don't interrupt the speaker, but let people see the excitement in your eyes and body language.

If you have questions, save them until after the meeting. This way, the newest person or people can ask any questions they may have.

THE MEETING FORMAT

There are three primary objectives for showing the plan. The first is very important—to uncover a need, a dream, a "Why?" inside each person in attendance. The second is to show how the Amway Sales and Marketing Plan will fill that need, dream and "Why?" Then, you should follow-up and follow-through by getting the prospect around your upline or the next upline activity (open meeting, seminar and rally or major function).

Just understand that the main purpose of showing the plan is finding a need. People get into the business because they see a way to fill a need they have: more time, more money, more security, less pressure, a business of their own, a better lifestyle or one of a thousand other reasons. People don't want to get into the business, but they want the results that the business can provide. You need to focus on what they want and how the business can help them get it.

With that in mind, let's go directly to the meeting. Your sponsor will use his or her own style of presentation, but the following format will serve as a guide:

(1) Introduction of the speaker (2 minutes).

(2) The speaker sets new prospects at ease with small talk about appropriate current events and a little humor (2 minutes).

(3) Comparison of the 5-10 year plan and the 45-year "rut" system (8-10 minutes).

(4) Dream session—goals and the importance of setting aspirations into a specific time-frame. Paint a picture of the dreams each prospect can have by reaching goals. Unless the people who are present have a dream, or can get one, they won't need the plan (10-15 minutes).

(5) Presentation of the sales and marketing plan (15-20 minutes).

(6) History of the Amway Corporation (5 minutes).

(7) Building credibility in the line of sponsorship and relating to the prospects. Show the Profiles of Success. Talk about your Upline, their children, previous occupations and background information (5 minutes).

(8) Wrap-up and possibly another short dream session. Offer first night INFORMATION PACKS for those who are serious about the business and seem open to listening to tapes (5-10 minutes).*

(9) Follow through: The plan is not over until you have set some appointments within the next 24-48 hours and/or booked the next plan. (More about this in a few pages.)

CLOSING THE MEETING

During the refreshment break, the hosts should have everybody serve themselves at a snack table. This tends to get everyone mixing together. Don't serve people where they are sitting. Here is where you begin your follow through program.

Generally, those who are interested will start asking you or your sponsor questions. Listen to the way your sponsor answers. Questions do not always indicate antagonism or disbelief. They often signal interest and a desire to know more.

Above all, keep the conversation on the business. Don't get sidetracked talking about the children or how the local football team is doing.

As their questions persist, suggest:

For those who would like us to, we will stay to answer questions and provide information about how to get started.

Remember not to pressure your prospects. They may think that you desperately need them. This approach often repels potential associates.

For those who are interested, set the next meeting while your sponsor and your prospects are together. You can say to a prospect, for example:

---

*We recommend introducing the *Amway Sales and Marketing Brochure* (SA-4400) at this time, as it should be made clear to **all** distributors that **all** prospects **must** be given this piece of literature.

We've been drinking coffee at our house tonight. How about if tomorrow night we drink some coffee at your house so we can both get another look at this business?

Or,

There's another get-together at my sponsor's house Friday night. It will be a great opportunity for you to meet some other people who are in business with us, and you can look at the plan again. Jane and I can pick you up at 7:30. Is that time okay for you?

You want every prospect to walk out the door excited about seeing the circles again. You also want each to leave with a sense of urgency—that NOW is the time to build toward the future, and NOW is the time to act.

Perhaps one of the most important things you do during the entire first meeting is to lend each prospect the First Night Opportunity Pack.* Many people, unmoved by the presentation, catch a dream while listening to the tapes or reading the literature in the packet.

Also, you may opt to send a few products home with people to try, and possibly include a copy of a *Lifestyle Showcase* pamphlet.* Point to a few pictures and share an anecdote or two from the stories which are highlighted.

Most of all, let each person know before leaving that you are excited about building the business together.

---

*These items are strongly recommended and available through your Upline. However, business support materials are optional and not required.

HOLDING YOUR OWN MEETINGS

Any motivated person will see soon that his or her business will not grow until getting "on board." Your sponsor will undoubtedly be glad to continue showing the plan for you, but that person's time is limited. If you are truly serious, you must begin to show the plan ("draw the circles") as quickly as possible. One of the easiest ways to start is by using the Presentation Manual (TL 287).*

Study the marketing plan, but don't get "hung up" on trying to be perfect before you attempt a presentation. Otherwise, you may never start.

Make notes. Listen to several different people present the plan, if possible.

Then practice giving the entire opportunity plan aloud. Get used to hearing your voice going through the format over and over again. Sure, you will make mistakes, both in practice and during actual meetings), but everyone does!

Just before you are ready, if possible, draw the circles for your sponsor or someone in your upline. Take any constructive criticism this more-seasoned veteran can suggest.

Prepare well. Any good presentation generally has an interesting introduction, an identifiable body and a strong conclusion. So it should be with your plan. Obtain or make some show-the-plan cards and possibly practice on someone who is already getting into the business.

Gain and hold attention by:

• Being natural and real

• Being relaxed

• Setting an atmosphere that is conducive to listening (avoiding distractions and making sure the room is a comfortable temperature)

• Looking your best

---

*These items are strongly recommended and available through your Upline. However, business support materials are optional and not required.

- Establishing your credibility and sincerity from the beginning

and

- Speaking to the needs of your audience

You can inspire your listeners to be involved in what you are saying through:

- Asking questions,

- Using humor

- Keeping your speech lively

- Being somewhat more animated than usual

- Talking loudly enough to be heard by everyone in the room

and

- Using variety in your voice (slow to fast, higher to lower, louder to softer)

In addition, use terms familiar to your audience (don't speak "down" to an audience, and neither should you "snow" them—be yourself.

During the plan, you will need to plan to handle the most common objections:

Time

Fear of Failure

Fear of Other's Opinions

The objections are not stop-signs; they are indications of interest and inquiries for more information. Practice dealing with these objections. Preparation is crucial.

Close with the FOUR QUESTIONS in your Presentation Manual:

(1) Do you really want these dreams you've listed?

(2) Are you willing to work (consistent and persistent effort) to achieve these dreams?

(3) Are you willing to make time available to accomplish these dreams?

(4) Do you have an alternative way to reach these dreams in the next five-to-ten years?

Don't forget to give each person who sees the plan an SA4400 and other appropriate literature, such as a FIRST NIGHT PACK (TL 47). Then set a date and time for the follow-through. Tell them you will be giving them a call tomorrow to answer their questions.

Finally, respect time limitations. If your audience finishes before you do, you have failed. Quite frankly, *the most important part*, especially the first time your prospect sees the circles, *is the dream.* Get the prospects dreaming enough that they will get into the First Night Pack and review the materials seriously. You could say:

Sally, please don't take this information unless you will listen to at least half of one of these tapes tonight.

The dream, the literature and especially the tapes sponsor more people than a lengthy discussion which details everything down to the last statistic. Your job, more than anything, is to get that man and woman dreaming and then excited about their future!

FOLLOW-THROUGH

If a follow-through is important in tennis, golf and basketball, it makes sense that it is even more crucial in this business. Of all the steps in the process of building a successful, profitable business, the follow-through (which is sometimes called the follow-up) step is the most important by far. Study Section Six in the Pocket Calendar for details.

The follow-through is the natural conclusion to the entire process of a new person's introduction to the business. It begins from the moment of your approach, continues throughout the contacting and inviting stage, then through showing the plan and signing the new prospect up, and continues through the same stages with the new distributor's prospects and downline. It is not a one-time shot that happens after a person sees the plan for the first time.

However, for the sake of this chapter, let's spotlight the part of the follow-through process that applies to helping your prospect who has seen the plan become either a successful distributor or a customer.

You need to set up a follow-through meeting with the prospect who has just seen the circles. Ideally, this should be set up at the close of the first meeting.

Do not ask, "Are you getting in?" or "What have you decided?" Instead, assume that the prospect is ready to get started.

Ask questions that cannot be answered with a simple "yes" or "no"—such as:

> *Curtis, how many names have you already started putting in those circles?*
>
> *What's the most exciting thought or dream you've had since the last time we talked, Don?*
>
> *Sheila, what did you like best about the business opportunity?*
>
> *After seeing the circles and having some of your questions answered, Loyd, would Tuesday or Friday be best for you and Glenda to have a get-together in your home and get some good things started for you?*

Always set up two meetings. One might be an open meeting for follow through, and one or more should be in the person's own home. Never, ever ask them when they want a meeting—most people will procrastinate. Offer a couple of alternatives. Go over the approaches—especially with AD PACKs, as well as contacting and inviting techniques. Discuss the meeting preparations briefly, including how to introduce you.

After you set up the meetings and confirm them by telephone, you need to continue the follow-through process. Here's how:

(1) Do the follow-through yourself.

> Probably your upline will help with this at first, but by the time you begin showing the plan, you

should follow up. You already have credibility with the prospect and have knowledge about him or her that will help as you discuss future plans.

As you start doing the plan for downlines, don't expect brand new distributors to follow-through. They may not be sure what to do or say.

(2) Do the follow-through in person.

Unlike the follow-up to your initial contacting approach, you should never use the telephone for a follow-through with a person who has seen the plan.

In fact, you should set a date and time for getting back together when you finish showing the plan.

Then, as mentioned previously, you can use the telephone simply to reconfirm the follow-through meetings.

(3) Build the friendship.

Begin to establish a relationship when you show the plan by taking a sincere interest in the individual or couple. As you develop a mutually-advantageous relationship with them, they will be more apt to respect you and listen to what you have to say.

Don't just be interested in getting their name on the dotted line of the application. Nothing magic happens just because someone gets a kit. We are in the people business, and relationships are what will build your organization.

(4) Give information.

Excitement without information can be frustrating. Help your prospective distributors and downline people by keeping up with what is happening both with Amway and the marketplace. Amway and InterNet have a wealth of business-building materials available. (Consult with your upline.)

The information you give about the business

builds understanding. Understanding can be the basis for great relationships.

(5) Build the dream.

We refer to this in virtually every chapter of the book—for good reason.

A person's dreams are directly related to his or her decisions about whether, when and how big to build this business. The dream will serve as that person's motivation to achieve.

(6) Follow-through within 24 to 48 hours during peak excitement time.

Waiting longer may allow the dream-stealers to move in. Be aware of the fact that the person who has seen this plan may be susceptible to others who "know all about this Amway thing!"

Seek to get the interested person started by giving more information, tapes and an opportunity to get together to see the plan again. (Ideally, this should be an open meeting where they can continue their positive experiences in the business as they meet other excited distributors.)

(7) Be prepared.

This was a step that we mentioned during the contacting section of the book, and preparation certainly applies here.

On all follow-through efforts, have the following items available (out of sight to use as needed):

• An Amway Sales and Product Kit (AD-2000)

• A Network Toolbox

• Extra AD PACKs

• Your calendar (for setting at least two more meetings)

Your attitude should be thoroughly professional. This could be the chance of a lifetime—for them and for you.

(8) Be a leader.

Be confident. Be excited. Be open. Be responsive.

Ask questions such as, "What did you like best about what you saw?" or "What interested you most about the concept?"

Any thinking person will usually relate some things he or she did like and things that might have seemed negative. Focus on the positive things.

When they show interest, say:

We're glad you're joining us.
We'll have great times together.

Realize, of course, that not everyone will decide to get involved with you immediately. **Regardless of a prospect's interest, you should view every person who sees the plan as one of the following:**

- A DISTRIBUTOR: This is an active associate who is going to build the business with you.

- A CUSTOMER/CLIENT: Even if he or she doesn't want to get started right now, the person can begin using basic products and services from your distribution system. Then, who knows? Many successful network marketing distributors got interested through using our company's excellent products.

- ONE WHO GIVES REFERRALS: If the person doesn't want to build the business, ask if he or she knows anyone who might be interested in adding a diversified income. Again, who knows? He or she might even reconsider, rather than losing out on the chance to sponsor friends or associates. One suggested phrase is:

Richard, I know the timing might not be good for you right now to build your mutual-benefit marketing business, but would you know a couple of people who sincerely might be open to making a couple of extra thousand dollars a month?

For those who do decide to get involved with you, you must realize again and again—throughout the follow-through process—that just purchasing a kit hardly insures success in this business. You must help each new distributor by setting up meetings and showing the plan to their friends and family. Help them become very **wide** and as **deep** as possible.

Don't forget the value of the system. Get them into books, tapes and functions. Call to make sure each new distributor is going to the next get-together; better yet, take them. Seminars and rallies are essential for growth.

OBJECTIONS

Whenever you show the plan to people and throughout the follow-through process, you may hear a zillion reasons why people choose not to get involved with you. Assuming you have done a good job throughout the entire process, however, there are generally only two core reasons why people do not get into the business:

False pride

or

Fear of the unknown

Actually, since false pride is actually a disguised fear, reasons for not getting into the business relate to a relatively low self-image. Your growing confidence in the business (through books, tapes and functions) and the constantly increasing credibility of Amway can help them get past fears. Just glancing through the *Profiles of Success* should remind any prospect that he or she can build this business.

Still, you will face objections. As mentioned earlier, objections are often requests for more information. Don't argue with people who raise questions, and don't minimize inquiries that are important enough for them to verbalize.

Use the **feel, felt** and **found** method of handling objections.

*I know how you **feel**. I **felt** the same way, but here's what I **found**…*

You are agreeing with them, but then you are turning their objections into a reason for getting involved with network marketing.

When someone says, "I simply don't have enough time," you can reply:

*I know how you **feel**. I **felt** the same way, but here's what I **found**—the people who build this business are generally the ones who don't have hardly any extra time. In fact, that's why they build it, because they don't want to spend the rest of their lives with little time to do the things they want to do. I've also **found** that one of the greatest benefits of this business is the time-duplication aspect. Many people have doubled and tripled their incomes by duplicating what little time they have and investing it in building their own mutual-benefit marketing business.*

Now, if time were no problem, who would you want in business with you?

When a person offers, "I really don't know enough people," you can joke:

*I know how you **feel**. I **felt** the same way, but here's what I **found**—when it became important for me, I discovered that I knew a lot more people than I thought I knew. In fact, if I were to give you $100 for the name of every family member, friend, acquaintance, business associate and person with whom you deal, how many names could you give me?*

If a person says, "I don't want to take any more time away from my family," point out:

*I know how you **feel**. I **felt** the same way, but here's what I **found**—this is a family business and can actually bring your family closer together. When I really got down to my real priorities, I **found** that my loved ones were the reason I wanted to build financial flexibility through this business.*

If a prospective distributor says, "I don't have the money to get started," you can reply:

> *I know how you* ***feel****. I* ***felt*** *the same way, but here's what I* ***found****—not having enough money is one of the main reasons for getting into this business.*

When they reach into their arsenal and bring up a $64 word, "What about saturation?" you can say:

> *I know how you* ***feel****. Many have* ***felt*** *the same way, but here's what I* ***found****—even after nearly three and a half decades, we still only have two million distributors worldwide. In checking population figures, I* ***found*** *that with five and a half billion people around the world and 250,000 babies being born every single day, saturation seems impossible, doesn't it?*[5] *The truth is, no matter how wonderful an opportunity like ours is, only a relatively few people make the choice to do whatever it takes to develop a better lifestyle.*

What about "It's just not my cup of tea!" comments? You should say:

> *I know how you* ***feel****. I* ***felt*** *the same way, but here's what I* ***found****—this business is mainly about making money and helping others. Which part didn't you like—making money or helping others?*

When they say, "I know it will work for you, but I'm just not very outgoing," a good reply would be:

> *I know how you* ***feel****. I* ***felt*** *the same way, but here's what I* ***found****—this business has been built by lots of people who are outgoing, but it is mostly built by people who are more reserved.*

> *Now, if not being outgoing were not a problem, who would you like to have in business with you?*

Here's the point: No one wins an argument. If you try to blast away at the person's objective, he or she will probably try to fortify that objective with even more.

---

5. Lori Fagan, "Population," *The 1992 World Book Year Book (Chicago: World Book*, 1992), p. 371.

Agree with the person who raises any objection, then turn it around by relating your own experience through **feel, felt** and **found.**

NOBODY IS PERFECT

No matter what you do—throughout the entire process—one of the hardest facts to face is that some of your closest friends, family and work associates may:

(1) Laugh at you.

(2) Not get in business with you.

(3) Freely dump horror story after horror story about Aunt Margaret—"She swears Amway soap puts holes in your clothes!"

(4) Tell you about "a friend of a friend" who lost lots of money in THAT business.

(5) Wonder, "Why in the world would you, with such a wonderful job, want to do that *Amway thing?*"

or

(6) All of the above.

As hard as it is to understand or believe, not everyone will want to get involved with you. In fact, not everyone will be happy with your choice to build your own business. We shouldn't isolate that merely to network marketing, since not everyone was ecstatic with your other decisions to improve yourself either.

Undoubtedly, there were people who downplayed your plans about a college degree, or that new position which required you to move across the nation, or that new car or even joining a tennis club. People simply resist change—in themselves or others.

Plus, many people are not ambitious enough to want this opportunity. When you realize this, you eliminate some of the heartache and disappointments that will undoubtedly be part of the inner growth on your way to success.

Not everyone is going to come to hear the opportunity. As mentioned earlier, the Diamonds in the *Profiles of Success* are there because they have had more "no-shows," among other things, than you have.

Again, not everyone who sees the circles is going to get into the business (despite the incredibly fantastic job you do showing the plan!). Like it or not, people naturally tend toward the negative.

Says Dexter:

> *As a Crown Ambassador Direct Distributor, I still have people look at me, eyeball to eyeball, and say flatly, "I'm not convinced it will work."*

Unbelievable!

So? What are you going to do if all your family and friends laugh at your dreams? You either quit, or you get gutsy and decide to prove them wrong!

Discouragement and lack of persistence are the two greatest enemies you will face. Determine, from the beginning, that you will overcome and go on. The rewards at the other end are too exciting to let a few "stubbed toes" keep you from realizing your dreams and goals.

Perhaps this will help get the proverbial monkey off your back: Once you have shared the opportunity with someone and have helped those you sponsor to the limit of your knowledge, ability, and time—then it is up to them to pick up the ball and run with it.

Just remember, it is much easier to build the business fast, rather than wallowing around the mundane ruts into which others tend to drag you.

A FINAL NOTE

One of the greatest (and perhaps scariest) parts of this business is that you set your own pace. YOU are ultimately the one who makes it happen. You get out of your business what you put into it.

So work smart! Give your time to all the people you sponsor, but concentrate on those who ask questions, who "chase" you, who follow the success system and who are excited about building their own business.

One final point: Don't ever call up a new distributor and talk solely about how much he is selling or why he or she is not doing more in terms of handing out AD Packs. That negates the positive part of network marketing. We don't downplay the importance of retailing, but we don't pressure people into selling (on the other hand, we do **encourage** them to merchandize a little or a lot). Permanence comes through emphasizing sponsoring and effective building activity.

When you ask them about the retailing part of their business, it makes them wonder about your motives:

> *Did he sponsor me just so I can move products, or is he genuinely interested in helping me build my business big?*

When you discuss retailing, talk about it in terms of merchandising (which will be explained in the next chapter).

Additionally, when you telephone downline people, let them feel that you are sincerely wanting to help them, not merely "checking up" on them. We are not in *direct sales.* We are in a *network marketing* business. We should always be aware of the difference.

Sure, there are many details—many construction steps—on your way to building a massive distributorship.

Not once in this book have we said it would be easy—just worth it!

Keep remembering that you can have anything in the world that you want when you help enough other people to reach their goals and obtain their dreams.

It takes organization, dedication, perspiration, and anticipation. And you can do it.

You can develop the skills
which are necessary to
BUILD YOUR OWN SUCCESSFUL
INTERACTIVE DISTRIBUTION BUSINESS!

BUILDING BLOCKS:

We have a great life, and this dream lifestyle has been made possible through Amway. We believe this business is the wave of the future, and tomorrow holds so much for those who understand the power of duplication, distribution and dreams.

Is it any wonder why we are so excited about this business? Our excitement stems from the potential. The potential motivates us to keep growing and sharing.

DAVE HAMBY
Former University
Administrator
Diamond Direct
Distributor (USA)

The spirit of venture is lost in the inertia of a mind against change.[1]

ALFRED P. SLOAN
Former General Motors
President (USA)

---

1. Alfred P. Sloan, *My Years with General Motors* (Garden City, NY: Doubleday, 1964).

When we first got involved in Amway, we kept thinking that it was too good to be true. Our thoughts changed completely when we attended our first major function. The excitement was unbelievable. The quality of the people was so exceptional. I'm not sure what we were looking for when we went to the get-together, but what we discovered was a large group of ambitious men and women. We came away from the meeting knowing that we wanted to spend more time with those people. It was the relationships with our newfound friends that fueled the fire that kept us going toward Diamond.

LUIS COSTA
Former Paint Store
Deliveryman
Diamond Direct
Distributor (Spain)

It is not the critic who counts, not the man who points out how the strong man stumbled, or where the doer of deeds could have done them better

The credit belongs to the man who is actually in the arena; whose face is marred by dust and sweat and blood; who strives valiantly; who errs and comes short again and again; who knows the great enthusiasms, the great devotions; who spends himself in a worthy cause; who, at the best, knows in the end the triumph of high achievement; and who, at the worst, if he fails, at least fails while daring greatly.

THEODORE ROOSEVELT
(1858-1919)
Twenty-sixth President
of the United States

As we built this business, we thought it was to give us a nice lifestyle. But you never really know why you are building it. After returning from our Diamond trip on the Enterprise yacht, my husband was killed in an automobile accident.

The greatest reward in this business is the unseen things—people helping people. My children and I received so much love and support during the tragedy. Our lifestyle didn't change, and I was able to continue building the business as a single.

I'm just so thankful that my husband saw the future financial security that this business could provide.

HELEN HUEBNER
Homemaker
Double Diamond Direct
Distributor (Canada)

The person who wins success is the one who makes hay from the grass that grows under the other person's feet, and who doesn't restrict his efforts to the hours when the sun shines.

READER'S DIGEST

We make our own decisions in life. We are not totally helpless. We determine our own direction! Success takes work and faith.

BIRDIE YAGER
Former Air Force Base
Keypunch Operator
Crown Ambassador
Direct Distributor (USA)

Success in business is a time-honored process involving hard work, risk-taking, money, a good product, maybe a little bit of luck, and most of all a burning commitment to succeed.

JOHN H. JOHNSON
President of Johnson
Publishing Company (*Ebony,*
Jet and *Black World*) (USA)

We were going through all kinds of problems when we first saw this business. Louie was a professional air traffic controller and was in the middle of a nationwide strike. Previously, we had a nice lifestyle, but we were suddenly reduced to working at low-paying jobs. This business came into our lives at the right moment. Thankfully, we wanted to be free from financial worries and job difficulties, so we were ready. When our upline said to hold meetings, we held meetings. When they said to follow-through, we followed through. We were so hungry to be free that we were willing to do whatever it took.

KATHY CARRILLO
Former Waitress
Executive Diamond
Direct Distributor (USA)

Each is given a bag of tools,
A shapeless mass,
A book of rules;
And each must make,
Ere life is flown,
A stumbling block
Or a stepping stone.

R. L. SHARPE
American Poet

I was pretty cautious about this business when Pat and I first saw it. She was excited, but to me the Amway plan seemed too simple to work, or perhaps it was my engineering background that made me more skeptical.

Then as we met more and more of the people who were in the business, it clinched it for me. They were positive and upbeat. I wanted to be around them even more. That's the secret of what makes this business work—the simplicity of the plan and the people. Those two components form an unbeatable combination.

GREG HOWARD
Former Engineer
Diamond Direct Distributor (USA)

The vitality of thought is an adventure. Ideas won't keep. Something must be done about them.[2]

ALFRED NORTH WHITEHEAD (1861-1947)

We are rewarded in direct proportion to our service for others. If we do little, then we will not prosper. However, if we go the extra mile, give a little more and encourage others more—our businesses will grow.

BOB McEWEN
Former U.S. Congressman (Ohio)
Amway Distributor (USA)

---

2. Quoted from the *Harvard Business Review*, July-August 1969.

You don't concentrate on risks. You concentrate on results. No risk is too great to prevent the necessary job from getting done.

CHUCK YEAGER
Test Pilot and Bestselling
Author (USA)

The reasons for building this business are as individual as the men and women who get involved. For us, Jenny and I wanted to continue our medical research. Later, our dream was to start our own biotechnology research company.

Thankfully, because we have paid the price to build our business using the proven success system. Our research is now largely funded through our business.

But our reason is important primarily to us. What is your "Why?" Once you decide your true reason for building your business, you can then put an action plan to your dreams and goals.

ROLAND MCGREADY
Medical Research Scientist
Diamond Direct
Distributor (Australia)

Some people like people who win. Some people hate people who win. But people who win will never go unnoticed.[3]

MIKE KRZYZEWSKI
Duke University Basketball
Coach (USA)

---

3. This statement was spoken by the coach of the defending national champion team on April 3, 1992 in Minneapolis, during a pre-Final Four press conference—Coach K's fifth straight Final Four appearance and sixth in seven years.

You have to find a reason for building this business. For me, time was the reason. I had no time when I was teaching school. With this marketing business, you learn to leverage your time. By investing those hours wisely, you start to get time back. You build equity as you build an organization, instead of merely trading time for dollars. That's the difference between working hard—which I had always done before—and working smart. That's also the starting point for gaining your freedom.

TIM BRYAN
Former Teacher
Diamond Direct Distributor (USA)

Additions

...Your Advanced Sales
and Marketing Directions

Generally, we recommend using the bulk of your business time building your network. Still, you will have opportunities to offer products and services to friends, family or people who have seen the circles but have not yet decided to get involved.

"Offer?" you ask, "as in **selling?**"

We may or may not like to be called salespeople, but in Amway, as with any effective network marketing system (or any business, for that matter), selling is involved.

Need some cash? Sell products. Do you need a lot of money? In addition to sponsoring people, develop a merchandising system. As you sponsor new distributors, teach them how the program works.

One follow-through for the prospect who decides (at least for the time being) not to join you is to use the catalogs and product "shopping list" (available through your upline) to talk about the items they may need in the future. For starters, you can mention:

- Amway has a wide range of products and services.

- The company's quality is recognized throughout the industry.

- Amway provides economy through concentration.

- Amway offers a 100% money-back guarantee.

  and

- We provide the added convenience of shopping at home.

Specifically, in the United States, Amway has:

PRIORITY SERVICE (order SA-330 for sign-up information)—Get your customers to order products directly from the company, and you get credit automatically.

PRIORITY SERVICE PLUS (again, order SA-330 for sign-up information)—You and your customers can sign up for automatic shipments of products (such as regular monthly deliveries of home care items and food supplements) from the company.

DIRECT CATALOG ORDERING—Over 4,000 brand name consumables, clothing, housewares and electronic products are available in the *Personal Shoppers* Catalog. In addition, the company offers several speciality catalogs. When your customers order, every item is credited to you.

CREDIT CARD PAYMENT—Your customers may use their major credit card for purchases, or you can sign them up for the Amway VISA card (SA-6536) and you can earn bonuses on their charges.

COUPONS—Have the magazine, *Just Among Friends*, mailed directly from the company (SA-1465), and encourage your customers to save cash with each order by using the valuable coupons.

SPECIAL PRODUCT OFFERS—At times the *Amagram* features a variety of products which are discounted. You can pass these savings to your customers.

LITERATURE—Many of the company's brochures are printed and sized specifically for you to mail. Your customers will enjoy reading the eye-catching materials.

VIDEOS—Certain products and services are featured in company videos. Drop these handy helps off and let the magic of television do your selling.

Merchandizing is an important part of your overall business, so treat it professionally. Know your products. Keep Customer Record Cards (SA-316). There are also specialized product-training videos which can help in developing your presentations.

YOUR FIRST TASK—
SELL YOURSELF ON SELLING

Because selling is sometimes not respected by the general public, for reasons already mentioned, even top-flight salespeople tend to become defensive about the way they earn their living. As a consequence, many high calibre salespeople fail to live up to their potential and eventually leave the sales profession altogether. In fact, numerous research studies have shown that at least 60% of all salespeople fail in their first year. Even veteran sales personnel experience burnout and fail because they get discouraged and lose their focus.

That is sad, because selling, of all the professions, should be the most respected. Selling, despite the "bad apples" in our industry, is absolutely crucial to our society. As our friend Ty Boyd says, "Nothing happens until somebody sells something to someone." Selling is vital to the success of our economy.

Virtually every job in the world relies upon some form of sales or marketing. Inventors, engineers, factory workers, accountants, clerical people, truck drivers, managers and executives—all are dependent on salespeople.

Cavett Robert, one of the world's leading sales educators, once said:

> *The selling profession is absolutely necessary in today's marketplace. A major thrust in business today is to innovate, to develop breakthrough products and services. But cashing in on those breakthroughs, however, requires salespeople to translate these improvements into benefits for consumers.*

Is it no wonder, then, that so many salespeople are paid so handsomely, in comparison to their research and development co-workers?

Therefore, selling generally means providing solutions for a lot of people. Specifically, selling means putting the customer's best interests first. When this happens throughout the marketplace, the economy flourishes.

That is why you, Mr., Mrs. or Ms. Distributor, are extremely important. That is also why—to succeed merchandising a little or a lot—you must first sell yourself on selling.

SELF-MERCHANDIZING

We have so many products that the bulk of your initial sales may be to yourself, but there is no reason why you cannot also begin to retail merchandise to customers within your first month or two.

To know how to sell your products, you must first know them. This one factor is the major reason for ordering several new products each week. You are simply replacing competitive, negative (!) merchandise, but you are also becoming familiar with and excited about your own line of products. You must know the advantages of your merchandise, as compared to the disadvantages of the competition, before you can become proficient at explaining the selling features.

Our corporate sponsor continues to do a masterful job of providing distributors with product information. As your organi-

zational sponsor, we also provide access to several cassettes and other business support materials which focus on distributors' experiences in successful selling.

Your job is to convert that raw knowledge into understanding the benefits which your customers can enjoy through the products you sell.

There are several major reasons people buy anything:

- Pride in the benefits of whatever you are selling (such as cleaner clothes), and value in services such as MCI, Amvox, or the Motoring Plan.

- Economic advantages by buying your products (which explains why so many people are experiencing tremendous profitability through selling our home improvement, health and fitness, and security items).

- Love and acceptance (better health of one's family)

    and

- Comfort (which you can provide through conscientious service).

To sell, you must build on these reasons.

While it is true that financial flexibility comes through building a large organization (in depth and width) rather than through retail sales, there should be a balance. Organizational growth helps keep your business expanding, but the retail sales throughout that organization can fuel tremendous excitement and profitability. Quite frankly, it is hard to get discouraged when you are making a lot of immediate income and sponsoring new people.

If you, personally, would develop ten regular retail customers, it could increase your monthly profits by approximately ten times, since each family uses approximately the same amount of products that you use in your home; they either use Brand X or the AMWAY products you sell to them.

Now, multiply that profitability times the number of people in your organization. Imagine if each of them developed ten new retail customers!

Especially with such high PV and immediate profit items as the AMGARD® security system, QUEEN™ cookware sets, and water treatment systems, for example, it just makes good sense to retail a growing volume of products.

Make the time you devote to this very efficient. Keep organized as a professional so you don't end up spending all or most of your time in this area.

MARKETING

While this book is not a primer on all the products which distributors can make available to their customers, it is an attempt to remind you of the most important and basic factors in making a sale.

First, when you sit down with that prospective customer, remember certain points, but stay away from a memorized speech. Your upline has a line of generic product-related brochures you may use to prospect a customer.

Next, it is important that you let them know from the beginning that you are interested in them as people, not merely as consumers. Ice-breaking small-talk should center on them, their children, things they are interested in, and their needs. Ask questions and listen, **really** listen. Listening is an important part of assessing their needs, finding common interests and helping them relax.

Once you establish a rapport, use what you learned from the questions to your advantage. Together, determine your client's needs. Ask about specific cleaning problems or make-up preferences. If you are attempting to sell an AMGARD® Alarm System, let them share certain fears or interests. When you let them express their needs, you are well on your way toward making a sale.

As you sense and determine that person's needs, it is up to you to show how your products can meet those needs. You must focus your attention upon the benefits, advantages, uses, and money-saving features of your merchandise. This is where your own belief and product knowledge makes the difference. Demonstrate those products. Provide proof for your claims.

Develop the need into a want. He or she may need the products you are showing, but until you change that need into a want, you will probably not make a sale. Use as many of the human senses as possible. Help that person visualize the benefits, the value and the service.

Don't sell products, sell delicious tastes (as with NUTRILITE™ food supplements and drink mixes), aromatic smells (colognes), beautiful sights (jewelry), and attention-getting sounds (AMGARD® Alarm systems). Sell health benefits, not NUTRILITE® vitamins or water treatment systems. You get the picture, don't you?

One way to get the customer to anticipate buying is to write his or her name at the top of the order form before presenting the product.

Then make the transaction. Practice handling the money questions. Visualize your customer signing that check. Don't be afraid to ask for the money. Simply ask for the order. There are many ways to do this, and your upline can help you with advice on specific business support materials on selling.*

You can ask for the order knowing that all of our products are priced fairly. You will find this to be true, especially with such high-tech products as the water treatment and Amgard™ protection systems.

Remember that our corporate sponsor's 100% money-back guarantee is even better than a free sample because the customer's satisfaction is based upon using the entire product, not just a small amount. Some companies give a 10 or 30 day guarantee, usually with a lot of forms to fill out, but with our products, the customer can return products to us **anytime** for **any reason.**

---

*These items are strongly recommended and available through your Upline. However, business support materials are optional and not required.

And if they ever want to return something, do it without a fuss. Ask questions. Seek feedback. You may actually make additional sales just because you are willing to listen to a person's complaint (legitimate or not).

When you talk with a customer, answer any questions which he or she may have. Pinpoint any objections which may come up in the conversation. Again, as with objections to the sales and marketing plan, use the **feel, felt** and **found** method of handling objections. Challenges are usually just questions for more information, not real objections.

Don't make the mistake of talking your client out of buying because of your own feelings of inadequacy as a salesperson. Continue to visualize the transaction taking place.

A FINAL NOTE

Once you make a sale, build on it. Establish the client as a regular customer. Ask for referrals. If that person enjoys certain products, he or she will not be able to keep quiet. When people talk about their new "find" to others, you can quickly add new clients to your list. You may even want to offer premiums or incentives for referrals or for a dollar volume of purchases.

Before long, you can even suggest to your original client that those referrals could be their customers, then proceed with setting up an appointment to show the Amway Sales and Marketing Plan to them!

Above all, be consistent. Establish 10 to 20 regular repeat customers. Service them at least twice a month. Establish a pattern of calling each customer regularly. Provide "shopping list" pads (available through your upline).

Remember, customer loyalty only goes so far. If a person keeps running out of SA8 because you forget to call, he or she will probably pick up some other brand on the next trip to the grocery store.

Done right, your merchandizing efforts can become an effective, money-making factor as you meet each person's needs.

Using merchandizing as an important, profit-generating method, you can build your own SUCCESSFUL NETWORK MARKETING BUSINESS.

BUILDING BLOCKS:

I will greet this day with love in my heart.

For this is the greatest secret of success in all ventures. Muscle can split a shield and even destroy life but only the unseen power of love can open the hearts of men and until I master this art I will remain no more than a peddler in the market place. I will make love my greatest weapon and none on whom I call can defend against its force.

My reasoning they may counter; my speech they may distrust; my apparel they may disapprove; my face they may reject; and even my bargains may cause them suspicion; yet my love will melt all hearts liken to the sun whose rays soften the coldest day.[1]

OG MANDINO
Former Publishing Executive
Bestselling Author and Speaker (USA)

The root of all lasting motivation is faith. Faith and motivation are interchangeable parts of the success system which you can use to build this business. Anyone who has faith and motivation who chooses to apply them to the system can succeed. It all comes down to making a commitment and trusting God to guide you.

BRIAN McCONNELL
Former Minister of Music
Diamond Direct Distributor (USA)

---

1. Og Mandino, *The Greatest Salesman In the World.*

Man is not a balloon going up into the sky, nor a mole burrowing merely in the earth; but rather a thing like a tree, whose roots are fed from the earth, while its highest branches seem to rise almost to the stars.

G. K. CHESTERTON (1874-1936)
British Philosopher

Everything about building this business becomes so simple when you plug into the success system. It comes down to developing a positive attitude, habits and relationships, and the system can help you. One of the smartest things Marge and I did was learning—quite early in the business—to follow the pattern. I just figured that if we did what was working so well for others, we would reach our goals.

DAVE LEWIS
Former Grocery Manager
Diamond Direct
Distributor (USA)

In the 1990s, the successful sales professional will be a master at needs analysis and application selling. Needs analysis is understanding and selling to the buyer's needs, rather than selling a product or service to meet a quota. You must shift your focus to place the customer's needs at the top of your list. Application selling is what you do with the information that you gather through needs analysis.[2]

BILL BROOKS
Speaker, Author
and Consultant (USA)

---

2. Bill Brooks, *Niche Selling: How to Find Your Customer in a Crowded Market* (Homewood, IL: Business One Irwin, 1992), p. 16.

Have patience. All things are difficult before they become easy. This certainly relates to the network marketing business. Learning a skill and perfecting your presentation is always more of a struggle in the beginning—then it becomes second nature.

MJ MICHAEL
Homemaker
Diamond Direct
Distributor (USA)

I don't know that anyone has ever succeeded in any business without having some unselfish sponsorship or mentorship, whatever it might have been called. Everyone who succeeds has had a mentor or mentors. We've all been helped. For some the help comes with more warmth than for others, and with some it's done with more forethought, but most people who succeed in a business will remember fondly individuals who helped them in their early days.

LES BROWN
Speaker, Author and
Talkshow Host (USA)

When Denise and I saw this business, we thought we didn't need anything else. We were comfortable and felt we had a good life. Still, when we saw the plan—really saw it—we got fired up. I was so competitive, anyway, so I liked the idea of a challenge. We mainly saw Amway as an opportunity to get completely out of debt. Thankfully, getting out of debt was just the beginning!

ALAN DECKER
Former Motorcycle
Racer and Salesman
Diamond Direct
Distributor (Australia)

Three days' neglect of study leaves one's conversation flavorless.

CHINESE PROVERB

Learn to focus on people's needs, especially when it comes to selling to them. If you are only concerned about doing a certain volume, the customer will see it in a minute. But if you are truly interested in what he or she needs, and if your sales efforts are geared that way, it will shine through like gold!

FRANK DELISLE, JR.
Former Architectural Engineer
Second Generation Amway
Double Diamond Direct
Distributor (USA)

Man does nothing by himself. There is always a cause, either internal or external, that moves him.[3]

DENIS DIDEROT (1713-1784)
Author and
Philosopher (France)

A debt-free lifestyle, travel, luxury, time to use as we choose—all these benefits from building our business are wonderful, but the best part is that today we have the opportunity to share the same success system with people from every walk of life. That keeps our life very interesting.

HULDA DUNLAP
Former Livestock Auction
Owner and Operator
Diamond Direct Distributor (USA)

---

3. Denis Diderot, *Thoughts on the Business of Life.*

A man's reach should exceed his grasp, or what's a heaven for?

ROBERT BROWNING (1812-1889)
British Poet

Anyone can duplicate this system once you identify who really wants to reach their goals and achieve their dreams. That's really the secret.

*Help your prospects get a dream that motivates them— something that they can't get from what they are presently doing. Whether it is financial flexibility or economic freedom or material possessions, as long as people have a dream that is bigger than what their current income can provide, they **will** find a way to build this business.*

PETER MCKENNA
Former Air Traffic Controller
Diamond Direct
Distributor (Australia)

The purpose of a business is to get and keep a customer.[4]

THEODORE LEVITT, Ph.D.
Professor, Harvard
Business School
Bestselling Author (USA)

You must believe in and be moved by principles larger than yourself. In the end, I believe that's the only way you can find real self-worth and happiness.

ANGEL DE LA CALLE
Former Casino Operator
Diamond Direct Distributor (Spain)

---

4. Theodore Levitt, *The Marketing Imagination* (New York: MacMillian, 1983), p. xii.

In the beginning stages of building this business, one of the hardest things to understand is the fact that other people really care about your success. In how many other businesses or pursuits does that happen? I knew I would never quit no matter how long it would take. I knew I would have to be willing to change and overcome all my fears, but the thing that kept drawing me back was the relationships. The team attitude I found was unlike anything I had ever seen before. We were in this thing together. Other people got as excited about your successes as you did. It's the relationships that bond everything together. Build strong relationships and you will build a strong organization.

BOB HOWARD
Former House Painter
Executive Diamond Direct Distributor (USA)

Cement

...Building Toward Direct Through Strong Relationships

President Franklin Delano Roosevelt once said:

It has always seemed to me that the best symbol of common sense was the bridge.

As you will be both a success and a leader, you must learn to creatively build bridges in all of your relationships with people. Such important elements are a unique part of our business. Relationships develop out of friendships, and enough close relationships build Directships. The system which builds these lasting relationships is also the system which cements your growing business as you focus on going Direct.

POINTING TOWARD DIRECT

Let us refer to two things in the previous paragraph. First, the operative word in the final sentence is "growing." One of the most basic rules of this business relates to the fact that **you can't mark time.** Either you are **growing** or **slowing**. If any, not much gray area exists between the two.

Now, let us repeat another phrase that you just read: **Relationships develop out of friendships, and enough close relationships build Directships.** As you start growing, one of the best ways to begin cementing your relationships with your distributors is by realizing that you must set the example in every area of your business, including building enough relationships and friendships to permit you to go Direct.

There are many ways to do this, but before getting into a discussion of several components of building and cementing your Directship—being a good example, width and depth, edification, loyalty, close friendships and living the Golden Rule—let us give you a definition of what it means to go Direct.

When we say "going Direct," we refer to a distributor who has built an organization that produces a minimum of 7500 PV at least six out of twelve months of Amway's fiscal year. Going Direct not only puts you into the 25% Performance Bonus level, but also gives you an opportunity to receive additional bonuses and trips.

Going Direct is especially important, because it is the first major step toward going Ruby, Pearl, Emerald, Diamond, EDC and so forth. If you can put together a Directship, you can certainly turn around and help downline people in six, nine and eventually twenty or more legs do the same thing.

The following is a chart which gives a quick overview of a plan to achieve Direct in six months:

SET A GOAL TO MAKE
DIRECT IN SIX MONTHS (or less)
Use this chart as an outline. Your actual growth may vary.

CONSECUTIVE MONTHS	1st MONTH	2nd MONTH	3rd MONTH	4th MONTH	5th MONTH	6th MONTH
TOTAL MONTHLY POINT VALUE	600 P.V.	1500 P.V.	2500 P.V.	4000 P.V.	7500 P.V.	10,000 P.V.
TOTAL NUMBER IN GROUP	15	40	60	80	125	150
PERSONALLY SPONSORED	6	10	12	14	16	18
NUMBER OF PERFORMANCE BONUS CHECKS PAID	4	8	10	12	14	15

In very simple terms, to go Direct in six months, you need to reach GO-GETTER each month, do QUICKSILVER twice, focus on three primary groups, and break three QUICKSILVERS in width. Ideally, at Direct, your organization should have approximately the same number of distributors in attendance at the monthly seminars and rallies and other functions as you have weekly SOTs.

BUILDING AND CEMENTING YOUR DIRECTSHIP BY BEING A GOOD EXAMPLE

"But," you may be saying, "how in the world do I motivate others to do all those things?"

It's a fair question, and it is one that every Diamond has asked himself or herself hundreds of times. In very simplistic terms, you can only motivate your downline to help build your Directship through two basic ways:

- THE SYSTEM OF BOOKS, TAPES AND MEETINGS

   You must plug each new distributor into the learning and empowerment system that has motivated thousands of others toward their goals. In a sense, the system is a mobile network marketing university staffed by professors with combined years of hands-on experience. These teachers are from every economic, occupational and educational background, and they are willing to pass on their accumulated years of learning to every person in your growing organization.

- PERSONAL CONTACT

   You may wear many "hats" as you build your business—executive, counsellor, manager, tutor, parent-figure, coach, tear-wiper, communicator and more. One of the most important "hats," however is role-model.

You lead best through modeling what you want to happen among your downline associates. Lead the way through **personal goals** such as these:

- Listen to a tape every day. (You will want to listen to some again and again.)

Nurture your own appetite for knowledge and inspiration available through your upline.* You can't promote what you aren't willing to do yourself.

• Read from a book every day.

Nothing improves your people skills more than reading. We've suggested many books in previous chapters, including *The Magic of Thinking Big, The Double Win, How to Win Friends and Influence People, Think and Grow Rich, Skill with People, The Greatest Salesman in the World and Ordinary Men...Extraordinary Heros.* *

• Read the Eight Step Pattern from your calendar every day.

It is the pattern for success. Learn it. Live it. Love it. Those eight steps will change your lifestyle as you build your Directship.

How about **business goals** that you need to model? Consider these:

• Sponsor five during the next 90 days and help put ten more in depth (QUICKSILVER), then repeat the process.

• Begin to show the plan on your own, pointing toward at least fifteen times a month (GO-GETTER).

• Especially during the first six months, seek to double your numbers every month at seminars and rallies (from one new person to two, then to four, eight, sixteen, etcetera).

• Promote **every** upline function.*

• Sign up for SOT and Go-Getter's tapes.*

• Order products every week, both for personal use and merchandizing.

• Keep adding to your list.

• Use the AD PACKs.*

---

*These items are strongly recommended and available through your upline. However, business support materials are optional and not required.

- Become a telephone professional.

- Teach people how to show the plan.

- Become a follow-through expert.

- Focus on dreams—yours and your downlines.

As mentioned previously, you lead best through modeling what you want to happen among your downline associates. If you want them to gain knowledge by listening to more cassettes, then YOU must listen to more. If you want your people to stop nitpicking, then take an honest look at the words you have been saying and the attitude you have exhibited. If you expect your downline men and women to use as many products as they can, then you must set the standard. If you expect your group to retail more effectively, then you should be able to teach from experience.

If you find yourself with an abundance of people who don't want to do anything, then let them see you blazing a fresh trail by sponsoring more associates and working the business feverishly.

Somehow your downline people will know if you are being hypocritical. They will automatically tend to pick up anything negative that you do or say. Therefore, don't expect your associates to do something that you are not doing.

If you are to be an example, you must seek to keep your men and women informed with what is happening. Some of them will not bother to check the calendar or our organizational newsletter, *DREAMBUILDERS REVIEW* (an absolute necessity if you want to be aware of meetings in both your organization and others; a subscription form is provided in this book), to see that a seminar or rally is coming up next Saturday. They may forget about Tuesday's opportunity meeting. It is up to you to remind them.*

---

*These items are strongly recommended and available through your upline. However, business support materials are optional and not required.

And, as one who models the proper pattern, it is important that you get your downline men and women around other growing distributors. Excitement breeds excitement. One of the most important ingredients in this business revolves around the sense of belonging to the most exciting organization in the world.

Do whatever you must to get your associates to all the major functions. Make sure they are making new friendships with other distributors.* Be certain that they are recognized and awarded for each new pin level. Make the business *theirs* through buy-in and emotional ownership.

Isn't that the reason why people go to sporting events and motion picture showings when they can easily stay at home and watch the same things on television? The EVENT or happening is so important. People want to be an integral part of something that is challenging, rewarding, exciting and energizing.

As you lead by example and get your organization involved in the success system of books, tapes, literature and meetings, your people will duplicate what you do.

---

*Avoid discussing or planning specific business-related subjects with distributors in organizations other than yours. This is called "Crosslining" and is a violation of the Amway Code of Ethics.

Setting an example means that you must continually keep growing. You will have "chasers" running behind you. But, believe us, when you are getting new pins and seeing your people receive new pins at the same time, the rewards overshadow the struggles.

BUILDING AND CEMENTING YOUR DIRECTSHIP THROUGH WIDTH AND DEPTH

We believe very strongly that you should build your organization in two directions as you point toward going Direct:

• WIDTH for profitability

and

• DEPTH for long-term security.

These phrases should become permanently imprinted in your mind.

Still, there are some myths and misconceptions about building your business with width and depth. For starters, some people think they have to know thousands of people personally to be able to develop a gigantic organization. That just is not true.

By the fourth downline generation (as discussed in Chapter Six), you may have thousands of distributors associated with you; still, *you will be working primarily with three wide and three deep at a time*, not hundreds or thousands. No one could work effectively with that many people.

The key is *duplication*. We say that building your network marketing business boils down to teachers teaching teachers to teach. There is more truth to that than most people realize.

Another myth concerning duplication is that by sponsoring a person, you have just duplicated yourself. Nothing could be farther from the truth. You have only begun to reproduce yourself until that new person is becoming successful at:

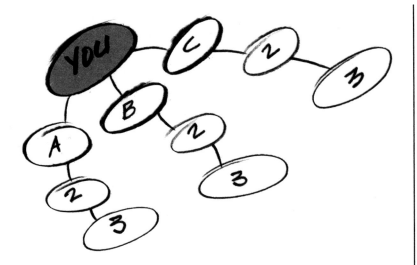

(1) Sponsoring and building an organization

(2) Moving products

and

(3) Teaching.

Just like you!

Granted, instilling these principles takes time and effort, but without your instruction, you merely sponsor "orphans." Needless to say, a disjointed, untaught business will not see much volume or growth, and certainly not Direct.

Ideally, we teach that you should sponsor "legs," not just individuals. To do this, you must first develop leaders (teachers teaching teachers to teach—remember?). The leader may not be your frontline/personally-sponsored distributor, but may come from downline in your organization. Back up your leaders with more leaders. As you learn this system, you will teach this system throughout your network as your Upline does now.

Of course, you can go out, sponsor lots of frontline distributors, move a lot of products and call yourself a network marketing genius. Plenty of people do that. But until *you are building depth, you are merely involved in direct sales*. With this set-up, your income will always depend directly upon your month-to-month efforts, not on a growing organization.

Width without depth will prove temporary. Width builds profitability and recognition, but depth brings security. While you always need to continue adding width, your focus should be on building depth. Depth is vital, since once you sign new distributors up, you need to focus on building an organization underneath them (we call this "driving depth").

Dexter says:

> *Since 1964, when Birdie and I signed the application to start our own Amway business, we've personally sponsored less than seventy people, yet out of those have come thousands upon thousands of Directs and hundreds of Diamonds and above. So you can see the benefits of building width, but as importantly, of driving depth.*

> *If, within the first year or so, you are paying out twelve to eighteen bonus checks, then you are building a foundation for higher pins. After all, without width, you cannot go on to higher pins.*

> *Still, in the long run (actually, right from the beginning), driving depth is where you build your financial security.*

When you are building in depth, the income will almost always be two to three months behind your growth. In other words, you may not reap the profits from working downline nearly as quickly as with frontline sales.

Randy Haugen, a very astute Executive Diamond, says:

> *Sometimes when you are working in depth, driving the leg deep, the business seems to grow so slowly. At first it doesn't appear to be as dramatic as personally sponsoring a lot of frontline people.*

> *Then, I've found that all of a sudden, every time you add a few more people at the bottom, you will start to see the kits moving. Twenty kits. Fifty kits. A hundred kits.*

When you continue to work in depth, and when the momentum builds and the leg really takes off, you will see a thousand kits going out. That's when it gets exciting.

That—and when the checks start coming in from the product movement among all those people down in depth.

Working depth seems so slow, but when it takes off, it really accelerates throughout your organization.

You must understand that as you point toward going Direct, you are building the foundation for a lifelong business. Keep working width and depth—in balance. Don't be discouraged if you are not reaping incredible financial rewards during the first months. Keep sponsoring. Keep retailing. Keep working downline.

You will obviously have to learn to budget your time as more and more people enter your organization. As mentioned, you should ideally work three legs wide at a time. Notice my use of the word "ideally."

It may not work out that way initially. You must always concentrate most of your efforts in these three legs, and you should continue to go deeper than those three leaders to find leaders who back up three leaders, and so on.

You have to slow down for some distributors, speed up for some and let others stay on the "back burner" until they are ready to make their move, and always encouraging them in a friendly, loving and positive manner.

So the question is: How do you know where to spend your most valuable resource and possession, TIME? (We will share more about using this priceless commodity wisely in Chapter Fourteen.)

Quite simply, invest the bulk of your hours each week working with the people who "chase" you. Potential leaders will hound you at times, asking lots of questions about the business. They will inquire about buying a board and easel like yours.

They will talk to you about holding meetings for them. They may ask:

What should I do in this situation?

What do you recommend with this person?

How do I get these distributors to a meeting in another state?

You should "chase" your upline ("chasing" with respect for his or her time, but not monopolizing it) and teach your distributors to do the same, always keeping a list of questions for your upline. This maximizes the time when you are together with him or her. This same principle should be followed when you call on the telephone or leave an AMVOX message. Get right to the point!

Also, a leader will inevitably start repeating things he or she has heard from the cassettes or read from the books. A person who gets immersed in positive materials quickly is a learner, not a leaner. Learners generally make great leaders.

A "chaser" will be excited about the business, wanting to know everything about it.

You will notice that a leader will take notes. He or she will write down goals and dreams. The eager person will show you a growing prospect list and a full calendar of meetings. You will not have to constantly encourage the "chaser" into doing the simple things.

A leader is also someone who is positive about life (or quickly makes the turnaround in that direction). One excellent signal is a man or woman who consistently builds up people and the network marketing business, rather than nitpicking and fault-finding. Another indicator is a person who is fun to be around—one who attracts others, both inside and outside of the business.

A leader will seek time with you and want to be around other successful network marketing people. He or she will attend the meetings and functions. The "chaser" will be there, with or without a new prospect. Most of all, he or she will keep asking questions.

When you find men and women with these traits, spend time with them. Don't ignore the others who are less motivated, of course, but you should always "fan the flames." Use time most profitably by teaching those who are the most willing to be taught.

Your time is money, so utilize it to the fullest by working smart, building depth AND width and by looking for leaders.

Most of all, don't just sponsor distributors. Build strong legs.

In this business, however, you cannot build anything worthwhile, nor can you attain higher levels, unless you are willing to teach others everything you know. You succeed best when you duplicate yourself. The better your downline distributors do, the more profitable your business becomes.

However, there are challenges, just as in the corporate world. Since you should know your business better than anyone in your group, it is important that you become a student of how the business works.

You've heard it said, "Information is power." Actually, information is only powerful in the way you use that information.

Therefore, use your knowledge about the business as you take risks with people. You cannot lead your organization by the negative methods that leaders often use in corporate settings—belittling people (including your spouse) in front of others, using foul language, instilling fear, controlling creativity and restricting advancement.

Face it, you are in a unique business!

BUILDING AND CEMENTING YOUR DIRECTSHIP THROUGH EDIFICATION

It is probably obvious by now that network marketing (and Amway, more specifically) is slightly different from the corporate world, where one often attains higher and better-paid positions by stepping over, around and on people as one climbs to the top.

Network marketing is more a people-based business than most companies view themselves. It is difficult to build a large networking organization without developing a true love for the men and women with whom you are associated.

For us, the love which cements our business together is the best benefit of all! That love should cause you to desire to be the best leader you can be as you strive to go Direct. (You will read more about leadership in Chapter Eighteen.) One of the ways your love shows is through edification.

Talk to anyone who is building a successful network marketing business, listen to almost all of the cassettes which are suggested by your upline,* and the term "edification" will surface. Why?

As with loyalty, edification creates the best environment for growth. Let's face it, we live in the "me" age in a society that places little emphasis on the team concept. For most, the refreshing part of joining the network marketing "team" is starting to hear people being built up.

Edification has to start in the home. Amazing things can happen in a person's business when he or she begins learning to

---

*These items are strongly recommended and available through your upline. However, business support materials are optional and not required.

complement and encourage the spouse and children instead of criticizing and blaming them. When family members understand the necessity of building up each other's strengths and overlooking weaknesses, they are well on their way to getting it together, **together**!

The next form of edification is toward your upline. That kind of dedication may require you to do what is being taught without totally understanding why, at first, but it only makes sense to realize that your Upline has your best interests in mind. Of course, for those teachings that seem more difficult to comprehend, a simple question or discussion with your upline will help. He or she would be foolish to hinder your growth, especially since his business can't grow unless yours prospers. You don't have to always agree with your Upline, and neither should you believe that he or she is perfect, but why discuss those disagreements and beliefs with anyone else?

Saying the negative creates doubt. Doubt causes confusion. Confusion stops growth. Lack of growth causes failure and fear. Why not replace those negatives with faith. Faith, after all, is the essence of edification.

Edification of your downline is also extremely important. Verbalize encouragement:

Mark, you've got what it takes to build this business... you're great at dealing with people.

Few Diamonds would have made it without encouragement and edification, especially at those critical moments when

the voice inside them was screaming, "Can I do it? Do I have what it takes?" Often your people will build their business on the pure strength of your belief in them, even when they don't believe in themselves yet! Plus, when they see you edifying both your upline and downline, they will naturally follow the pattern.

Edification is one of the most important ingredients to duplicate throughout your business!

BUILDING AND CEMETING YOUR DIRECTSHIP WITH LOYALTY

Leading by example requires huge amounts of rock-solid loyalty. What do we mean?

The dictionary defines loyalty as follows:

...to be constant and faithful in any relation-ship; employing trust or confidence.

More to the point, Elbert Hubbard wrote:

If you work for a company, in heaven's name work for it!

We would say that if you work for yourself, it makes sense to do everything you can do to make it work for you!

Loyalty is a "cement" that must be solid in every area of your life.

As we have mentioned previously, we teach that it is best for your network marketing business to be a secondary income, at least until your checks are twice as much as your current salary and you can put your current full-time income in the bank for at least six months (in **most** cases but not **all**). Then, through counselling with your upline, you can decide whether you want to continue in your chosen profession or not.

Regardless, while you are still an employee, determine to be the best worker in your company. Especially when you start building your own business, you should be an example of dependability and loyalty to your employer. Give more than you are expected to. Don't use your time on the job to contact and invite. Don't show the plan at work, no matter how interested another worker might be. Don't make telephone calls or other networking-related endeavors during your on-the-clock time. Not only is it dishonest to cheat your employer, but these activities shed a bad light on ALL fellow distributors, especially when it is clearly stated.

If nothing else, your heightened loyalty to the company will make your employer miss you even more when you "get free" and leave one day!

Likewise, in every area of your life, be loyal. If you are going to work for yourself (on your own time, of course), then do it. Don't play self-sabotage games. Build yourself up.

Loyalty to God, to your church, to your nation, to yourself, your profession, your spouse, your family, your networking business, your Upline, your business associates—these are so important and should never be downplayed. Without loyalty, you will see little progress.

Granted, you will always have reasons to find fault with things. But as Teddy Roosevelt once quipped:

> *One man in the arena is worth ten, a hundred, a thousand harping critics.*

Negativity and disloyalty seem to go hand and hand. One who is either negative or disloyal is almost always eliminated from the race to success.

By the same token, loyalty is one of the greatest marks of a leader. To be a success in this business, you would do well to seek loyalty as a character strength. Since you have already undertaken the task of building this business, you should commit allegiance to it.

Your loyalty makes you radiate enthusiasm. It lights up your entire personality, puts a sparkle in your eyes and pours money into your pocket. In fact, loyalty should be as much of a motivation for you as money.

BUILDING AND CEMENTING YOUR
DIRECTSHIP THROUGH CLOSE FRIENDSHIPS

In the beginning of this chapter, we wrote:

> *Relationships develop out of friendships, and
> enough close relationships eventually build Direct-
> ships.*

It is true. We can say that, since we have seen it happen to thousands of people who have become successful in network marketing.

But it goes beyond mere distributorships. In fact, one of the most wonderful parts of this business is the relationships you will form through the years.

In our mobile society of impermanence, one by-product has been the loss of lasting relationships. For many coming into this business, one of the most shocking, disturbing realizations comes at finding out one's lack of true friends. When they laugh at you, try to discourage you, or fail to believe in you—many times, but not always, they lose the term "friend" by default.

You have a chance to make a difference. When you make contacts for your business, seek first to be a friend.

When your new distributor has his or her first "no-show" ("me-show"), and has just found out that not all his or her pals are friends, you are the one who has the power to build or destroy, through your relationship.

Verbalize to your friends what you like about them and how thankful you are for their presence in your life. Delight in their talents and applaud their successes.

Be honest. Open communication is the essence of friendship, so it is okay to express your feelings on occasion. However, there is a tactful way of even disagreeing. Of course, it is wise to be aware that, at times, some things are better left unsaid.

Treat your friends as equals. In true friendship, there is no Number One, no room for showing off how smart and successful you are, no room for envy, nor for feeling either superior or inferior.

Trust your friends and associates. We live in a messy, important world which is made up of imperfect people. Trust, despite imperfections, is essential to building lasting relationships.

And be willing to take risks. One of the obstacles to developing close relationships is the fear of rejection and being hurt. A person cannot build his or her business without being vulnerable at times, but unless we dare to love others, we condemn ourselves to a sterile, unsuccessful life.

There are many ways to nourish friendships. Permit people to be themselves—imperfections and all. Don't feel threatened if their opinions and tastes sometimes differ from yours. Friendships happen, but they must be nurtured and fueled.

BUILDING AND CEMENTING YOUR DIRECTSHIP THROUGH LIVING THE GOLDEN RULE

Nothing can illustrate the foundation for lasting relationships, friendships and Directships than the passage recorded in Matthew 7:12:

> *In everything, do to others what you would have them do to you, for this sums up the Law and the Prophets.*[9]

Building this business really can be that simple. Treat other people the way you would like to be treated, and good things will come your way. The Golden Rule is the best mirror to reflect your thoughts, acts and motives.

Without being a good example, width and depth, edification, loyalty and close friendships—all tied directly to the Golden Rule—you will encounter a very difficult struggle in building a successful distributorship.

A FINAL NOTE

All the principles discussed in this chapter are cement which bonds all the building blocks together as you move toward Direct. These principles all point toward the need for you to make the right kind of choices.

---

9. New International Version (Grand Rapids: Zondervan, 1978).

You can develop the kind of character it takes to make this business work. You can be a good example. You can build width and depth. You have what it takes to edify your spouse, your family, your upline, your downline associates (or, at least, edify better!). You can be loyal. You can nourish close friendships. Sure, there are risks, but what are the alternatives?

You tap into unlimited potential when you make the decision to go Direct.

You can live your dreams
as you build toward going Direct in your own
SUCCESSFUL REFERRAL-BASED
DISTRIBUTION BUSINESS!

BUILDING BLOCKS

This is a lonely world without people to experience the great times with, but this business offers the opportunity to share your best times with others—in some of the greatest places around the world.

Sure, winning pins and achieving dreams is wonderful, but that's not as important as the relationships. There is simply no way success or fame can replace the close friendships we've found through this Amway business!

TYLER LIBBY
Former Soil Conservation
Service Manager
Diamond Direct
Distributor (USA)

So long as we love, we serve; so long as we are loved by others I would almost say that we are indispensable; and no man is useless while he has a friend.

ROBERT LOUIS
STEVENSON (1850-1894)
British Novelist
Author of *Treasure Island*

When you get completely caught up in something as wonderful as Amway, you become less aware of the challenges that you face and more aware of the excitement of reaching goals.

When you are this involved in your vision, you find that your creative imagination is released. You find ways to succeed that you never thought possible before.

DELAINE RUPE
Former Elementary
School Teacher
Diamond Direct Distributor (USA)

You can make more friends in two months by becoming interested in other people than you can in two years by trying to get other people interested in you.[1]

DALE CARNEGIE (1888-1955)
Speaker and Bestselling Author
Founder of the
Dale Carnegie Institute (USA)

People wonder sometimes why I am so sold on network marketing and interactive distribution. I know what a difference this business has made for my family. It took me from the clutches of bankruptcy and helped me to rise to new levels of prosperity. No one can put a price on an opportunity that can do so much.

LUC MIERESONNE
Former Grocery &
Furniture Store Owner
Diamond Direct Distributor (Belgium)

1. Dale Carnegie, *How to Win Friends and Influence People* (New York: Simon Schuster, 1936 & 1964), p.63.

Life is either a daring adventure or nothing!

HELEN KELLER (1880-1968)
U.S. Social Worker,
Speaker and Writer

*Once we got involved in the Amway business,
and once we saw the dream of financial freedom, we never
questioned the fact that we would build this business.*

*The knowledge that some of our friends wouldn't or
couldn't see the dream just made our "burn" get hotter- to show
them, to prove to them that we made the right decision.*

COLOMBO DISALVATORE
Former Construction
Business Owner
Diamond Direct Distributor (USA)

*Nice guys may appear to finish last, but usually they're
running in a different race.[2]*

KENNETH BLANCHARD
Bestselling Author of
The One-Minute Manager (USA)

*I believe that you start becoming successful when you take
your eyes off yourself. I've heard it said so many times—"If you
help enough other people achieve success, you will be successful." I know it's true, for it happened to my husband and me
when we truly understood what this business was all about.*

EFFIE REID
Homemaker
Diamond Direct
Distributor (USA)

2. Kenneth Blanchard and Norman Vincent Peale, *The Power of Ethical Management* (New York: William Morrow, 1988).

Discipline means doing what has to be done, doing it when it has to be done, doing it as well as it can be done, doing it that way all the time.

BOBBY KNIGHT
Head Basketball Coach of the
National Champion Indiana
University Hoosiers (USA)

When we realize that we are utilizing only a very small percentage of our potential, that thought can drive us past any fear, and it can propel us forward to the attainment of our goals.

Unlimited abilities, coupled with a proper attitude toward others, brings action. Action causes success. Nowhere is this more true than in this business!

GEORGE PEINTNER
Former Insurance
Agency Owner
Diamond Direct Distributor (USA)

You cannot teach a man anything. You can only help him to find it within himself.

GALILEO GALILEI (1564-1642)
Italian Astronomer
and Physicist

Stay consistent... be persistent... and you will achieve your goals! Consistency and persistence are two of the greatest "secrets" for success.

VALORIE HAUGEN
Former Records Technician
Executive Diamond
Direct Distributor (USA)

These six principles—the value of the worker, walking and talking in the trenches, responsibility and the pursuit of excellence, the value of training, dollars and sense, and working to serve—sound simple enough, but if applied sincerely they can revolutionize the workplace in America.

Now, restoring the sense of significance, overcoming the alienation and cynicism is not going to be accomplished by presidential proclamation or self-esteem commissions that so many states are ludicrously establishing, nor by new labor-management agreements or policy manuals. But these attitudes can be changed when we regain our sense of respect for the dignity of the individual...[3]

CHUCK COLSON
Bestselling Author of *Born Again*
and *Why America Doesn't Work;*
Served as Special Counsel to
President Richard Nixon;
Chairman of Prison Fellowship

There isn't much time in this business (or in any other, for that matter) to step back to admire your work or to wonder if you're headed in the right direction. Of course we should be thoughtful, we should learn from our mistakes and from our failures, but there is no time to brood. When you succeed, pat yourself on the back, take a five-minute break to celebrate, then get back to work. When you fail, have a good cry and then wipe your tears away. There is work to be done. There are frontiers to be explored. There are new limits to test and incredible victories to be won.[4]

RICH DEVOS
Co-founder, Amway
Corporation
Bestselling Author
and Speaker
Owner of the Orlando Magic NBA Team (USA)

3. Chuck Colson and Jack Eckerd, *Why America Doesn't Work* (Dallas: Word, 1991), p. 175.
4. Rich DeVos, *Compassionate Capitalism: People Helping People Help Themselves* (New York: Dutton Books, 1993), p. 236.

Leader-led training and mentoring provide an opportunity to encourage corporate values, while the close relationship gives management a chance to spot troublesome attitudes and practices and nip them in the bud.

True value is not just the worth of things. It is not just an appreciation of tangible assets tallied on a balance sheet. It is also the value of people, the worth of their individuality. A well-trained, enriched, and empowered work force is the direct link between true productivity and true profit.[5]

JACK ECKERD
Founder and former CEO of
the Eckerd drugstore chain;
Bestselling Author of *Finding
the Right Prescription*

Maybe it sounds like a simplistic phrase, but freedom and belief and dreams are really what this business is all about. People who have those vital ingredients will find a way to make it happen.

JOAQUIN LUCAS
Former Union Steel Worker
Diamond Direct Distributor (Spain)

Folks are generally as happy as they make up their minds to be.[6]

ABRAHAM LINCOLN
U. S. Statesman and
Sixteenth President

---

5. Chuck Colson and Jack Eckerd, *Why America Doesn't Work* (Dallas: Word, 1991), p. 162

6. Eleanor L. Doan, *The Speaker's Sourcebook* (Grand Rapids, MI: Zondervan, 1960), p. 120.

People everywhere are looking for freedom. It's true here in this country. It's true in Europe. It's true in Asia. It's the same all around the world. People simply want the opportunity to achieve their dreams and reach their goals.

This business gives people—no matter where they live or work now, and despite what background they are from—to break free from whatever is holding them back. This business offers a step-by-step system for developing the lifestyle that you want.

It's no wonder why Amway is growing so fast in virtually every free market country. And the best part is that we are just beginning to understand what the future holds for those of us who are willing to share this opportunity with people who want to be free!

FRED HARTEIS
Former High School Teacher
Double Diamond Direct Distributor (USA)
Past ADA Board Officer

Views

...Your Long-Distance and International Sponsoring Efforts

When you wrote out your prospect list (Chapter Eight), you were encouraged to develop a number of "long-distance," "distance" or "out-of-town" names. Distance, you were told, refers to people who live three or more hours away, which would generally require an overnight stay when you work that group.

So, dutifully, you listed your Uncle Calvin who lives on the other side of the state, your high school buddy Larry who moved somewhere out West, your ex-neighbors George and Martha who now live in Paris (as in France, not Texas or West Virginia!). You've kept adding a number of names to that list.

"Now," you ask, "when do I get to start building distance groups?"

It is a fair question, but one that has many answers. For starters, you shouldn't consider working distance until you:

- Are reasonably confident at sharing the plan, both with the Presentation Manual or on the board;

- Can answer most of the questions that come up when the plan is shown;

- Are willing to travel to work with a distance group (unless you are foster sponsoring in a foreign country—more about that toward the end of this chapter) at least one or two weekends a month for the next year;

  and

- Check upline for counselling and advice on plugging your distance distributors into the system.

With this framework in mind, let's move on to discuss the benefits of, drawbacks of and guidelines for building long-distance legs. Since we consider international groups to be in this category (with a few differences), we have prepared a discussion of sponsoring in foreign countries at the end of this chapter.

ADVANTAGES

First things first. Why should you consider sponsoring distance groups?

For starters, you probably don't have a choice. We've never known anyone who has built this business solely with local groups. We live in a transient society. It's not unusual anymore for people to move across town, across the state or province, across the nation or even into a neighboring country. Frankly, because we are so nomadic, you and many of your new distributors may know more out-of-town people than those who live within a three-hour radius.

With that in mind, let's discuss the advantages of sponsoring long-distance groups:

(1) Distance sponsoring helps weatherproof your business.

Consider this: What if you had built your business exclusively in Charleston or Charlotte during September 1990 when Hurricane Hugo hit, in Osaka, Japan during September 1991 when the horrible typoon swept through that country, in south Florida during August 1992 when Hurricane Andrew devastated the area or if you had built your business primarily in the upper Midwest states during the floods of July 1993? If so, your business would have undoubtedly nosedived for days, weeks and even months while residents (including all of your distributors) dug themselves out of the devastation caused by these weather-related disasters.

When you focus your efforts exclusively in one area, you make your business more susceptible to weather-related upheavals which tend to be geographic in nature.

As you build in more than one area, however, the weather problems in one community, state or even country don't affect your income so drastically.

(2) Building distance groups also helps solidify and diversify your business to protect you against economic downturns.

As with weatherproofing your business, the same principle applies to any area that is hit hard by economic downturns, such as with strikes, plant downsizings, military base closings and any other potential financial disaster.

No geographic area or marketplace niche is immune from unthinkable circumstances that can slow down or shut down the economy for a given period of time.

In fact, a quick glance at the front page of the *Wall Street Journal* or *USA Today* should convince you that business downturns are a fact of life. With most traditional businesses, you are dependent upon so many things which are out of control.

This business is different. In fact, Amway's growth often runs counter to conventional wisdom, actually exploding during recessionary times. That makes sense, since economic downturns force people to face the fact that job security is a myth and that they need to look for other ways to recession-proof their income.

Long-distance sponsoring allows you to avoid putting all your eggs in one basket, so to speak.

(3) If you are married, one of the best benefits from building long-distance legs is the fact that you get to spend time with your spouse.

Granted, going out of town a weekend or two every month may seem as if it would be challenging to a marriage. Depending upon your job situation, age of your children and other factors, you will probably have to spend some of the distance-building time away from your spouse and family. However, if you plan well, you should be able to travel out of town with your husband or wife at least part of the time.

Distance-building can also be a time of marriage-building. Not only can you grow together as you work the business and counsel downline people, but you can also have mini-honeymoons away from home and spend travel time talking about your vision, dreams, goals, action plan and habits.

Don and Nancy Wilson, one of the closest couples you will ever meet, point to long-distance sponsoring as a relationship-builder. He says:

When we got involved in this business, we were going in two different directions. I had a full schedule as a teacher and coach. Nancy somehow balanced careers as a registered nurse, homemaker and mother. What we didn't have a lot of was time with each other.

Once we really understood the potential of this business and got committed to building it, we also began working distance groups.

At first, we saw distance-building as a sacrifice, but our perception soon began to change.

Sure, these efforts sometimes took us away from each other and our kids, but those times also began to help us get free.

Best of all, we soon saw that Nancy and I were getting closer than we had ever been before.

Today, because of the tapes we've listened to, the books we've read, the functions we've attended and the time we've spent around people like Dexter and Birdie, and also because of so many hours we've spent traveling together, we have added a dimension to our marriage relationship that we didn't have before we got into this business.

(4) Another benefit of traveling while working distance groups is the education you receive.

Not only do you get to work with a growing circle of people who come from diverse family, economic and geographic backgrounds—that's a wonderful education in itself—but you can also spend lots of time listening to business-building cassettes.

The people who have become long-distance champions soon learn to distinguish **trip time** as **tape time.** Before long, you will begin to measure distance in a completely new way—not three hours, but "My new group is six tapes away."

(5) Building distance groups will force you and your group to use your time more wisely.

You will read more about distance-group time management in Chapter Fourteen, but suffice it for now to say that you will often discover that your out-of-town people will organize their telephone calls better, work harder toward getting people to meetings and listen more readily than your local distributors.

This principle is true, not only with this business, but in virtually every other area of life. In fact, isn't it interesting that the greatest Teacher who ever lived once said, "Only in his home town and in his own house is a prophet without honor" (Matthew 13:57, NIV).

Now, don't take this to mean that you can't build your business with a number of local groups. But balance it out. The fact remains that people from your local area don't always respect you and your time as much as others who are distance legs.

For example, you will find that local downline distributors will call numerous times to ask questions or seek counsel, and even though these calls don't cost money, perhaps, they can be costly in terms of your time. Long-distance people, however, tend to avoid adding lots of calls to their phone bills, so they will tend to make only one or two calls compared to a local person's ten calls. As you get your nine or more personally-sponsored legs, multiplied by dozens of downlines—that 10:1 ratio can quickly tie you permanently to the telephone (all the more reason to get on AMVOX, which we will discuss in the next chapter).

One of the added benefits of working distance is that your local legs often begin to esteem you and your time more. There is nothing like a little competition, if you want to call it that, to get people to realize that you are moving on in this business, with or without them.

With all these benefits, you can see that, done correctly, building distance legs can bring a brand new scope to your business and make you more effective with both long-distance **and** local groups.

CHALLENGES

Just as there are many benefits to building long-distance groups, there are also a few potential adjustments for which you should prepare.

As if you don't already know this, traveling costs money. The farther you travel, the more it costs.

Building distance groups can also be a challenge to your attitude, however if you have been listening to cassettes, a long-distance no-show, for example, won't faze you nearly as much.

In fact, it is during those moments when you decide whether you are willing to do whatever it takes to build this business or not.

It was during one of these moments, as they drove toward yet another meeting, that Diamonds Ron and Toby Hale made a life-changing decision. She remembers:

> *We were headed to show the plan to an out-of-town group. Ron stopped by the side of the road. We were both very tired. We had gone through some disappointments. But we had also been listening to tapes and reading books.*
>
> *Frankly, we were in a turmoil. It was at that moment, beside the road, that we realized we had a choice. Either we would get back on the road and go to the next meeting, or we would turn the car around, go home and forget the whole thing.*
>
> *It was that black-and-white. As we talked, we knew it was one or the other. There was no middle ground.*
>
> *Thankfully, the dream won out. All the things we had heard from Dexter and Birdie and other leaders came back to us. We began thinking about the people*

who were already in business with us—we knew we couldn't let them down.

We've thought about that moment beside the road many times since then. How different our life would have been if we hadn't made the right choice.

Everyone in the *Profiles of Success* has achieved Diamond or beyond because they have been willing to make the sacrifices to build a strong organization with both local and distance groups.

All of your leaders have faced "impossible" challenges, but they learned to do the impossible while traveling mile after mile.

Like Jerry and Cherry Meadows or Jack and Effie Reid, they learned to take turns driving while changing clothes. As with Don and Ruth Storms or Dave and Marge Lewis, they somehow found a way to show the plan and counsel downline without letting anyone know about their own personal upheavals going on back home. Like Kenny and Donna Stewart, Ed and Charlotte Courtney, Randy and Valorie Haugen, Jim and Linda Brollier or Merritt and Beth Wiese and many others, they learned to sleep in their cars and eat peanut butter sandwiches because they didn't want their distance downline distributors to know that they were going through financial disasters. As with George and Ruth Halsey or Joaquin and Marian Lucas, they found a way to squeeze in a few more one-on-ones before heading back home for a couple hours of sleep and yet another Monday morning. Like Dwight and Margaret Ann Smith or Bob and Bonnie Howard, they have frequented lots of all-night truckstops and downed gallons of coffee. As with Dick Hopper, Karen Yamada, Gerry Betterman or Helen Huebner, they have often had to travel alone—alone except for their dreams of bringing hope to hundreds and thousands of lives.

You get the point. The heroes of this business have paid the price for success. If you want to reach Direct, Emerald, Diamond and beyond, you must be willing to realize the fact that with building your business—distance or otherwise—there is a price to be paid in terms of time, money, hobbies, entertainment and other personal sacrifices.

GUIDELINES

With benefits and challenges clearly in view, let us offer these principles for building long-distance businesses:

(1) Distance sponsoring should be face-to-face, whenever possible.

Use an AD PACK, with either audio or video cassettes, to prospect and qualify, but you should sponsor primarily when you can show the plan in person or ask for upline assistance.

Granted, with the network of opportunity meetings available in most cities and towns throughout your country and abroad, you can sponsor people by sending AD PACKs, determining interest and having them attend an open in their area. However, unless you or your upline can make the commitment to go in and work with that distributor, you lessen the chances for success dramatically.

Sure, there are stories of people who were "orphan" distributors who built big organizations, but those accounts don't reflect the bad experiences of so many others who purchased a kit and were never given any direction or empowerment.

(2) Distance sponsoring requires a two-way commitment.

You must be willing to dedicate yourself to helping your distance downline build his or her business, in terms of time and money, but your prospect must also be willing to make a commitment. Work with a group as fast as you can, but be careful about pushing too much at first. Still, out-of-town people generally have to assume leadership roles more quickly than local distributors.

(3) When distance sponsoring, hold at least two meetings on your first visit.

Do one meeting to get things started, then hold another to begin cementing your group together.

(4) From the first visit on, teach distance groups how to **build** the business.

Your goal should be to teach them to contact and invite, draw circles, plug into the system and order products on the very first visit.

(5) Make a commitment to the distance group.

Be prepared to return at reasonable intervals. If the group is within driving distance, you should make a minimum of one or two visits every month during the first year; more frequent trips may be necessary within the first two to six months. When flying is required, someone in your upline may be willing to share that responsibility.

(6) Pack lots of tools for each visit.

For each new group, take several AD PACKS, 10-20 training and motivational tapes and throw in a few business-building books. Take a few extra Presentation Manuals, an extra easel and board (don't forget the erasable markers) and warehouse authorization forms (when instructed by your upline Direct).*

(7) Point your people to both open meetings and seminars and rallies in their area.

Subscribe to *Dreambuilders Review* and your upline Diamond's newsletter to find the nearest locations for scheduled meetings.

Above all else, seek your upline Direct Distributor's guidance. With something as crucial to your business as long-distance sponsoring, why try to do everything by yourself?

Your Direct may already be building a leg in the same area in which you have a prospect. Not only may you be able to tap

---

* These items are strongly recommended and available through your upline. However, business support materials are optional and not required.

into your upline's existing efforts, but he or she may also be able to travel with you at times to reduce expenses and multiply counseling time.

Never forget one over-riding principle for building groups—distance or otherwise: The object of sponsoring should always be to develop a Direct Distributor with maximum return on your investment of time and money. You need to be guided by this principle, but your decisions should also revolve around the fact that you are building relationships. Relationships are THE foundation for a large, profitable, long-term business.

This is an area where counselling upline will make the difference between success and failure. Ask for lots of advice from the people who are actively building long distance groups.

INTERNATIONAL SPONSORING

All Amway distributors have the opportunity to expand their businesses into other countries—for good reason. **The playing field for business is now the world.**

In his book, *Making Global Deals: What Every Executive Should Know About Negotiating Abroad,* Jeswald W. Salacuse, Tufts University professor of international law and member of Harvard's Program on Negotiation, writes:

> *Spectacular technological advances, especially in computers and communications, and profound political changes, like those in Europe and the Soviet Union, are causing the "globalization" of business. Companies in all countries are shifting from a national to a world-wide field of action and—especially—of vision.*[2]

Unlike most other direct sales or network marketing businesses, Amway offers an alternative in international sponsoring for those distributors who have both the income and the time to build an international business, much in the same way they build their businesses within their country. As a result, thousands of lines of sponsorship have already crossed international boundaries.

---

2. Jeswald W. Salacuse, *Making Global Deals: What Every Executive Should Know About Negotiating Abroad* (New York: Times Books, 1991), p.1.

Amway publishes a colorful four-page brochure, *International Sponsoring Guide* (SA-891), which answers most of the questions you will have about this exciting opportunity.

Please understand that there are two primary ways to sponsor people in other countries—either travelling to that country and establishing your business there or by utilizing the international sponsoring procedures to introduce a prospect as a "foster sponsor." For most people, we recommend the latter, since travelling to another country and building a business there can be complicated, more challenging, costly, and—in some cases—prohibited to non-residents of the country. Through the fostering method, however, your international group has a foster sponsor in the other country; that person takes full sponsorship responsibilities and works personally with a new distributor to insure a more successful start in building his or her own Amway business. However, let us note, if you are able to fulfill the business and legal requirements of travelling to and establishing a business in another country, you also have that opportunity. Check with your upline Direct for more information.

Since most people who read this chapter will opt for the foster sponsoring route, let's focus on that method. The procedures are relatively simple.

When you are ready to begin your international sponsoring efforts, start by following these basic guidelines:

(1) Counsel with your upline Direct Distributor before contacting your international prospect.

(2) Get the facts straight.

Don't destroy your credibility and chances with a prospect by making undocumented claims or offering wrong information.

For example, while Amway is spreading to a growing number of free market nations throughout the world, we are not in **all** countries. An Amway business may only be conducted in the countries where Amway has established a corpo-

rate operation or has authorized distributorship activity.†

(3) Make the initial prospecting contact yourself.

Usually, the foster sponsor will not make a "cold contact" for you.

(4) Contact your prospect in one of two ways:

• Telephone

Contact your prospect and determine if he or she would be interested in knowing more about a business that you are building. Let the prospect know that there you plan to expand into that person's country, and that you are looking for someone who would like to participate in this expansion. Ask if they would be interested in listening to a tape that will explain more about the business. Then send an AD PACK* with a

---

† Contact your upline for information about countries in which you may do business.

* Some AD PACKs and sponsoring information are available in a variety of languages. Check upline for details.

short note asking for a response either by telephone or letter.

- Letter

     When you cannot contact a prospect by telephone or if you prefer to do so by letter, send an AD PACK and write a short note explaining the expansion prospects outlined in the previous paragraph. Again, ask for a response either by telephone or mail.

(5) Once you get a reply of interest from a prospect, contact your upline Direct.

     Your Direct will help guide you through the process of filling out an "International Sponsoring Prospect Report Form."

     Follow the instruction on the form, then send it to the address listed. Preferably, a copy of the letter of interest from your prospect (or a detailed note from you confirming a phone call of interest) should accompany the form.

(6) You will receive information from your upline about whom your prospect should contact and any other pertinent details.

     You will need to write a letter or make a telephone call to give this information to your prospect. Encourage him or her to make that contact as soon as possible.

(7) If the prospect decides to get involved in building his or her own business in that country, you will receive a letter from Amway confirming that you have been recorded as the international sponsor.

After the prospect gets started, send letters of encouragement and maintain contact with all international legs so you can be aware of the progress, but leave all business-building techniques to the Foster Sponsor.

     One final note to people who know U.S. military personnel who are stationed in countries where Amway has an affiliate: You have an excellent opportunity for international sponsoring, but you should follow the proper procedure. Service men and women may operate on a military base as a U.S. Distributor, provided that they have permission from the base commander. Amway products for personal use **only** may be sent to these service personnel by you through the APO/FPO mailing address. Products for resale must be shipped by regular shipping methods. Military personnel (or spouses) who are U.S. distributors may contact prospects in foreign countries, but should then follow the procedures previously explained for international sponsoring.

We encourage you to enjoy the prestige and increased income of expanding your business internationally through the international sponsorship Program. Thanks to people, both at Amway's corporate headquarters and with each overseas affiliate, and thanks to the distributors who have sacrificed time and money to go into these countries, the world of network marketing and interactive distribution has become a profitable international opportunity.

A FINAL NOTE

Unlike most "traditional" businesses—retail, franchise or discount—you are not limited to a specific location or territory with your Amway business. In the world of commerce, that fact is a tremendous advantage.

At the same time, you do not have to "invent the wheel" as you seek to develop distance groups, either in your country or internationally. You already have a proven, workable pattern to follow. The international sponsoring program—coupled with our system of books, tapes and other business support materials, and meetings—form an unbeatable combination for giving you the opportunity to develop a worldwide business.

Now it is up to you. Develop your list. Keep adding out-of-town and international prospects to that list. Encourage your downline to do the same. Pay the price. Above all else, celebrate the breakthroughs.

**You can solidify your organization with
powerful long-distance and far-reaching
international groups as you
BUILD YOUR OWN SUCCESSFUL
DISTRIBUTION MARKETING BUSINESS!**

BUILDING BLOCKS:

I don't understand those who keep trying to do things to hurt and hold back entrepreneurs. As far as I am concerned, the future of this country and the entire free world is people who believe and participate in free enterprise. Nothing embodies freedom more than entrepreneurs.

JACK KEMP
Former NFL Quarterback
U.S. Statesman
Co-founder of **Empower America**

Traveling and working with people in different countries has added an entirely new dimension of belief in this system. We find that people are basically the same, no matter where you travel. We are just separated by customers and territories, but everyone seems to have the same hunger for freedom. With the Amway business, we can offer that opportunity for financial flexibility and emotional freedom.

PEDRO LIZARDI
Former Computer
Programmer
Diamond Direct
Distributor (Puerto Rico)

...nothing in life just happens. It isn't enough to believe in something; you have to have the stamina to meet obstacles and overcome them, to struggle.[1]

GOLDA MEIR (1898-1978)
Israeli Stateswoman and
Prime Minister

People ask me what it's like to reach Diamond and beyond. There is no way to describe the lifestyle. The travel, the freedom, the time to be together, sharing things, personal growth, excitement—that's what this business is all about.

The best part is that you can share it all with others and help them attain this lifestyle, too. What could be better?

BONNIE HOWARD
Former Dental Assistant
Executive Diamond
Direct Distributor (USA)

Common sense is genius with its working clothes on.

THOMAS JEFFERSON (1743-1826)
Third President
of the United States

The best part about working distance groups now is that it allows you to be with people who think like we think—who inspire us. What a difference it is to be around men and women who are even bigger dreamers than we are. That's exciting.

ED KNICKMAN
Former Computer Salesman
Executive Diamond
Direct Distributor (USA)

---

1. Golda Meir, *My Life* (New York: Putnam, 1975), p.26.

One pound of learning requires ten pounds of common sense to apply it.

HORACE GREELEY (1811-1872)
U.S. Journalist,
Politician and Educator

When we got involved in this business, we didn't have a lot of money, credibility, fancy clothes or expensive cars, but we did have a "want-to" that helped us focus on getting the job done. We were tired of being broke, and we made a commitment to do whatever we had to do.

LOUIE CARRILLO
Former Professional
Air Traffic Controller
Executive Diamond
Direct Distributor (USA)

I do not want to talk about what you understand about this world. I want to know what you will do about it. I do not want to know what you hope. I want to know what you will work for. I do not want your sympathy for the needs of humanity. I want your muscle. As the wagon driver said when they came to a long, hard hill, "Them that's going on with us, get out and push. Them that ain't, get out of the way." [2]

ROBERT FULGHUM
Bestselling Author
and Philosopher (USA)

---

2. Robert Fulghum, *It Was on Fire When I Lay Down on It* (New York: Villard Books, 1989), p. 109.

The best part of building this business is our personal freedom. What we've sacrificed to reach this point is nothing in comparison to being free from debt, free from life's ruts and free to continue building our future.

LITA HART
Former Travel Agent
Executive Diamond Direct
Distributor (USA)

If you're going to attempt something new, don't try it, do it. Go full out. If you're going to make a mistake, make a big one. Good entertainers do that all the time. They barrel ahead. It's worse to be wishy-washy than to be wrong.[3]

CAROL BURNETT
Comedy Legend and
Actress (USA)

The secret to building this business is the size of your dream. In fact, we reached Double Diamond because our dream was that big, but then we plateaued for awhile. Getting new dreams got us going again. For us, those newfound dreams were to help more people achieve the economic and emotional freedom we had developed. Once we got started again, we were already on our way to Triple and our organization was spreading quickly throughout the United States, Europe and Asia.

KAY SHAW
Former School Teacher
Triple Diamond Direct Distributor
(USA)

---

3. Quoted from Walter Anderson, *The Greatest Risk of All* (Boston: Houghton Mifflin Company, 1988) p. 23.

All our dreams can come true—if we have the courage to pursue them.

WALT DISNEY (1901-1966)
Visionary U. S. Film Producer,
Animator and Theme Park Pioneer

A lot of people want personal freedom and financial flexibility, but they just don't have the avenue to get there. This business provides a step-by-step plan. The fast growth throughout the free world is proof of that.

When you decide to get involved, be aware that the secret to starting your own business is getting precise with your dreams and goals. Put dates on your dreams.

SERGE VALLEE
Former Sales Representative
Diamond Direct
Distributor (Canada)

The hardest victory is victory over self.

ARISTOTLE (384-322 B.C.)
Greek Philosopher

The best part of building our Amway business, in addition to the financial flexibility, is that now our family actually spends time together. That seldom happened before.

TIM KLINE
Former Appliance Store Owner
Diamond Direct Distributor (USA)

The secret to building this business is belief. One of the hardest things to do, especially in the beginning, is to believe that the things you do and the time you invest will someday pay off. It's so easy to look at those who are Diamonds and beyond, and to say, "Sure, I know it will work for them—after all, they have a great lifestyle and plenty of time to enjoy it, but will it work for me?"

During the first weeks and months, you've simply got to make your choices based on belief. You've got to invest your energy and time based on that belief. But when you make the right choices—based on belief—you soon begin to enjoy the rewards.

Because the Diamonds in this business made the right choices, they have lots of time to do the things they want. But in the beginning, they were each just like you—with belief and choices.

DARRELL RUPE
Former Optometrist
Diamond Direct Distributor (USA)

The Time Clock

...Your Personal and Professional
Management Skills

You are probably already struggling to balance all the areas of your life. In fact, you have also probably wondered, "How in the world am I going to fit my business-building activities into an already-rushed schedule?"

It is a fair question. After all, life is fragmented for most of us.

However, unless you find a way to manage the precious resource known as time, you will probably never learn to manage your future.

PRIME TIME

The major television networks diligently guard the hours from eight to 11 each night. They know this is when they have the largest audiences and, thus when they can make the most money from selling commercials. They call these hours "prime time." Prime time for the distributor, for example, is the precious intervals each day spent actually showing the plan.

Now that you are involved in network marketing, you need to be aware of your prime time, as well. You can build your business virtually any time of the day or night, but you will find that some hours are more profitable than others. Certain times of each day and week, generally during evenings, offer greater opportunities than any other time. During those hours, everything else should take a lesser priority.

But you can't use your prime time effectively if you let other things—we call them time-bandits (more about these thiefs later in this chapter)—rob you of your peak hours.

First, just how valuable are your hours?

TIME VALUE CHART

IF YOU WANT AN ANNUAL INCOME OF	EACH HOUR IS WORTH	EACH MINUTE IS WORTH	AN HOUR\A DAY FOR A YEAR IS WORTH
$20,000	$10.32	$.1728	$2,518
$25,000	12.81	.2134	$3,125
$30,000	15.37	.2561	$3,750
$35,000	17.93	.2988	$4,375
$40,000	20.64	.3596	$5,036
$50,000	25.62	.4268	$6,250
$75,000	38.42	.6404	$9,375
$100,000	51.22	.8538	$12,499

NOTE: The table is based on a typical year of 244 working days of eight hours each. You can project the value of your time by viewing it over 45 or more years. Generally, by saving one hour each working day during a normal career, you can add the equivalent of six years of productivity.

Obviously, time is important. But how do you keep the time-bandits from robbing you of your prime time?

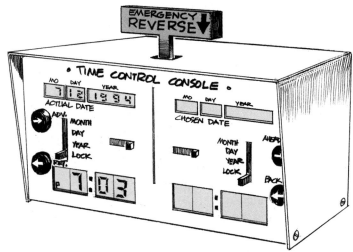

TIME MANAGEMENT

Technically, you can't manage time because you have no control over it. And since you can't manufacture more hours in the day—especially during your prime time—all you can do is learn how to manage and prioritize your use of time. Therefore, when people speak of time management, they are actually talking about self-management.

To be successful at avoiding time-bandits, you must focus on your **goals,** not on **activities.**

If you constantly feel rushed and are still short of time, chances are pretty good that you need to do something about your personal time-management habits and practices. This is something that you can, and must, change!

But how?

TIME HABITS

The first step in managing your life is knowing precisely where your time goes. Most people have a general idea—so many hours are spent working, sleeping, eating and enjoying recreation. But exactly where do the hours go?

Time management experts suggest a very effective tactic for analyzing your time habits: keep a detailed time log for each 30-minute period of your working day and carefully analyze what you do with your time.

Candidly, this is a bothersome exercise, but when you take the time to do those things that add value, you multiply your results!

TIME BANDITS

Once you investigate trends in your schedule, you will also see that time-wasting habits can rob you of your most vital possession—time—and give little or nothing in return in terms of profitability.

In a time-management study released by *USA Today*, research showed that during his or her career, the average American worker spends:

- Six months sitting at red lights.

- One year searching for belongings amid the clutter of home or office.

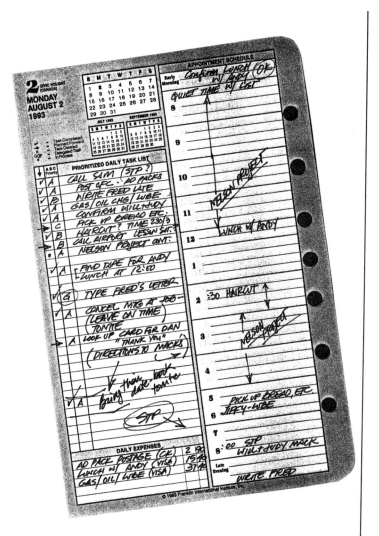

- Eight months opening junk mail.

- Two years playing "telephone tag."

- Three years attending meetings.

- Five years waiting in lines, and

- Six years eating.

6 MONTHS

A YEAR!

8 MONTHS

2 YEARS

5 YEARS

3 YEARS

6 YEARS

From the time-log that you keep, you will probably begin to see a pattern of "bandits." Watch specifically for the notorious "dirty dozen":

(1) Procrastination—the worst!

(2) Unnecessary routine tasks done because of habit

(3) Distractions or interruptions

(4) Inefficient use of the telephone

(5) Needless or lengthy meetings

(6) Excessive socializing

(7) Unclear organizational goals

(8) Inability to say "No!"

(9) Trying to do too much or over-committing

(10) Red tape and paper shuffling

(11) Poor delegation

(12) Waiting for work to be finished by others

You may be able to add several time bandits from your lifestyle to our "dirty dozen." Brainstorm with your family and upline associates as you identify and begin to eliminate the time-bandits which are most prevalent in your life.

Remember, you can rationalize all time-bandits, but you cannot hide the fact that those moment-depleters make unmistakable statements about your goals, philosophy, values, intentions and needs. Simply stated, they will keep you from reaching your goals.

APPLY TIME-MANAGEMENT TECHNIQUES TO YOUR BUSINESS

One of the most important things in life and in this business is learning to major on the majors and minor on the minors.

What do we mean?

Majoring on the majors implies a learned skill at determin-

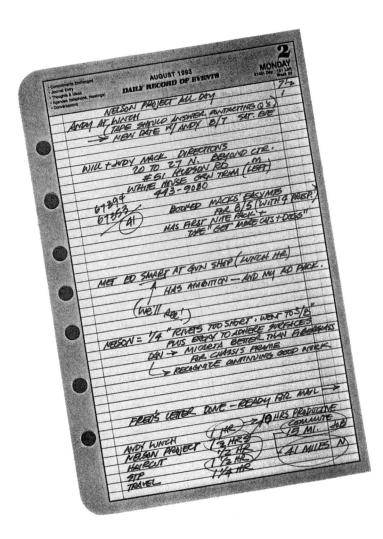

ing the most important tasks you must do to reach your goals.

To define our "major-on-the-majors" time management philosophy, let us offer these nineteen basics:

(1) For starters, below is a list of 12 daily activities that will lead you to success in this business. Use forms available through your upline to check the appropriate box each day of the month as you complete that task and head toward your 30-day objective.

The "Daily Dozen"

"DAILY DOZEN"	1	2	3	4	5	6	7	8	9	10	11	12	13	14	15	16	17	18	19	20	21
Give Thanks																					
Family Time																					
Review Goals & Dream																					
Read 15 Minutes																					
Listen To Tape																					
S.T.P. & Follow Up																					
Exercise																					
New Contact																					
10 Phone Calls																					
Vitamins & Use Amway																					
List — Things To Do																					
Positive Statement																					

RGETTING + REACHING + PRESSING x VISION = SUCCESS

(2) Next, make a list every day and prioritize your activities.

As you develop your list, put a number in front of each one. Number one is what must absolutely be done today. As you go down the list, get the major ones out of the way. Then, if you miss the minors, you can put them on tomorrow's list. You may even find that numbers fifteen and sixteen have taken care of themselves, and you can discard them altogether.

(3) Use time-saving devices such as the AMVOX voice-mail messaging service by Amway.

Two things are important with tools such as AMVOX—**when** you answer and **how** you answer.

One includes staying up with the messages. We both start in the morning—while we are getting ready and even when we hit the road—to go through our messages. Twenty minutes on the road is twenty minutes of messages off the AMVOX. We try to keep up with them during the day. And before going to bed—no matter what the day's activities have included—it's a good idea to clear out any remaining messages.

The second part is to be as organized as possible with your messages and to make it easy for the person on the other end to answer you. Once your business really starts to take off, these two tips can help you be so much more effective. An instructional "Tips and Tricks" list is available from AMVOX.

(4) As you build your business, realize that you can't do everything perfectly.

This gets back to majoring on the majors—and it certainly relates to time management for people who are serious about this business.

There are a lot of repetitious things that can be done less often. Now, we are not saying that you should completely let your house and lawn go neglected while you build the business, but dust is still dust. Grass is still grass. You can dust your house and mow your lawn every single day, while taking valuable time away from your business. Putting some busy-work off or doing repetitive things less is sometimes the wisest thing you can do.

(5) Cluster activities in twos and threes.

This seems so simple, but you might be surprised at how many people waste so much time by doing only one thing at a time. Listen to cassettes while you are driving, for starters. Discuss important things with your spouse over dinner—things that are happening with your family and your business. Use dream-session time with your distributors, as you look at luxury cars and walk through new homes, to counsel and teach.

(6) If you are married and have children, get everyone involved.

Don't try to do everything by yourself. Discuss ways to break down some of the responsibilities—all the way from paying bonus checks to handling products. This gives everyone in the family a better understanding of what you are trying to do together. Your kids won't be ruined if they have to give up some play time to pitch in an hour or so every day. In fact, by sharing in the business and learning a good work ethic, they learn to be better time managers, too!

(7) Use wisdom in building your long distance business.

Once you start distance groups, make a commitment to spend a weekend once a month for the next year with each one.

When you are only available once a month, your distance distributors tend to put more of an importance on your time.

Hold as many meetings as possible during your time, then be willing to spend late-night hours counselling with people who are already in the business.

Don't forget to work on dream-building with the people in your group. Perhaps you can stop by a car dealership on your way to a meeting or tour a home during lunch.

Here is the bottom line: Time away from your family is extremely valuable. Use it wisely as you build long-distance groups.

(8) Schedule quiet time for yourself to get things done.

If you don't make time to be alone, you will constantly be at the mercy of others.

(9) Analyze your schedule.

Ask yourself what would happen if you didn't get certain things done; if "nothing" is the answer, stop doing them.

(10) Allow flexibility in your day.

Plan some time for the unexpected. Tasks often seem to take longer than you initially expected. Be realistic by being flexible.

(11) Learn how to say "No!"

Be gracious with people, but firm with your time. Time management often means setting your priorities and sticking with them.

(12) Eliminate as many mistakes as possible.

Do things right the first time, even if it takes a little more time.

(13) Spot negative trends.

If crises and hurtful patterns keep reoccurring, learn to be proactive instead of reactive.

(14) Eliminate, shorten, modify, combine or otherwise improve paperwork.

Try to handle paperwork only once. When materials hit your desk, you have only two questions to ask yourself: (1) "Do I need to keep this?" and (2) "Where do I put it right now?"

Keep clutter under control—as much as you can—or it will control you.

(15) Take time to be a good listener.

> This one skill is invaluable, for it usually saves time and almost always prevents problems.

(16) Show people your respect for their time.

> They will usually return the favor.

(17) Conquer procrastination.

> Force yourself to make decisions **now** and ACT **now** upon those decisions.

(18) Be accountable to someone.

> Your upline is someone who can help you be focused and on-track.

(19) Take time for yourself.

> Don't forget to refresh, care for and be good to yourself.

The most important time management concept is the over-all realization that people build the business. The more time you can spend with people—prospecting them, building relation-ships, showing the opportunity to them, counselling them, dream-building with them—the bigger your business will grow.

Unfortunately, there are so many busy-things you can do that tend to keep you away from the most important things. So, to spend time with people, you have to learn to manage time better than ever before.

Time management is one of the most important keys to building a great business. The schedule book pocket calendar and the Franklin Planner are great tools for managing your time.*

A FINAL NOTE

There has never been a system devised that will work, unless you make it work.

Begin by keeping a time log. Analyze your time habits for the next two weeks. Then develop strategies to get better con-

---

* These items are strongly recommended and available through your Upline. However, business support materials are optional and not required.

trol of your time usage. Starting now, you can maximize your greatest assets in the weeks and years to come.

Primarily, let us encourage you to balance time in all aspects of your life:

- Spiritual

- Family

- Career/your own business

- Social

- Physical and emotional wellness

- Self-development

Balance is the foundation for your career as a network marketing professional, and you can do it.

You can become more organized and accomplish more worthwhile goals as you BUILD YOUR OWN SUCCESSFUL REFERRAL MARKETING BUSINESS!

BUILDING BLOCKS:

There are many people who own their own businesses and who have worked long, hard hours in the most difficult situations, and who still have very little to show for their efforts.

But this business has so many success stories that we can point to. We have a proven system to follow. We have long-term potential, and an opportunity that has the best parts of the most up-and-coming trends, but without the worst parts of traditional businesses.

As far as I am concerned, I can't see doing anything else. Why not travel a proven road of success?

CARROL REA
Former Optician
Executive Diamond
Direct Distributor (USA)

Things do not change; we change.

HENRY DAVID THOREAU (1817-1862)
U.S. Naturalist and Writer

This business has many benefits. One of the greatest rewards has been to better understand why we were put here and what our purpose is. Another is that you are surrounded with people who believe in you—who get excited when you reach your goals.

*One of the best advantages, however, is much more personal. Jerry and I have grown more close as a couple. We've built this business **together**. We've learned to be better mates and parents.*

Not long after we got involved, we heard someone say that this was so much more than a business. It's true! It's a great, positive and fulfilling lifestyle.

POLLY HARTEIS
Former Registered Nurse
Diamond Direct
Distributor (USA)

If time be of all things most precious, wasting time must be the greatest prodigality, since lost time is never found again; and what we call time enough always proves little enough. Let us then be up and doing, and doing to a purpose; so by diligence shall we do more with less perplexity.

BENJAMIN FRANKLIN
(1706-1790)
U.S. Inventor, Printer,
Diplomat
Author and Statesman

We knew how to work hard when we got in this business. We had already spent a decade taking care of a dairy farm. You haven't lived until your entire life centers around 135 Holstein cows!

But there's a big difference between working hard and working smart. No matter what we did, in terms of our dairy, it all had to be done all over again the next day. The secret of this business is that you can stop trading time for dollars. You can invest your time and energy, and can eventually reap a tremendous harvest in terms of time and money. The only thing holding you back with this business is the size of your dreams!

ED COURTNEY
Former Dairy Farmer
Executive Diamond
Direct Distributor (USA)

The day you take complete responsibility for yourself, the day you stop making any excuses, that's the day you start to the top.

O. J. SIMPSON
Pro Football Hall of Fame Member
and Broadcaster (USA)

One thing at a time well done is worth one thousand things started, but unfinished. To succeed in this business, you have to learn to be a finisher. It's one thing to prospect people, but you must also get them in front of the plan and follow through. It's one thing to get people in the business, but it's another thing to get the business in them. It's not enough to just get a person's name on the application; you also have to be willing to counsel and work with them. Being a finisher requires an ongoing commitment, but without that dedication, I don't think you can ever enjoy great achievements.

CONNIE FOLEY
Homemaker
Triple Diamond
Direct Distributor (USA)

Successful people are influenced by the desire for pleasing results. Failures, on the other hand, are influenced by the desire for pleasing methods. Failures are often satisfied with whatever results can be obtained by doing only the things they like to do. Successful people are able to do the things no one else likes to do because they have a strong purpose. Their purpose is strong enough to make them form the habit of doing things they don't like to do in order to achieve the purposes they want to accomplish.

DR. LARRY BAKER
Educator, Author and
Time & Management
Consultant (USA)

We had such powerful reasons for building our business. I wanted to have the freedom and time to train extensively as a triathlete. Anna always wanted to be able to breed and show her boxer dogs. You don't do either of those things without money and time. This business gave us both, but not before we were first willing to spend lots of time and energy doing the things that others are often unwilling to do. Sure, it took commitment to our action plan. It was a sacrifice. But we had already learned a lot about discipline through athletics. It helped us develop the consistency and persistency that we needed to keep going. That's the secret—it all comes down to your reasons, your dreams, your commitment and your willingness to invest your time and energy.

CRAIG DEANE
Triathlete
Executive Diamond
Direct Distributor
(New Zealand)

You've got to have a plan and the best time to complete it is the night before. That way you'll wake up motivated and you won't be floundering around for half a day just defining what you want to accomplish.

TOM HOPKINS
Sales Trainer, Speaker
and Bestselling Author (USA)

Some   ple have asked us about our secret of success. I believe that ue way to succeed in this business is simply taking your eyes off yourself and focusing your attention on the success of the people in your organization.

When you think about it, it's really no secret at all. You just have to do it!

LYNNE MADDISON
Former Secretary
Diamond Direct
Distributor (USA)

Time is the scarcest resource and unless it is managed, nothing else can be managed.

PETER DRUCKER
Economist, Educator
and Bestselling Author (USA)

One of the great things about this business was the one thing I had trouble understanding at first. We didn't have enough time as it was, so investing more time in a business didn't make sense.

Thankfully, Ron and I learned firsthand the value of time-compounding. By investing time and by building equity in our growing organization, we began to develop more time.

*Now, time is on our side. We have the option of getting up in the morning when **we** decide. If we want to go skiing or fishing or whatever, it's up to us.*

This wonderful benefit—freedom of time—is available to anyone who makes the right decisions and who decides to plug into the system.

MELANIE RUMMEL
Former Business
Consultant and Teacher
Diamond Direct
Distributor (USA)

Take time to live;
  it is one secret of success.
Take time to think;
  it is the source of power.
Take time to play;
  it is the secret of youth.
Take time to read;
  it is the foundation of knowledge.
Take time for friendship;
  it is the source of happiness.
Take time to laugh;
  it helps lift life's load.
Take time to dream;
  it hitches the soul to the stars.
Take time to worship;
  it is the highway to reverence.
Take time to pray;
  it helps bring God near
  and washes the dust of earth from our eyes.

UNKNOWN

Our vision of this Amway business has expanded over the years. At first, it was a secondary income. Now it has become our primary vehicle for financial growth and stability.

Also, our view towards time has changed. In the beginning, we were so busy that we only had a small amount of time to dedicate to this business. But we kept investing time here and there, leveraging what we did have. Now, because the leveraging principle works so well, we have all the time we want to do whatever we want.

When you pay the price, your vision and view of time will keep expanding!

CURTIS LEDBETTER
Former College Professor
Double Diamond
Direct Distributor (USA)

The surest way to make customers fall in love with your business, come back for more, and tell others how wonderful you are is to practice the "and then some" principle. Your products do all that you said they would do—and then some. Your service is as prompt, reliable, and courteous as you promised it would be—and then some. If the customer needs your help after the sale, you provide that help—and then some. It's the willingness to go that extra mile that separates the true champions from the also-rans.[1]

MICHAEL LEBOEUF, Ph.D.
Bestselling Author, Lecturer and
Professor of Management at the
University of New Orleans

---

1. Michael LeBoeuf, Ph.D., *How to Win Customers And Keep Them for Life* (New York: Berkley Books, 1987), p. 123.

Treat your business like a big business, right from the beginning. The potential is there. You can grow and expand— far beyond anything you can conceive right now—but only if you understand what you have in your hands, and only if you do whatever it takes to build your business on a strong foundation. Be committed to your business. Refuse to take shortcuts. Again, treat your business like a big business—from the way you deal with people to the way you market the products and use the tools. Done wrong, your business won't grow. But done right—as you follow the system—your business can be as big as you want it to be!

RON HALE
Former Air Force Recruiter
Diamond Direct Distributor (USA)
Past ADA Board President (1990)

Wading Through
The Red Tape*
...Your Legal and Ethical Policies

One of the great benefits of starting and building your own network marketing business is that you don't have the tremendous start-up costs of the typical retail business (including a wholesale or discount enterprise).

Legal costs for those "normal" businesses, for example, can run into megabucks just to set up a company.

The beauty of network marketing, by contrast, is that you don't have to spend thousands upon thousands of dollars in legal and corporate fees. However, there are some elementary things that you should consider, depending upon tax laws which cover your specific country, state/province and city.

---

*This tax information is intended only for general and resource purposes. It is neither legal nor accounting advice, nor should it be regarded as substitute for professional counsel on tax and business matters from your CPA, tax advisor or attorney.

TO INCORPORATE OR NOT?

It is imperative that you follow the simple legal guidelines set forth by Amway in the materials you find in your sales and marketing kit.

In addition, you may need to make decisions during the coming years concerning the question of incorporating.

In many free market countries, there are several advantages of incorporating. One is the limited liability a corporation offers. Another consideration is the subject of taxes. Corporate tax rates have historically and generally been lower than individual tax rates. That advantage, however, has been decreased in the United States somewhat by the Tax Reform Act of 1986 and the February 1993 home-office ruling by the Supreme Court.

Still, one of the best ways to pay less taxes is still owning a full-time or part-time business (more about this later in the chapter).

In the United States, you can elect to run your business in one of several ways:

• A traditional "C" corporation

• A "Subchapter S" corporation

The "S" has traditionally been used during start-up years in which you expect to lose money. Both income and losses flow directly through to the individual shareholders. These losses may be used as tax write-offs by these individuals.

Regardless of your choice, you must file a Form 1099 statement of earnings at the close of each tax year. You should be careful to reserve sufficient funds for your tax payments from ongoing earnings.

If you operate as an unincorporated sole proprietor, you must file Schedule C of Form 1040.

Needless to say, seek professional counsel before deciding on the type of business organization you select. Your upline Emerald should be able to help with your decisions. (Most Distributors usually opt to incorporate at Emerald or above).

U.S. TAX ADVANTAGES

Many of the generous tax breaks remain for part-time or full-time business owners after the 1986 Tax Reform Act, but the real advantages come from advance planning, not after the fact.

Operating your personal business opens up numerous tax-saving opportunities.

Owning and operating your own business continues to be one of the very best, perfectly legal tax advantages. Use the laws to your benefit, but be prudent. Always check with a lawyer or accountant if you have any questions.

383

YOU AND THE IRS

One of the great benefits of operating a home-based business in the United States is the opportunity to deduct business expenses from your gross income, just as any other business does.

Based upon eligibility, these legitimate business expenses may include a percentage of the following **(as they relate to your business)**:

- home repairs
- property taxes
- utilities and services
- insurance

- telephone

- rent

- casualty losses

- mortgage interest

  and

- mortgage depreciation.

You may even be able to claim partial deductions for purchasing, installing and maintaining some Amway products such as your own Amagard® home security system!

However, there are strict guidelines. In the wake of a monumental February 1993 U.S. Supreme Court ruling, the Internal Revenue Service has issued new guidelines. Tax analysts say the new rules are, if anything, even tougher than the old ones.

The issue: When is a home office your principal place of business? According to the IRS, only if you spend most of your time there, earn most income there and have most of your business equipment there.[2]

Generally, you may take deductions for your home-based business ONLY if the business portion is used exclusively and on a regular basis as either:

(1) the principal place of activity for your network marketing business

   or

(2) place where you meet or deal with customers or clients in the normal course of your network marketing business.

"Exclusive use" is the key phrase, and it means 100% business use. In other words, the areas or storage places that you use may only be used for your network marketing activities or inventory.

If part of your home or storage space meets these criteria, you can divide the expenses of operating your home between

---

2. Bill Montague, "IRS Redefining the Home Office," *USA Today*, February 9, 1993, p. B1.

your business and personal use. That percentage can vary, but is generally calculated by dividing the square feet in your house or by segmenting the rooms used for business.

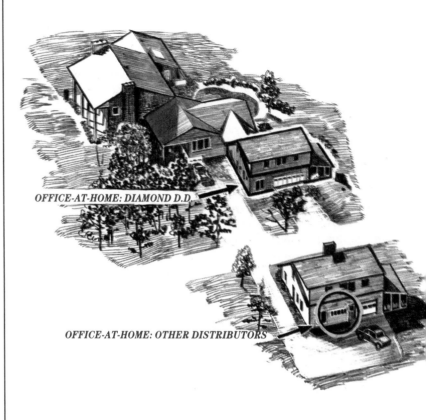

OFFICE-AT-HOME: DIAMOND D.D.

OFFICE-AT-HOME: OTHER DISTRIBUTORS

You may also be able to depreciate the portion of your home and furnishings used exclusively for your business, plus certain automobile expenses. In addition, you may be able to write off any home computer or office equipment, as well as travel and business-related entertainment expenses.

A FINAL NOTE

Let us end with a word of caution: This chapter is certainly no thorough treatment of the intricate legal details of owning your own business, especially since readers hail from a multitude of free market countries. Still, we have sought to offer a few starting points and have used the U.S. laws as a reference.

Regardless of your pin level or the country in which you reside, remember to always check with professional and competent individuals whom you use to assist in preparing your tax returns. Also, check with your upline about tax preparation materials which are available through the network.*

Above all, deal with these details from the beginning; then you can be free to concentrate on building your business correctly.

**As you understand the
legal aspects and seek wise counsel,
you can BUILD A SUCCESSFUL
INTERACTIVE DISTRIBUTION BUSINESS.**

---

*These items are strongly recommended and available through your Upline. However, business support materials are optional and not required.

BUILDING BLOCKS:

First we must understand that there can be no life without risk—and when our center is strong, everything else is secondary, even the risks. Thus, we best prepare by building our inner strength, by sound philosophy, by reaching out to others, by asking ourselves what matters most.

ELIE WIESEL
Nobel Prize Winning Author and
Holocaust Survivor (USA)

The biggest risk in life is not risking. When you refuse to take any chance of losing, you eliminate the possibility of winning. That's no way to live.

JIM MARTIN
Former Veterinarian
Diamond Direct
Distributor (USA)

*When you talk to people about themselves, you are rubbing them the right way, you are working **with** human nature. When you talk to people about yourself, you are rubbing people the wrong way and working **against** human nature.*

Take these four words out of your vocabulary: "I, me, my, mine." Substitute for those four words one word, the most powerful word spoken by the human tongue—"you." [1]

LES GIBLIN
Bestselling Author and
Speaker (USA)

When people ask me how to make it in this business, I always have three points ready—being the minister I am. One, know that you were created to succeed. Two, plug into the Yager networking system, because it is the best you'll find. Three, do whatever it takes for as long as it takes. Period!

TEDD FISH
Minister
Diamond Direct
Distributor (USA)

The success of companies is based, in large part, on the integrity of their leaders. For over 30 years, Amway has led the way in network distribution, and they have provided a free enterprise opportunity for literally millions of people around the world.

I'm proud of my association with this great company, and I urge you to consider the Amway opportunity as a business of your own.

TOM LANDRY
Legendary Former Head
Football Coach,
Dallas Cowboys (USA)

---

1. Les Giblin, *Skill with People* (Wyckoff, NJ: Giblin, 1985), p. 3.

No matter what your dreams are when you get in this business, you can reach them. I had always wanted to travel, so it was exciting to look through pictures and imagine what it would be like when we reached Diamond. It has all come true. We've traveled to the most beautiful places in the world— Hawaii, Jamaica, New Zealand, Tahiti and Paris.

What are your dreams? For some, it's just to be able to buy a new dress without feeling guilty. For others, it's having enough money to be able to afford to send their children to the school of their choice.

Whatever your dream is, you can achieve it. Everything comes down to the decisions you make and your dedication to following the success system. You really can see your dreams come true!

LAURITA BERLAND
Homemaker
Diamond Direct Distributor (USA)

Five percent of the people think. Ten percent of the people think they think. The other eighty-five percent would rather die than think.

THOMAS EDISON (1847-1931)
U.S. Inventor (with more than
1000 patents)
Founder of Edison Electric Light
Company (later the
General Electric Company)

Free enterprise is one of the greatest blessings anyone can know. Network marketing is one of the purest forms of free enterprise. The opportunities throughout this business provide unlimited potential.

To me, one of the greatest breakthroughs came when I realized that if I built this business, I would never have to work for anyone else again!

JIM AGARD
Former Auto Body
Shop Manager
Diamond Direct
Distributor (USA)

Thinking is the hardest work there is, which is probably the reason why so few engage in it.

HENRY FORD (1863-1947)
U.S. Automobile Pioneer
Founder of the Ford Motor Company
"Father of Mass Production"

What I like most about this business is that the people who get in today have the opportunity to build a bigger, more profitable organization than ours. That's the beauty of Amway. No one holds you back but yourself.

Who knows what will happen in the next five or ten years? Mainly, it is obvious that this business will continue to explode, and Jody and I are more glad than ever that we are a part of it.

KATHY VICTOR
former Bookkeeper
Crown Direct Distributor (USA)

I love the man that can smile in trouble, that can gather strength from distress, and grow brave by reflection.

THOMAS PAINE (1737-1809)
British Writer and
Political Theorist

Amway is built on a proven process of duplication. You avoid problems such as large investments, employee situations and location difficulties. Plus, this marketing and distribution concept is spreading throughout the free world.

The system works, but you have to make a commitment to never give up on your dreams!

BUBBA PRATT
Former Automobile Salesman
Diamond Direct
Distributor (USA)

Be more concerned with your character than with your reputation, because your character is what you really are, while your reputation is merely what others think you are.

JOHN WOODEN
Legendary UCLA Head
Basketball Coach
Author and Speaker (USA)

The ideal Amway prospect should have a want, a need, a dream, a desire or a void. That person needs to be trustworthy, hungry, willing to work and willing to listen. Most importantly, that prospect must be willing to change.

Does that list apply to everyone you meet? Of course not.

Does it apply to some? Definitely! That's what makes this business so exciting. You never know.

BRIG HART
Executive Diamond Direct
Distributor (USA)

There are no secrets to success. It is the result of preparation, hard work and learning from failure.[2]

GENERAL (ret.) COLIN L. POWELL
U.S. Commander during Desert Storm

There is always a price for success, but with this business, there is such a proven track record which lets you know that the sacrifices will pay off handsomely.

CONSUELO HERNANDEZ
Former Marketing Consultant
Diamond Direct Distributor (Mexico)

---

2. Colin L. Powell, "Success," *The Black Collegian*, November 1991, p. 4.

In any undertaking it is difficult to have faith when you haven't seen results yet. Obviously, a lack of results can affect your attitude about building the business. But if you can only understand how important your attitude is to your future, you will do whatever it takes to develop a great outlook on life.

That's why this system works so well. There are plenty of people who believe in you when you don't believe in yourself. You have leaders who have a great attitude, and you can spend time with them—through counselling sessions, meetings and tapes—until their attitudes begin to rub off on you. They will be there to say, "You can build this business."

Still, it is up to you to understand how important your mindset is, and it is up to you to develop a tremendous attitude, even when you face challenges.

FRANK TENEROVICH
Former Engineer
Diamond Direct Distributor (USA)

Thomas A. Edison, as a young man.
Edison's work often resulted in success,
but nothing succeeded by accident.

"I never did <u>anything</u> worth doing by accident."

Better Buildings
...Your Positive Attitude

Some years ago, a researcher decided to find the secret of success. After months of study and countless interviews, he finally gave up.

"There's no secret," he said, "it is all related to hard work. One must climb the ladder to success, not just be lifted on an elevator."

It's true! Any achiever knows that. Thomas Edison, for example, was provoked when people related his success to chance. He said:

> *I never did anything worth doing by accident. nor did any of my inventions come by accident.*

So it is with anything worthwhile, especially your Amway business. It takes work to:

- Make progress-checks

- Tabulate your organization as it exists and what you want it to be each month

- Seek counsel upline about your progress

- Confer with and encourage downline distributors concerning their efforts

- Set new goals

  and

- Maintain a sense of urgency in sponsoring and a professionalism in retailing.

All those elements of your business take much more perspiration than inspiration.

Likewise, it takes great effort to teach the pattern for success-to first learn, then teach, then teach the teachers to teach. The plan only works if you work it.

There are however, ways to work smart.

THOUGHTS

Thinking is the basic process to becoming successful and building your Diamondship. What you achieve in this business (or in life) is a direct result of what you think, so it is important to develop right mental attitudes. Thinking wrong, believing wrong, and confessing wrong always leads to an unhappy, unprofitable way of life. Don't take that direction.

To think success, to become better and to believe BIG, you must develop the right kind of mental processes.

David J. Schwartz, Ph.D., in his book, *The Magic of Thinking Big*, wrote the following:

> *Persons who reach the top rungs in business management, selling, engineering, religious work, writing, acting, and in every other pursuit get there by following conscientiously and continuously a **plan for self-development and growth.***

Likewise, Ralph Cordiner, Chairman of the Board of the General Electric Company, said this to a leadership conference:

> *...we need from every man who aspires to leadership—for himself and his company—a determination to undertake a personal program of self-development. Nobody is going to order a man to develop... Whether a man lags behind or moves ahead in his speciality is a matter of personal application. This is something which takes time, work, and sacrifice. Nobody can do it for you.*

You have been programmed to be negative, to disbelieve, to be skeptical. But you can change. Those negative experiences, the minuses, can be transformed into positives and pluses simply by changing your attitudes.

We teach that you can change your thoughts by changing the input. What goes in must come out. You control the future because you have the power to control your thoughts.

We've always said that success is just a decision away. That is true, since it IS the first step. But that decision must be backed up with solid effort.

You are in a business with tremendous, unequaled opportunities. Your growth potential, return on your investment, reward for your efforts and personal independence are limited primarily by your vision and desire. In other words, your *thoughts*, in a very real way, control your destiny.

What can you do to change your thoughts?

BE ENTHUSIASTIC. You have a lot to be excited about. Verbalize that excitement to yourself in the mirror, to your family and to your associates. Remember, building a professional image requires doing things—including developing enthusiasm—that less-successful people are not willing to do.

BE POSITIVE. You should develop a habit of reading positive mental attitude books the first thing every morning, during the day and immediately before going to sleep. The list of available materials is almost unending:*

---

* These items are strongly recommended and available through your Upline. However, business materials are optional and not required.

The Bible,

The Magic of Thinking Big,

Skill with People,

Acres of Diamonds,

Compassionate Capitalism,

Don't Let Anybody Steal Your Dream,

How to Win Friends and Influence People,

Believe,

The Go-Getter

Attitude, Your Most Priceless Possession, etc...

Read anything penned by Og Mandino, Dale Carnegie, Robert Schuller, J. Paul Getty, Norman Vincent Peale, Dr. Denis Waitley and Zig Ziglar.

Paul Conn's books about Amway are superb. The growing list of books authored by Dexter and Birdie have been written especially for you. Ask your upline for suggestions about the books you should read.

What I am saying is that you have a tremendous array of books* which can help you be the positive person that you want to be or continue to be.

BE TEACHABLE. The cassettes which are available through your upline can be powerful educational tools. It is as if a banner beckons, "Welcome to Network Marketing and Interactive Distribution University... where financial flexibility can be yours!" You have the opportunity to invite the most successful distributors and business leaders to ride along with you. Through a cassette, you can receive personal tutoring in the best ways to build your own business.

BE INVOLVED. You become like the people with whom you surround yourself. Why not spend time with success-oriented men and women? Just as the hottest, glowing chunk of burning coal

---

* These items are strongly recommended and available through your Upline. However, business materials are optional and not required.

quickly becomes a dying ember when separated from the furnace, so you destroy your own "burn" when you avoid the rallies, open meetings, training sessions, seminars and weekend functions which are available to you.* Networking in person with other positive associates helps you and your downline people to keep your eyes on the big picture. It builds your faith in the success system when you see it working for so many others. You must associate with positive people to build this business.

BE SPONSORING AND WORKING IN DEPTH. "Now," you ask, "what does this have to do with a positive mental attitude?"

You may have heard the phrase, "Nothing succeeds like success." The words certainly apply to your business. Reading books, listening to tapes and going to meetings are all necessary motivators, but their value is diminished unless you see real results in your business.

When you actually get out and sponsor your nine or more distributors, then help each of them bring in their four or more people, then those four get two or more—all of this excites and motivates everybody up and down the line of sponsorship.

If you doubt this, watch what happens when new people are sponsored. You cannot help but get excited when your downline people go out and start finding "hot" distributors. New blood always breeds excitement, especially when everyone's checks are increasing!

Observe yourself very closely as you begin developing positive mental attitudes and mastering the principles of success. Watch what happens to the "fire" in your eyes. Notice how your financial status improves. See how your personality becomes a true asset.

Success comes to those who become success-conscious. That happens only when you control your thoughts through the proper input.

---

* These items are strongly recommended and available through your Upline. However, business materials are optional and not required.

WINNING

A winning attitude is vital. Quite simply, people want to associate with winners.

Merely knowing the difference between winners and losers can help put a ton of gold in your pockets:

A winner respects those who are superior and tries to learn something from them; a loser resents those who are superior and rationalizes their achievements away.

A winner says, "Let's find a way," while a loser whines, "I don't think there is a way."

A winner cuts through a problem; a loser tries to go around it.

A winner shows he's sorry by making up for his mistake; a loser may say, "I'm sorry," but he often does the same thing again.

A winner works harder, yet usually has more time, while a loser is always "too busy" to do the necessary things for success.

A winner is not afraid of losing, but a loser is often secretly afraid of winning.

A winner makes commitments; a loser makes empty promises.[4]

We have found that winners also refuse to pin the blame on others for personal failures. They share the credit for successes. They look for solutions, not excuses. They are less concerned with status than with accomplishment. They listen to the best advice, but they make decisions based on their own authority and character.

Winners want the accomplishment, not just the prize. Here is why: Winners realize that the difference between winning and losing often comes down to the choice of not quitting—even when no one seems to care and when beset by impossible odds.

A FINAL NOTE

We loved the Rocky movies, all five of them. Especially memorable is the tense scene in Rocky II when the bloody, battered character played by Sylvester Stallone looks across the ring at his shimmering adversary, Apollo Creed, and grunts to his manager, "I ain't goin' down no more!"

The reason we are mentioning this is that you will be faced with quitting many times. Things won't go right. You will get your feelings hurt. You may have to make sacrifices. The proverbial bottom line is this: Are you a quitter or a winner?

Will you quit because you are afraid to dial the telephone? Will it be when a respected "friend" or "loved one" laughs at you? Will that moment come when you have to talk in front of a group of potential distributors, or will it happen at 2 A. M. as you speed toward home on a deserted highway after traveling several hundred miles for a "no-show?" Will you quit when nothing seems to be working, and when no one, not even your spouse, believes that you have what it takes to "do that Amway thing?"

---

4. From the book, *Winners and Losers* by Sydney J. Harris.

British Prime Minister
Winston Churchill,
July 1945

Years after the second World War, he gave this
speech to a graduating class (quoted in full):
*"Never quit.   Never quit.   Never, **never** quit."*

What will make the difference between quitting and
going on?

We can tell you from experience that there will come a
time when the only thing that keeps you from giving up will be
all that stored-up positive input. Another great difference-maker
will be the friendships and relationships which will develop
between you and the other network marketing winners.

But there is one more factor that no one can measure. It
is that invisible ingredient that no one can define. It is that

unexplainable, gutsy component inside you that simply won't let you give up on your dreams for obtaining freedom, even when most other men and women would quit.

You will be faced with challenging moments, we guarantee it, and only then will you discover whether you have the ultimate courage to win.

Increase your odds by building the strongest, gutsiest, most positive mental attitude. Fortify your inner strengths now for the times to come.

We believe you can be a strong, positive winner. You can do it.

**You can build your own
SUCCESSFUL NETWORK
MARKETING BUSINESS
and experience the rewards that
you deserve as a winner!**

BUILDING BLOCKS:

The biggest lesson I have ever learned is the stupendous importance of what we think. If I knew what you think, I would know what you are, for your thoughts make you what you are. By changing our thoughts, we can change our lives.

DALE CARNEGIE (1888-1955)
Author of *How to Win Friends
and Influence People*
Founder of the Dale Carnegie
Institute (USA)

We believe that in a free society, it is our obligation to be as productive as possible. We totally believe in the free enter-prise system. Our own credibility depends upon what we've done, what we are doing, and what we plan to do. We believe we can help change the world for good!

HEATHER BRADLEY
Former Architectural
Draftsperson
Diamond Direct
Distributor (New Zealand)

As you read remember:
  Don't read to be big;
Read to be down to earth.
  Don't read to be smart;
Read to be real.
  Don't read to memorize;
Read to realize.
  Don't read to learn;
Read to sometimes unlearn.
  Don't read a lot;
Read just enough to keep yourself curious and hungry, to
learn more, to keep getting younger as you grow older.[1]

CHARLES E. "TREMENDOUS" JONES
Speaker and Author of
Life Is Tremendous (USA)

I like this business because it offers such flexibility. You
can share the Amway opportunity with **anyone**, *regardless of*
background, position or financial standing. Less advantaged
people can build it successfully, and very advantaged people can
build it, too.

I stay excited about this business because you never know
who you are going to meet the next time you share the plan. It
may be someone who isn't ready yet, or it may be that person
who will build a powerful organization.

And best of all—it's even more exciting to build this busi-
ness today than it was when I got started!

KAREN YAMADA
Homemaker
Diamond Direct
Distributor (USA)

---

1. Charles E. Jones, *The Books You Read* (Harrisburg, PA: Executive Books, 1985), p. 24.

This may shock you, but I believe the single most significant decision I can make on a day-to-day basis is my choice of attitude. It is more important than my past, my education, my bankroll, my successes or failures, fame or pain, what other people think of me or say about me, my circumstances, or my position. Attitude.... .keeps me going or cripples my progress. It alone fuels my fire or assaults my hope. When my attitudes are right, there's no barrier too high, no valley too deep, no dream too extreme, no challenge too great for me.[2]

CHUCK SWINDOLL
Minister, Broadcaster
and Bestselling Author (USA)

The success system builds the man and women, and that person then builds the business. We were able to go Diamond because we were able to tap into the vast empowerment and support system. Then we were able to bring along so many other people because we could help them plug into the system.

The books, tapes, meetings and upline support—the system is what makes this business work so well for people from all walks of life!

CHARLIE KRAZIT
Former Construction
Company Owner
Diamond Direct
Distributor (USA)

Never stop the parade to pick up a dime.[3]

H. JACKSON BROWN, JR.
Bestselling Author of
Life's Little Instruction Book

---

2. Charles R. Swindoll, *Strengthening Your Grip: Essentials in an Aimless World* (Waco, TX: Word Books, 1982), p. 207.

3. H. Jackson Brown, Jr., "Trust in God, But Lock Your Car," *Reader's Digest*, July 1993, p. 125.

Working with people is always surprising. Some who seem perfect for this business just never make the commitment, and others who seem to possess few people or entrepreneurial skills find a way to make it happen.

MICK CLARK
Former Dairy and Potato Farmer
Diamond Direct Distributor
(Australia)

Declare war on negative feelings. Don't let unrealistic worries eat away at you! When negative thoughts invade your mind, fight them. Ask yourself why you, who has every natural right to be happy, must spend your waking hours wrestling with fear, worry and hate. Win the war against these insidious twentieth century scourges.[4]

MAXWELL MALTZ, M.D.
Surgeon, Behaviorist and
Bestselling Author of
PSYCHO-CYBERNETICS (USA)

We give so much credit to our success in this business to our upline people. They were there to encourage us when we wondered if we could make it. They believed in us when we were short on belief. I don't think any of us truly understand what that kind of support means—especially compared to any other business or area of life.

ANNA DEANE
Champion Dog Breeder
and Showperson
Executive Diamond
Direct Distributor
(New Zealand)

---

4. Maxwell Maltz, M.D., *The Magic Power of Self-Image Psychology* (New York: Simon & Schuster, 1964), p. 88-9.

Winning is setting out to accomplish something even though you don't know for sure how much that effort is going to cost you in the long run. It means admitting to the world that you want to win, and then it's working so hard to meet your goal that you give yourself no excuse to lose.[5]

DENNIS CONNER
Founder of Dennis
Conner Interiors,
Captain of the U.S. America's
Cup Sailing Team
and Bestselling Author

So many people are looking for the secret to success in the Amway business. I tell them that there really aren't any hidden secrets. It all comes down to following the system. Listen to the tapes. Get to the functions. Read the books. Do what your upline recommends. Most of all, be open to change. If those are the secrets of building this business, then they certainly aren't hidden. Anyone can do them, but only a few will.

BRUCE ANDERSON
Former Medical Aviation Pilot
Diamond Direct
Distributor (USA)

The greatest discovery of my generation is that human beings can alter their lives simply by altering their attitude.

WILLIAM JAMES (1842-1910)
U.S. Psychologist
and Philosopher

---

5. Dennis Conner with Edward Claflin, *The Art of Winning* (New York: St. Martin's Press, 1988), p. xviii.

I've heard it said, "Barriers are those horrible things you see when you take your eyes off your goals." It's true! When your eyes are on what you want to accomplish, you don't have the time or energy to focus on all the challenges that would hold you back.

PEGGY FLORENCE
Former Special
Education Teacher
Diamond Direct Distributor (USA)

Great minds have purposes; others have wishes. Little minds are tamed and subdued by misfortunes, but great minds rise above them.

WASHINGTON IRVING (1783-1859)
U.S. Author

One of the best decisions you can make as you start building your Amway business is to be teachable.

After all, if you want to become successful, doesn't it make sense to listen to the advice of successful people?

This system offers mentorship—pure and simple. If you are willing to listen and work, there are many people waiting to share their success principles with you.

This system is also focused on education. First, you learn to think as an achiever, then work like one, and eventually you become successful.

This mentorship and educational program is already in place. It has helped hundreds and hundreds of people reach Emerald, Diamond and beyond. It can work for you, too, when you make the decision to become teachable.

CARLOS MARIN
Former Insurance
Agency Owner
Executive Diamond
Direct Distributor (USA)

As you share the Amway opportunity with people from all walks of life, you may find—as we have—that so many men and women are more concerned with what they can have right now, rather than what they can put together for the future.

That's one of the big differences between people who build this business and those who don't. When the challenges come and the hard choices have to be made, some people will say, "It's not worth the sacrifices and struggles." Other will say, "It doesn't matter what happens—I'm going to do whatever it takes to build a great future for my family and myself."

And the ironic part is that you really don't know what people will do until they are faced with the struggles. All you can do is believe in them and help them see that they have a tremendous opportunity in their hands. Still, it's up to them to keep going or to quit. Needless to say, lots of people in this business have kept going!

ROLAND HUGHES, Ed.D
Former Professor
Diamond Direct Distributor (USA)

Bent Nails, Broken Blocks and Shattered Glass

...Your Ability to Handle Struggles

Sometimes, it seems that life deals people bad hands.
Take the case of a six-year-old girl who was snatched from her family's eastern Poland estate by the Soviet secret police and shipped as a slave in a cattle car to a labor camp in Siberia. Case closed.

Or how about a young man who wanted to become a professional basketball player, but he stood only five-feet-four? It would seem as if he didn't have a chance.

If you think you have financial worries, consider the young Missouri homebuilder who was one of the largest developers in his city, but—simply because of a drastic downturn in the economy—suddenly had millions of **borrowed** dollars sitting in 40 unsold homes?

Or what about a young Cuban couple—an elite member of Fidel Castro's personal guard and the director of a school—who expressed a distaste for the dictator's policies and suddenly lost their positions?

It may seem that all five of these people were at dead ends, but not so. Here are the rest of their stories.

The six-year-old, Alicia, endured unimaginable hardships and cruelty, but eventually was able to get out of Siberia. She went from streets in Persia to Africa, and finally, reunited with her family, came to America in 1951. Eventually she married Hank Gilewicz, a professional engineer who spent most of his career with IBM. But that's not the only happy ending. During the early 1970s, they saw the Amway Sales and Marketing Plan, started building their own network marketing business and built a worldwide Diamondship.

The short basketball player is Tyrone "Muggsy" Bogues. We have not only sat with Free Enterprise celebration audiences as he shared his story, but have watched in awe as he used his small frame and speed in the National Basketball Association to outmaneuver opponents in a sport traditionally dominated by "giants." Muggsy has simply refused to let his size dissuade him from a basketball career. Even though he was a high school star with a perennial powerhouse team (Dunbar High in Baltimore, Maryland), virtually everyone told him that he could never play in college. Wrong! He became a star for Wake Forest University in the tough Atlantic Coast Conference. Then he was ridiculed for thinking that he could make the transition to professional basketball. Wrong again! Perhaps a novelty at first for the Charlotte Hornets, he quickly established himself as a mainstay point guard. Instead of viewing his height as a liability, Muggsy focused on his overall potential.

You may think the Missouri homebuilder got some bad breaks. Yes, he did. But let us tell you more about him. His name is Ken Stewart. As his construction business was reduced to ruins during the late 1970s, Kenny and Donna decided to build their own Amway business. Even as they began experiencing breakthroughs with their networking organizations, the bill collectors swarmed around to recoup construction debts. Few, if any, of his downline distributors realized his desperate straits, since he drove a nice car, nor did they realize that he often slept in that automobile as he built distance groups because he couldn't afford a motel room. Times have changed, of course, as the Stewarts became Diamonds only 28 months after signing their Amway application. Today, they are Crown Directs. Those days of stunning downturns are mere memories.

In 1963, the Cuban couple who dared to speak against the dictator lost their jobs. Two years later, they came to the United States on one of the now-famous "Freedom Flights." Juventino and Carmen Hechavarria's dream to be free led them first to Maryland, then to Florida. They built a highly-acclaimed chain of automotive businesses, then saw their enterprise plunged into an abyss when Tino was shot—he took a bullet intended for an employee. Here was a man and his wife who definitely hit rock bottom, but there is always a way back up, no matter how far or how hard people fall. The Hechavarrias heard about the Amway opportunity, eventually they sold their automotive chain (an economic downturn left little profit) and built a network marketing business that quickly spread from the United States to Mexico, Central America and around the world. Today, Juventino and Carmen speak to audiences about their once-broken dreams which have been turned into triumphs, and few people can listen without weeping.

Were these people just fortunate? Absolutely not! Each had to work hard to achieve success. Alicia Gilewicz, the little girl from Poland had to get past the scars of unimaginable terror. Muggsy Bogues had to develop his basketball skills—perhaps even more than many of his seven-foot-tall contemporaries. Ken Stewart had to rise above the unfairness of an economic downturn and had to develop himself as a businessman, motivator and dream-sharer at a time when his self-confidence was at an all-time low.

Juventino and Carmen Hechavarria could have quit many times, not only when they were persecuted in Cuba or when Tino was a victim of a senseless shooting, but even after they moved to Mexico to build their Amway business and had to endure a robbery as well as initial prejudice against the opportunity they desired to share.

No, these people weren't lucky at all. But they did know and act on the slightly-corny motto of all powerful people who have experienced adversity: If life gives you a lemon, make lemonade.

You see, no matter what life hands you, it is within your power to turn it into advantage.

Alicia Gilewicz could have given up or chosen to be a scarred, scared victim forever. Not Alicia! Anyone who knows her today can't help but be amazed at the fact that she has succeeded not only as a wife, mother and businesswoman, but regularly returns to her homeland and other formerly communist-bloc countries to share her faith and offer those individuals the same opportunity.

Instead of resigning himself to another line of work, Muggsy Bogues focused on developing his potential on the basketball court. As a result, his size actually became an asset, since it provided him greater maneuverability among taller team members.

Ken Stewart could have used his experience as an excuse to declare bankruptcy to stay down for the count. Instead, he used it to rise again, and he emerged a clear champion. He beat the economic downturn instead of letting it beat him.

The Cuban couple could have quit many times. In fact, they could have received well-deserved pity for life's inequities. Instead, they have remained faithful, hopeful and hard-working, using their unfortunate experiences to share their message about political and financial freedom.

What are you allowing to hold you back? Is there anything to keep you from achieving your vision of success? If so, those barriers are also holding you back from developing your potential, both personally and professionally.

DEFEATS

It would be wrong for us to write a book about success through building your own network marketing and interactive distribution business without a chapter on the realities of shattered hopes.

Life does not always grant your first dream, or your second, or fifteenth. Along with your triumphs and successes, you will face obstacles, heartbreaks, tragedies, hindrances and unavoidable problems.

While most people tend to lose heart and surrender their dreams during life's horrible times, go-getters learn these universal principles:

- You must discern the difference between temporary setbacks and permanent losses.

You learned in seventh grade science, "For every action, there is an equal and opposite reaction." If you do anything in life, anything at all, you will encounter opposition. It is a fact.

Still, you cannot turn back every time you run into a wall. It's not always easy to tell the difference between a stepping stone and a stumbling block, especially when the object seems to be ten feet tall.

Remember these lines from the Kenny Rogers song:

You gotta know when to hold 'em;
Know when to fold 'em;
Know when to walk away,
And know when to run.[1]

Nobody, but nobody, wins every skirmish or goes through life unscathed. If you cannot conquer every foe, the secret is to decide which victories are worth fighting for, and which are not.

- Obstacles are there to strengthen you.

When you misunderstand the purpose of struggles and allow them to breed discouragement, you de-energize the benefits.

In every man and woman's life there comes a time of ultimate challenge—a time when every resource we have is tested, when life seems unfair, when our faith, our values, our patience, our compassion, our ability to persist, are all pushed to our limits and beyond.

Some people use such tests as opportunities to become better people—others allow these experiences of life to destroy them.

- Obstacles offer progressive measurements of your growing strength.

---

1. From the song, "The Gambler" by Don Schlitz, Copyright 1979. All Rights Reserved. Used by Permission.

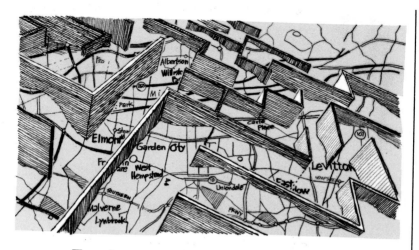

They give you an opportunity to see how far you have come. Any tennis star doesn't consider it unreasonable to work up through the amateur and professional ranks; likewise, you should look upon each problem as another chance to measure your inner muscle.

As difficult as it may seem, problems come to make you strong. Heraclitus wrote:

It is not good for all your wishes to be fulfilled. Through sickness you recognize the value of health, through evil the value of good, through hunger satisfaction, through exertion the value of rest.

One of Abigail "Dear Abby" Van Buren's columns included this powerful poem:

Cripple him, and you have a Sir Walter Scott.
Lock him in a prison cell, and you have a John Bunyan.
Bury him in the snows of Valley Forge, and you have a George Washington.
Raise him in abject poverty, and you have an Abraham Lincoln.
Subject him to bitter religious prejudice, and you have a Disraeli.
Afflict him with asthma as a child, and you have a

Theodore Roosevelt.

Stab him with rheumatic pains until he can't sleep without an opiate, and you have a Steinmetz.

Put him in a grease pit of a locomotive roundhouse, and you have a Walter P. Chrysler.

Make him play second fiddle in an obscure South American orchestra, and you have a Toscanini.

At birth, deny her the ability to see, hear, and speak, and you have a Helen Keller.

Today we have many champions who are tremendous overcomers:

- Sam Walton broke through walls of poverty and out-moded thinking among his peers to establish the immensely popular Wal-Mart and Sam's Club stores.

- John McCormack overcame bankruptcy and depression to build a multi-million dollar beauty salon empire, Visible Changes, and to write a bestselling book, *Self-Made in America.*

- Hal Gooch, though he operated a North Carolina furniture manufacturing business with his dad, was painfully shy when he was shown the Amway business (introverted then, but certainly not now). Susan, his wife, got excited about the network marketing opportunity, and soon Hal joined her enthusiasm. He forced himself, night after night, to show the plan. He somehow developed the courage to actually look at people while he talked, rather than staring at the floor. People who know him now as a self-assured, friendly, warm Double Diamond have trouble believing that he ever had a problem with extreme shyness.

- Mel Tillis spent a childhood of embarrassment as a chronic stutterer, yet has touched the hearts of millions as a country music entertainer.

- Dan Williams, another stutterer since he was five, got started with his Amway business with numerous disadvantages. Not only did he have to endure his embarrassing, grueling speech impediment, but was on-call 24-hours a day, seven days a week (leaving little time for showing the plan). His wife Bunny was suffering from a ruptured disc. Their children were small and required lots of attention. They lived in a tiny house. Their car was unreliable. Dan had ulcers. About the only thing the Williams had going for them was their dreams. That was enough! Within two and a half months, they were Directs. Within twelve months, they had sponsored four Directs. Two years afterward they reached Diamond. Double, Triple and Crown followed, and by 1979, they reached Crown Ambassador, Amway's highest honor.

The list could go on forever. The point is this: Difficulties actually accelerate your development, especially when you understand the value of opposition. Muscles never get stronger from inaction; much to the contrary, unused muscles tend to waste away.

FAILURES

In addition to defeats, mistakes are a valuable part of life, for in them we find another reason to keep dreaming, no matter what happens.

The attitude we take toward mistakes and failures, separates the successful person from the unsuccessful man or woman.

Chemist Paul Ehrlich discovered a drug to treat people who were afflicted with syphilis. It was named "Formula 606" because the first 605 tests had been unsuccessful.

Another man was viewed as a mild lunatic by most railroad executives when he suggested that a train could be stopped by using wind. Yet George Westinghouse persevered and finally sold what is now the Westinghouse Air Brake, a standard feature on American trains.

When successful people fail, they think about what went wrong and what they can do differently the next time. Frankly, most of us can deal with success, but how we deal with failure is the one thing that determines what we get out of life.

"Good timber does not grow with ease," wrote J. Willard Marriott (Founder of Marriott Hotels); "the stronger the wind, the stronger the trees."

People who fail seem to condemn themselves for every new failure. Dreambuilders know that it does not matter how many mistakes they make, or even how many times they fail. What matters is the concentrated attempt to learn from each failure and to improve performance the next time around.

Winners and leaders—anyone with personal power—understand that if you try something and do not get the results you want, it should simply be treated as feedback. What you need to do is use that information to make better decisions about what you need to do to produce whatever results you ultimately desire.

Granted, you may be allowed fewer and fewer mistakes as you move up the success ladder, but you can never reach the point where you stop taking risks.

Make mistakes, but never allow yourself to stay wallowed in your misery. You must be creative, not reactive. Strength only comes through life's lessons and character building. Say to yourself, "How can I make something good come out of this?"

PERSISTENCE

In every man and woman's life, there are times of summit-like challenges—either through defeats or failures. Relatively few people use such tests as opportunities to become stronger, better-equipped people. The majority, by far, allow these ordeals of life to destroy their dreams. Persistence is one of the most effective keys you can use to overcome these dream-killers.

Wrote President Calvin Coolidge:

Nothing in the world can take the place of persistence. Talent will not; nothing is more common than unsuccessful men with talent. Genius will not; unrewarded genius is almost a proverb. Education will not; the world is full of educated derelicts. Persistence and determination alone are omnipotent.

Persistence is a conscious decision. It is a choice which must be built on dreams, preparation and an attitude of achievement. It must become a way of life for you if you want to succeed in the world of network marketing.

BE CHANGE-FRIENDLY

Life does not always grant your first wish. So many fail because their first efforts miscarry; they lose heart and quit. That is sad.

Mark Twain once wrote:

> *We should be careful to get out of an experience only the wisdom that is in it—and stop there; lest we be like the cat that sits down on a hot-stove lid. She will never sit down on a hot-stove lid again, and that is well; but also she will never sit down on a cold one any more.*

We must learn that obstacles are in our way to strengthen us. When we misunderstand their purpose and allow them to breed discouragement—that is, when we cannot tell the difference between temporary setbacks and permanent failures—then we want to turn off our efforts and surrender our dreams.

It is necessary, as you build your own business, that you encounter hindrances and unavoidable problems. We call them "challenges." In fact, you will develop faster after you understand the value of opposition. You will get a chance to learn who you really are.

You will get tired building your business, but don't worry about that. Weariness does not come so much from overwork as from a lack of interest in what you are doing. With your dream always flaming, you may get tired, but never weary from boredom.

Is it any wonder why the Apostle Paul wrote these words?

> *And let us not get tired of doing what is right, for after a while we will reap a harvest of blessing if we don't get discouraged and give up* (Galatians 6:9, *The Living Bible*).

So exert those business-building muscles. The strongest oak tree in the forest is not the one that is protected from the storm and hidden from the sun, but the one which standing in the open where it must struggle for its very existence against the wind, rain and scorching sun.

Effort and struggle—mental, physical and spiritual—are ways by which we achieve. Success, you must understand, is not a comfort zone that you reach someday. It is a journey, a conquest, a series of challenges to be mastered.

As you build your own business, here are some construction constants which will help you succeed more quickly:

LEARN FROM EXPERIENCE. If you are unable to be taught by the past, you will be condemned to repeat it.

BE A DOER. Successful people are usually doing things already while others are still talking.

AIM HIGH. Your goals make the difference between aimless wandering and effective action, especially in the network marketing business.

CONCENTRATE ON PRODUCTIVE EFFORT. Most people spend the majority of their time on relieving tension and busy-work. You will become a Diamond, not just because of your efforts, but because of your *effective* efforts.

KEEP MOVING. Continually set new goals and dreams for yourself. Determine that your organization will grow wider and deeper. A lot of people are depending upon your actions.

No one else has as great a stake in your future and your family's future as you. That opportunity is worth every bent nail, broken block and shattered glass as you build your business.

A FINAL NOTE

Zig Ziglar has taught many people in our business how to make a dramatic difference in the way they face their struggles. He says to write these affirmative words on a note card:

I, _____ , have a magnificent self-image. I am a disciplined individual. I am teachable. I am honest. I have character and personality. I am fair. I have faith. I have complete integrity.

These are the qualities of the winner I was born to be.

Tonight is going to be a magnificent night, and tomorrow will be an absolutely wonderful day.

After you write these words, set them beside your bathroom mirror and read the sentences to yourself every night before going to bed.

Do it even if you don't feel comfortable. After all, if you are like most people, you have probably spent years reminding yourself that you are stupid, ineffective and unsuccessful. Worse, lots of other people have chimed in to agree with you. Therefore, it may take awhile to begin believing your positive affirmations.

But it can happen. You can develop the ability to handle incredible struggles—just ask Muggsy Bogues or Mel Tillis. You can achieve great things by becoming a great dreamer and self-affirmer—just ask John McCormack and William Sessions.

By learning to overcome problems and barriers, you can become a tremendous businessperson—just ask Alicia Gilewicz, Tino and Carmen Hechavarria, Kenny Stewart, Hal Gooch and Dan Williams.

You can overcome any challenge as you BUILD YOUR OWN INTERACTIVE DISTRIBUTION BUSINESS.

BUILDING BLOCKS:

The intelligent person is one who has learned how to choose wisely and therefore has a sense of values, a purpose in life and a sense of direction.

J. MARTIN KLOTSCHE
Philosopher

When it comes down to it, success isn't measured by how much money or possessions one accumulates, but by the true friendships developed.

SUSAN GOOCH
Former Computer Operator
Double Diamond
Direct Distributor (USA)

Your past is important because it brought you to where you are. But as important as your past is to your present, it is not nearly as important as the way you see your future.

DR. TONY CAMPOLO
Bestselling Author,
Educator and Speaker (USA)

Our greatest glory consists not in never failing, but in rising every time we do fail. All of history's great leaders have learned that failure is only the opportunity to begin again more intelligently.

This business system teaches how important challenges are to your overall success. Like it or not, we live in an imperfect world. Everyone fails. Every person meets unexpected turns and detours--whether they are single or married, old or young, educated or unschooled. It's what you do with those challenges and failures that will make or break you. And it's your dream that will take you past any barrier you face.

DICK HOPPER
Former Truck Driver
Diamond Direct
Distributor (USA)

In every rejection you learn something and I have learned that if you just go about your business and love people and not hate anyone that you ultimately gain a victory.

DR. NORMAN VINCENT PEALE
Pastor and Speaker
Founder of *Guideposts* Magazine
Author of *The Power of
Positive Thinking* (USA)

It's the desire for freedom that led us to build our Amway business, and that dream still motivates us to help other people achieve their goals. If anything, our successes have only made the dream burn brighter.

JUVENTINO HECHAVARRIA
Former Automotive Store Owner
Diamond Direct Distributor (Mexico)

God comforts. He doesn't pity. He doesn't commiserate. He picks us up, dries our tears, soothes our fears, and lifts our thoughts beyond the hurt.

How does God comfort us so masterfully? Five ways: (1) He gives us courage; (2) He gives us a sense of calm; (3) He gives us companionship; (4) He gives us compassion; and (5) He gives us a new set of commitments.[1]

DR. ROBERT SCHULLER
Minister, Broadcaster,
and Bestselling Author (USA)

*To live is to risk. The greatest disaster in life is to risk nothing. In fact, a risk-less man, woman or child **does** nothing, **has** nothing and **is** nothing.*

The risk-less person may appear to avoid suffering and sorrow, but will never learn to feel, taste, touch, smell, change, grow, love and live. Worse, the person who becomes willfully enslaved to a risk-free rut life simultaneously defaults in every area of life.

Only a person who knows risk can ever hope to understand true freedom.

DARRYL E. HICKS
Bestselling Author,
Media Consultant
and Direct Distributor (USA)

1. Robert Schuller, *The Be-Happy Attitudes: Eight Positive Attitudes That Can Transform Your Life* (Waco, TX: Word Books, 1985), p. 64.

If you're not willing to do whatever it takes to become successful, then, I guarantee you, you never will become successful.

JOHN McCORMACK
Bestselling author of
Self-Made in America
and Founder of
Visible Changes Salons

What do you do when you are faced with the kind of adversity that makes you want to give up?

It's a question that I have asked myself many times during my career in medicine. It's a question that I have asked myself over and over as we built our Amway business. It's a question that I've asked myself lots of times since I fell fifteen feet, changing my entire life, on that fateful day in 1993.

What do you do when you face seemingly "impossible" situations?

You keep going. You hurt, cry, pray and ask all the hard questions. Then you wipe away the tears and keep going.

In my case, I leaned on Don a lot. I also re-discovered what a great source of strength Amway people are.

One of the best parts of this business is that you have people around you who hurt, cry and pray with you. There is so much love flowing through this organization.

What happens when you face trials? You keep going, and you thank God for a business where people really do care about you.

NANCY WILSON
Former Registered Nurse
Executive Diamond
Direct Distributor (USA)

I made an analogy once of a plane going down and people jettisoning all the weight to keep the plane up. I think one of the first things to go as people's lives start to go down is their dreams.

Dreams should be the last thing to go—dreams are things you go down with. If you're left clinging to a piece of driftwood in the middle of the ocean, I'd put on it the word dreams.

KEVIN COSTNER
Motion Picture Star of
Bull Durham, Field of Dreams,
Robin Hood, JFK and
Bodyguard (USA)

The Amway business, though certainly not a breeze, is simple compared to the typical business. Barbara and I owned a "traditional" one, and it was no picnic. We were relatively successful, but the larger that business grew, the more headaches there were--from accounts receivables, bookkeeping and tax liability procedures, growing overhead, insurance problems and the constant wear-and-tear on our equipment.

When we were first approached about Amway, an acquaintance asked me if I would like to be in a business that had tremendous potential without the typical headaches. It sounded almost too good to be true.

After a decade of building our own business, I can tell you that there is nothing out there to compare with this opportunity. It's still seems almost too good to be true, but it works!

JOHN SIMS
Former Auto Towing
and Repair Business Owner
Diamond Direct
Distributor (USA)

Frequently, unpredictable and uncontrollable external factors derail a chieftain's plan of action. As a result, adaptability to circumstance is vital to a chieftain's success.[2]

ATTILA THE HUN

As someone who knows, having experienced the challenges of raising two children by myself after my husband died, this business offers something that you don't find anywhere else.

Whether it's because of the death of a spouse or through divorce, there are lots of families headed by single parents. If it had not been for the fact that we had built our Amway business, I would have probably lost my nice home, taken a low-paying job and stuck my children in a daycare.

The most exciting part of this business is that those who make a solid commitment—single or married, man or woman—will be rewarded. This has been proven over and over.

CAROL LARRIMORE
Former School Teacher
Diamond Direct
Distributor (USA)

We are not the sum of our possessions. They are not the measure of our lives. In our hearts we know what matters. We cannot hope only to leave our children a bigger car, a bigger bank account. We must hope to give them a sense of what it means to be a loyal friend, a loving parent, a citizen who leaves his home, his neighborhood and town better than he found it.[3]

GEORGE BUSH
Former Oilman, Congressman
(Texas), Ambassador to the
United Nations, Director of the
Central Intelligence, Vice President
and Forty-first President of the United States

---

2. Wess Roberts, Ph.D., *Victory Secrets of Attila the Hun* (New York: Doubleday, 1993), p. 36.

3. George Bush, "Inaugural Address," Washington, D.C., January 20, 1989.

Although it seemed to many people that Don—a chemical engineer—and I had very fulfilling jobs, we got involved with network marketing because we saw it as a way to eventually have freedom to work whatever hours we wanted to. But as we built the business, we found so many other benefits. We quickly fell in love with our newfound friends. We eventually developed the kind of income that helped us to become financially secure and debt-free. Best of all, this business has allowed us to be full-time parents to our daughter Kristen.

GRETCHEN SEAGREN
Former Flight Attendant
Executive Diamond Direct
Distributor (USA)

Every team has to learn that excellence is not a destination but a process that must be continually improved. One of our key players, when a reporter asked him why he only poured on the effort if we were in danger of losing, grinned and replied, "See me in March." he meant that he would save himself for play-off time, when the effort really counted. But if you believe you can turn your work ethic off and on at will, one day you will try to flick the "on" switch—and it might not respond.[4]

PAT RILEY
NBA "Coach of the Decade"
Head Coach of the New York Knicks
Former Head Coach of the World
Champion Los Angeles Lakers
Bestselling Author—*The Winner Within*

---

4. Pat Riley, "The Winner Within" *Success*, September 1993, p. 35.

One of the greatest parts about the Amway business is the teamwork it cultivates. Teamwork is essential in any area of life, for it is needed to develop the commitment and skills of each person on the team. I saw the value of teamwork in the corporate world, but nowhere is teamwork more valuable than in this business.

Thankfully, the system teaches true teamwork and strong leadership. The reason is simple: A good leader inspires other people with confidence in the leader, but a great leader inspires people to have confidence in themselves.

Time has proven that this system works, for it has changed the lives of so many people, and it has built strong leaders and powerful teams in the process.

DAN WILLIAMS
Former Dow Chemical Plant Superintendent
Crown Ambassador Direct Distributor (USA)
Past ADA President ('82-'83/'86 -'87)

Leadership
...Your Team-leading Vision

What is the difference?

What causes one person to fast-track up the leadership ladder and build a huge network marketing organization while another, apparently equally qualified individual, fails to get results?

Is the difference being in the right place at the right time? Luck? Fate? Educational background? Mentoring?

Obviously none of these answers is conclusive. The explanation rests not so much in the intellectual and technical capacity of the individual as in the qualities of leadership that he or she projects.

But these questions about leadership are not trite philosophic puzzles. Leadership affects each of us.

The leadership crisis is not an exclusive problem "at the top." All of us must be leaders and risk-takers if our organizations are going to be strongly balanced and future-oriented.

The overall leadership problem relates to a lack of commitment and identification, and it goes from the top to the bottom. The sooner we face this fact, the better off all of us will be!

We can start with the negatives: **six leadership myths** and **six reasons why leaders fail.**

MYTHS

A subject as important as leadership has been appraised, examined and bottom-lined so often that the findings have become cliches.

Some of the findings reach absurd levels, including one by John Byrne, a writer many years ago for London's <u>Director</u> Magazine. Byrne, quite seriously, suggested that a prerequisite for leadership should be a pear-shaped head, citing British Prime Minister Harold Wilson, and France's Generals Napoleon Bonaparte and Charles DeGaulle as examples. Byrne labeled this leadership characteristic "the Burgundy Bottle Look," and called it the key to success in business and politics.

Unbelievable! Byrne's theory resembles Swiss cheese when one considers the overwhelming majority of men and women, yesterday's and today's leaders, who had non-pear shaped faces.

Absurdities aside, it is apparent that any study about leadership must confront some of the reoccurring myths which always tend to "muddy the waters" and which often keep would-be leaders from grand achievement.

Upfront, let us present what leadership is not. Here are six of the most common leadership myths:

MYTH #1: **Some people are born leaders; the rest are born to be followers.**

Many of history's great leaders were quite human men and women who learned major leadership skills through trials by fire: Moses, Deborah, Christ, Alexander, Joan d'Arc, Christopher Columbus, George Washington, Clara Barton, Helen Keller, John D. Rockefeller, Sr., Eleanor Roosevelt, Margaret Chase Smith, John F. Kennedy, Martin Luther King, Jr., Ronald Reagan, Lee Iacocca, Rich DeVos and Jay Van Andel, Sandra Day O'Connor...

As a personal test, look back at your high school yearbook. How many "born" leaders are now locked into dead-end jobs? How many "nobody"-type followers are now entrepreneurial or corporate fast-trackers?

Stereotypes, especially the "born leader" myth, have no place in leadership descriptions.

MYTH #2: **Leadership is an isolated gift, enjoyed by only a few select people.**

Nothing could be more untrue. I have found that great, once-in-a-lifetime leaders such as Winston Churchill or Ronald Reagan are a rare breed, but everyone has leadership potential.

True, there is a scarcity of great leaders today, but we are impressed with a growing number of "ordinary" men and women in this business who are being transformed into extraordinary network marketing leaders.

MYTH #3: **The best leaders are always gifted with magnetic, dynamic, charismatic personalities.**

Some leaders are electrifying. Many are not, even though they have admirable qualities which translate into warmth and power.

Peter Drucker, best-selling author possesses interesting insight. He says, "Effective leadership doesn't depend on charisma. Eisenhower, George Marshall and Truman were singularly effective leaders, yet none possessed any more charisma than a dead mackerel!"[1]

1. Peter F. Drucker, "Leadership More Doing Than Dash," *The Wall Street Journal*, January 6, 1988, p. 3A.

Analogies aside, you should realize that the world's corporate boardrooms are filled with men and women who, underneath the tailored suits and custom-made shoes, are quite human. The same goes for Diamonds, Double-Diamonds, Triple-Diamonds, Crowns and Crown Ambassadors! They, like a cross-section of all people, are hardly stereotypical and not always charismatic. But if they have reached those lofty levels in this business, you can bet that they are true leaders.

We realize that there are numerous theories about leadership qualities, much like Byrne's hilarious pear-shaped face hypothesis, but our experiences have pointed in the other direction. Many men and women who are considered great leaders in this business have worked incredibly hard to compensate for a lack of natural charisma. Ironically, as they have striven to develop effective leadership skills, they also have developed an attractive, dynamic magnetism! People are attracted to success—not only in the Amway business, but in every area of life.

MYTH #4: **Once a leader, always a leader.**

False. Period.

People may be impressive leaders in one role, and yet be quite ordinary followers in another situation.

One of our corporate acquaintances is the epitome of assertiveness and leadership in the executive boardroom, yet he is content to develop menial assignments in his church and civic organizations.

On another level, remember Alvin Toffler's concept of the accelerated rate of change? What worked yesterday may work today, but it might not. Who knows if Spectrum Information Technologies John Scully's concepts or Pepsi-Cola's Craig Weatherup's hard-charging style will work as effectively seven years from now?

That's why we have to keep changing with the times and learning about up-and-coming paradigms.

MYTH #5: **Leadership, for better or worse, must depend on force and manipulation.**

H. Gordon Selfridge built up one of the world's largest department stores in London. He achieved success by being a leader, but not a controlling boss. Here is his comparison of the two types of administration:

The boss drives his people, but the leader coaches them. The boss depends upon authority, but the leader on good will. The boss inspires fear, but the leader inspires enthusiasm. The boss says 'I'; the leader 'we.' The boss fixes the blame for the breakdown, but the leader seeks help in fixing the breakdown. The boss knows how it is done, but the leader shows how. The boss says, 'Go,' while the leader urges, 'Let's go!'

Are Selfridge's comments too-simplistic? Perhaps, but listen to the words of an employee of the John Deere Company, speaking of William Hewitt, who took over the old-line corporation and turned it into a multi-faceted, global-oriented conglomerate: "Hewitt made us learn how good we were."[2]

Warren Bennis and Burt Nanus, authors of the excellent book, Leaders, made this pointed statement:

Leaders lead by pulling rather than by pushing, by inspiring rather than ordering, by creating achievable, though challenging, expectations and rewarding progress toward them rather than by manipulating, by enabling people to use their own initiative and experiences rather than by denying or constraining their expressions and actions.[3]

MYTH #6: **Leadership is a functional role, so it only applies to executives, managers and—in this business—to Diamonds and above.**

---

2. Warren Bennis and Burt Nanus, *Leaders* (New York: Harper & Row, 1985), p. 225.

3. *Ibid.*

This myth is disproven every day in network marketing.

People in leadership roles are absolutely necessary on **all** levels of modern corporations and organizations, from janitorial rooms to board rooms to drawing circles. That can include **everyone!**

In other words, you need to be a responsible leader in your organization, even if your organization only numbers a few. It begins inside you—by plugging into the system of books, tapes and meetings. It's not something "magic" that happens when you reach a certain pin level.

William Kieschnick, ARCO's CEO, has repeatedly mentioned that one of the biggest problems he faced was to inspire the entire multibillion-dollar corporation to understand the need for individual "ownership" and entrepreneurship. He said, "We need leadership at every single unit, at every level."[4]

That's certainly true in this business!

These six common myths can keep you from achieving your potential as a personal business owner. When those myths are dispelled, it becomes increasingly apparent that **being a leader is not a position or destination, it is a journey.** Leadership is not something you receive in a conveniently wrapped package. It is a process of talent recognition and skill improvement.

Myths aside, let us move into a discussion of why leaders fail.

SIX PRIMARY REASONS WHY LEADERS FAIL

Failure… it is every aspiring leader's secret nightmare. Whatever the reason for the failure, it is often easier to cover up past failures than to examine why they happened.

Of course, there are many unknowns which can cause disaster—the economy, wrong timing, unfortunate circum-

---

4. *Ibid.* p. 224.

stances—but more often, failure is self-related, rather than externally-caused—usually through one of these six primary causes:

(1) **Cannot get along**

Poor interactive people skills form the singlemost reason for the failures. Inability to get along with others is also the most fatal imperfection a person can detect and correct within himself or herself.

Weak leaders typically can't inspire and win the loyalty of underlings because they aren't good listeners, don't give or take criticism well and view conflict as something bad instead of something inevitable that has to be handled.

(2) **Inability to be flexible and change-friendly**

The inability to adapt to change is the fatal flaw of the person who clings to an outmoded, mechanistic, top-to-bottom or dictatorial leadership style.

We wish we had a dollar for every time we've heard someone declare, "Well, I don't care what anybody says—the old method worked in the past, and no one will ever make me change!"

We believe in the system of books, tapes and meetings—obviously—since we have pioneered a lot of it. We also believe in consistently looking at new techniques that grow and develop this business, but those that don't conflict with proven principles. That has led us to new tools, innovations and breakthroughs.

(3) **The Solo Syndrome**

Every leader wants to be recognized and rewarded for his or her efforts, but some become so preoccupied with individual pin-winning that they become useless to their organization.

Part of the blame, quite frankly, should be attributed to the success, power and leadership books, as

well as the training systems which push one-upsman-
ship, aggressiveness and manipulation to extremes.

It's incredibly wearing to have to work with someone who's constantly demanding recognition and inca-
pable of any selfless acts. Leaders have to be authentic
team players.

A large percentage of lonely-at-the-top leaders
stumble because they cannot lead others unselfishly.
Putting personal gain above their companies' most
important needs is the worst offense. Sooner or later,
as well-publicized downfalls have shown, arrogant and
selfish people somehow find a way to self-destruct.

(4) **Fear of action**

Leaders who fail may be limited by their inability to
put themselves on the line. They may be diligent workers with new ideas but without the passion or convic-
tion to sell them.

At the core of this lack of commitment is an even
greater fear of failure. Such so-called leaders try to
prevent a fall by avoiding action—but in doing so
actually accelerate their own ruin.

(5) **Unable to bounce back from failure or disappointment**

There are many overnight successes who do well
early in their careers—not just in this business, but in
every area of the corporate world—but are unable to
sustain their climb when faced with setbacks.

It is ironic that those who are unable to bounce
back after failures often seem quite the same as those
who have the ability to rebound. Both groups are often
very bright and ambitious, but those who don't (or
can't) recoup tend to react to failure by becoming
defensive, trying to conceal it or blaming others.

By comparison, successful rebounders almost
always admit where they have erred and then try to

correct it. We dealt with this more completely in Chapter Seventeen.

How you handle failures and disappointments can often be the thing that makes or breaks your leadership climb. If you learn from your mistakes, your leadership breakdowns may prove to be your greatest assets.

(6) **Lack of ability or willingness to support others**

We have seen hundreds of non-support situations which are invariably detrimental to a team. Lack of support comes in many forms, primarily in terms of undermining uplines or downlines.

Not nearly enough organizations foster support. Likewise, not enough organizations have leaders who are secure enough to support other people on their team.

You will find that this business is different. We thrive on support and loyalty.

One-Minute Manager author Kenneth Blanchard says, "Leadership is the process of influencing the activities of an individual or a group in efforts toward goal achievement in a given situation."

As such, success often means rising above failure and moving into a new understanding of what a leader can become. That's the purpose of the remainder of this chapter.

FIVE LEADERSHIP PRACTICES

We have already discussed leadership myths and reasons why leaders fail. Enough of leadership's down side!

Let's concentrate on ways you work toward leadership success while avoiding the traps. Several years ago, James M. Kouzes and Barry Z. Posner authored a book which has since become a classic. In *The Leadership Challenge*, they pointed toward an extensive study in which they uncovered five fundamental practices that enable leaders to get extraordinary things done:[5]

(1) Challenging the process

(2) Inspiring a shared vision

(3) Enabling others to act

(4) Modeling the way

(5) Encouraging the heart

Of course, these five leadership practices can be developed. They are, as Kouzes and Posner pointed out in the book, available to anyone who wants to accept the leadership challenge.

How?

By being aware of the five practices and by striving to make these practices second nature to you. You can incorporate these practices in the way you relate to your upline, your downline, your prospects, your family and your friends.

During the remainder of the chapter, let's go back through each of the five leadership practices, taking them one at a time, to define and explain specific ways to make these practices vital to your life, especially in relation to the ways you build your mutual-benefit marketing business.

CHALLENGING THE PROCESS

Leadership is an active process, not a passive one. People who make it in this business simply don't wait around for fate to smile on them. Those who succeed do so because they see a need and fill it. They refuse to accept the status quo.

In a very real sense, the leaders in this business are pioneers—people who are willing to step out into the unknown.

Says Kouzes and Posner in *The Leadership Challenge:*

The leader's primary contribution is in the recognition of good ideas, the support of those ideas, and the

---

5. James M. Kouzes and Barry Z. Posner, *The Leadership Challenge* (San Francisco: Jossey-Bass, 1987), pp. 7-13.

willingness to challenge the system in order to get new products, processes, and services adopted. In this sense, it might be more accurate to call them early adopters of innovation.[6]

The "system" we are challenging is the "rut" system (the corporate JOB route). The new system of books, tapes and meetings, however, provides the solutions to the traditional systems. Challenge the rut system, but plug in to the new one.

In relation to this business, the potent words from the authors of *The Leadership Challenge* seem to spotlight a Diamond's leadership position; their "challenging the process" role points toward finding new opportunities to make the system work for you. For the distributor who is moving from Direct to Diamond, "challenging the process" relates to helping downline people develop new dreams and plugging them into the system. For you, however, as you start building your Amway business, your "challenging the process" role should focus on learning and following the five-to-ten year plan to free you from the typical 45-year "rut" career schedule.

Thankfully, with this business, you have a proven system that helps you break past the old "rut." You don't have to put together the best products and services in the world—Amway already has. You don't have to develop a worldwide sponsoring and training system—you are already plugged into the best in the world of network marketing.

But what you can do, in terms of challenging the process, is to constantly look for ways to improve your progress, your growth and the degree to which you are willing to change and move out of your comfort zones.

Consider these positive ways:

• Creativity and Initiative

Because leadership means, literally, to "go in advance" (our translation: "to make it happen!"), it depends greatly on the leader's **initiative** (the ability to break away from dependence on the group) and **creativity** (the ability to look for opportunity).

---

6. *Ibid*, p. 8.

Examples of trailblazing exist in nearly every lasting enterprise—Ford pushed mass production into the forefront, Birdseye moved from canned into frozen foods, Xerox pioneered modern paper-duplicating methods, Polaroid revolutionized photography with the instant-print camera, Apple made personal computing affordable and Amway developed new worldwide distribution methods while making personal business ownership available to virtually anyone.

Good leadership fosters creativity and initiative, and creating an atmosphere that fosters these traits must flow throughout an organization for sustained success.

Admittedly, dreams are a dime a dozen, but it takes positive action to implement those ideas. (You may want to re-read Chapter Eight, in which we outline ways to develop your own action plan.)

(Not all ideas are worth a dime a dozen!)

• A willingness to learn

John H. Johnson, *Ebony* Magazine founder, was asked how he recognized leadership qualities.

> *By observing. I look for dedication and commit-*
> *ment, and willingness to learn. I think it's more the*
> *last than it is anything else, because an intelligent*
> *person can be taught almost anything that's not purely*
> *technical. So we look primarily for a desire to learn*
> *and a dedication to the job. If they have these, we can*
> *teach them the rest.*[7]

Studies show that leaders pursue knowledge from every available source. They read as much as possible. They listen. They observe. They are ever alert to opportunities for adding to their store of information relevant to their profession, ready to draw from it to gain an advantage in difficult situations.

This ability to be creative, as well as the constant pursuit of knowledge, used properly, is attractive to other people. It will draw people to you—others who want to challenge the status quo—so never lose your eagerness to move yourself and others ahead. Always look for the best way to do things, but never forget to seek upline counsel. Mainly, improve yourself and your skills.

Please realize the fact that "challenging the process" means that you will have to be gutsy enough to risk difficulties and sometimes even failure. "No pain, no gain" is more than a catchy sweatshirt phrase; it is a very real part of building your business (or doing **anything** worthwhile!). Says Ollie Bovin, a manager at Hewlett-Packard in Europe:

> *You have to be brave enough to fail as a leader.*[8]

Quoting again from *The Leadership Challenge:*

> *If this (risking failure) seems like foolish advice,*
> *recall the times you have tried to play a new game or a*
> *new sport. Did you get it absolutely perfect the first*

---

7. John H. Johnson, " 'Failure' Is a Word I Don't Accept," *Harvard Business Review*, March-April 1976, p. 124.
8. Kouzes and Posner, p. 8-9.

time you played it? Probably not. Experimentation, innovation, and change all involve risk and failure.

It would be ridiculous to state that those who fail over and over again eventually succeed as leaders. Success in business is not a process of simply buying enough lottery tickets. The key that unlocks the door to opportunity is learning.[9]

Anyone who succeeds at anything realizes that risk and potential failure is a natural part of the learning process.

INSPIRING A SHARED VISION

A leader must be able to create a vision, which is the reason we focused on this subject during Chapter Five. We quote from Kouzes and Posner:

Leaders spend considerable effort gazing across the horizon of time, imagining what it will be like when they have arrived at their final destinations. Some call it vision; others describe it as a purpose, mission, goal, even personal agenda. Regardless of what we call it, there is a desire to make something happen, to change the way things are, to create something that no one else has ever created before.[10]

But it is not enough to create a vision; you must also be able to share that vision with others. Again, quoting from *The Leadership Challenge:*

In some ways, leaders live their lives backwards. They see pictures in their minds' eyes of what the results will look like even before they have started their projects, much as an architect draws a blueprint or an engineer builds a model. Their clear image of the future pulls them forward. But visions seen only by leaders are insufficient to create an organized movement or a significant change in a company. A person with no followers is not a leader, and people will not become followers until they accept a vision as their own. You cannot command commitment, you can only inspire it.[11]

9. *Ibid*, p. 9.
10. *Ibid*.
11. *Ibid*.

How do you inspire others to share your vision? There are many ways, of course, but let us share a few of the most obvious:

• Develop your vision

Successful leaders almost universally live by a clear sense of mission. Leaders seem to have an unusually clear vision of their unique roles and limitations. This vision is communicated to others that the leader is a special person who deserves more than a routine effort.

Get a vision of where you want your business to go and grow. Your vision will touch other people because it offers a positive view of the future, inspires better performance and supplies courage in the face of the unknown.

• Energize your vision.

This should be no surprise, yet too few discussions of leadership spotlight this vital trait.

If you have leadership potential, you probably are already an active, energetic person—on your feet, moving about, working long hours.

Nolan Bushnell, who founded Atari, the electronic games company, put this trait quite simply:

The critical ingredient is getting off your chair and doing something. Not tomorrow. Not next week. But today.[12]

If you are an energetic person, you are probably also assertive. You seek out problems rather than letting them come to you. You are not afraid to make your ideas known. You use your energy to persevere where others might yield, to hold on to your convictions where others would be swayed or change their minds.

For example, anytime we ask people about leadership, such phrases as these keep coming up: "She is relentless in the pursuit of her goals," or "He just never gives up, no matter what happens."

Every organization, every movement, every building and every product begin with a dream. Amway was born in the hearts and minds of Rich DeVos and Jay Van Andel, and this dream continues to be the catalyst that creates the future for this business.

You can breathe life into the dreams and aspirations of others as you enable them to see the exciting possibilities that the future holds. You can get others to buy into your vision, as well as their own dreams, by showing how everyone can be served by sharing in a common purpose.

Since we were children, we have heard the phrase, "You can't light a fire with a wet match." Simply stated, you cannot ignite the flames of passion in others if you don't pour yourself into others. Your own belief, as you plug into the system more and more, will ignite many flames.

To do this, you must know your people. You must speak their language. You must understand their needs. You need to help them define their dreams. People must believe that you genuinely have their interests at heart. All of these are vital components of inspiring a shared vision.

---

12. Lester R. Bittel, *Leadership* (New York: Franklin Watts, 1984), p. 15.

ENABLING OTHERS TO ACT

As discussed in the previous section, you cannot achieve success by yourself. You must share your vision. Even more, you must learn to enable others to act on their dreams.

Quoting Kouzes and Posner:

> *Exemplary leaders enlist the support and assistance of all those who must make the project work. They involve, in some way, those who must live with the results, and they make it possible for others to do good work. They encourage collaboration, build teams, and empower others. They enable others to act. In 91 percent of the cases we analyzed, leaders proudly discussed how teamwork and collaboration were essential. Additionally, our data on others' perceptions of leaders indicate that this is the most significant of all the five practices.*[13]

How do you do this?

• Develop good communication skills

In numerous studies, including those cited in *The Leadership Challenge*, business leaders have been asked, "What qualities do you consider to be the most desirable for leaders?" Virtually everyone from every survey has picked COMMUNICATION SKILLS first.

When you think about the essence of leadership, this top-of-the-list emphasis is no wonder. Only men and women who can communicate their ideals effectively can attract others to "buy in" to those concepts. This is true in virtually every area of the network marketing and interactive distribution business—from drawing circles to taking orders, and from counselling with a few people to speaking in front of a filled coliseum.

Granted, people often associate intelligence, or any one of the other qualities with effective leadership, but unless a person develops persuasive oral and non-

---

13. Kouzes and Posner, p. 10.

verbal communication skills, other leadership abilities will probably be overlooked.

Good communicators include other people in the decision-making process. This is true on all levels, beginning with showing the plan.

Remember this: People are capable of doing things best when they join in for **their** reasons. **That is the essence of teamwork and enabling others to act.** Communication professionals know that their best chances of getting things done are tied to giving others a strong reason for being an integral part of what needs to occur. Remember this when doing **every** dream session. This kind of "mental ownership" and teamwork can only happen through effective communications.

• Let others know what you want to do.

General Dwight D. Eisenhower, Supreme Commander Allied Forces Europe. On an informal visit with paratroopers on the eve of "D. Day" June 6, 1944.

Share your expectations. Establish clear priorities and guidelines. Then have a two-way door. As part of this, encourage others to come to you, but you must also get out in their living rooms.

Enabling others to act helps them feel strong, capable and committed. People in your group must feel a sense of ownership. They must feel empowered. When they feel part of the team, they are more likely to use their energy to bring about outstanding results.

MODELING THE WAY

Great dreams, even when shared by a unified team, cannot come to pass until you follow a plan. To get people to follow, you must model the way.

Granted, in this business, your position as an upline, especially as you get to higher pin levels, gives you a measure of authority. It is your behavior, however, that earns the respect of others.

Here are a few starting points to model the way for the people on your team:

• Be organized.

Leaders must be better prepared, more organized and able to anticipate more effectively than others. Organization and planning skills are learned and are absolute musts to sustain long-term leadership.

• Be objective about the ups-and-downs you will face.

As a leader, you will have to weather stormy periods as well as sunny. You must guard against the ebbs and flows—an inflated ego that often accompanies a period of uninterrupted successes, and the damaged ego that accompanies disappointment and failure. Otherwise your judgement becomes distorted.

• Be dedicated to the cause.

Certainly, leaders must believe in something strongly and feel passionately about achieving it. Accomplishment must be a dominate motivation.

LEADERSHIP

Selfishness, on the opposite end of the spectrum, ultimately destroys achievement.

- Keep your promises.

Credibility creates trust. Trust builds strong organizations. Always tell the truth. Too many contemporary leaders have already learned that the trouble with stretching the truth is that it is apt to snap back!

Being a role model means paying attention to what you believe is important—for you and your team. You must model the way through planning and leading by example. It means showing others that your deeds are as good as your words— some call it "Walking the talk." True leaders act in ways that are consistent with their beliefs.

ENCOURAGING THE HEART

Quoting again from Kouzes and Posner:

The climb to the top is arduous and long. People become exhausted, frustrated, and disenchanted. They often are tempted to give up. Leaders must encourage the heart of their followers to carry on.[14]

What are a few simple ways to encourage the heart?

- Be people-conscious.

Create a climate that will lead to greater performance and satisfaction in your organization. Be a friend. Care about your people. Be there when they need you, not just when you need them. Know them so that when they need help you will know how to respond and what to recommend.

- Seek to give your distributors opportunities to grow.

Empowerment comes through a positive, people-building environment. Don't fight all their battles or handle all their problems. Let them be challenged, not bored.

14. *Ibid*, p. 12.

• Motivate others.

   True motivation moves beyond situational leadership. Good leaders make other people in the organization—upline and downline—feel important. They
encourage progress by letting others know what is
expected and by instilling pride. They work hard to
create a pleasant, energetic atmosphere. Great leaders
are almost always masters at recognition, giving credit
for downlines' achievements and praising them for
productive and profitable efforts.

• Pass the pride along.

   Empower people! Recognize them! Show prompt
appreciation for good ideas and good performance.
Look for ways to encourage them to keep on passing
out AD PACKs, showing the plan and building their
groups. Genuine acts of caring will endear others to
you and your vision.

   Encouraging the heart has special meaning in this
business. We recognize individual achievement by
celebrating with group activities such as providing
reserved seating areas, giving awards for 1000, 1500,
2500, 4000 and so forth, and with "little" things such as
postcards from exotic locales, personal thank-yous
and inspirational note cards which share the humor-
ous, sensitive and caring parts of building this business. The key word is encouragement.

   As you encourage others, don't forget that you need to
keep things in perspective. Remember to encourage your own
heart.

   Go dreambuilding. Don't get so wrapped up in everyone
else's goals that you completely forget to keep developing your
own dreams. Take time to go sit in that luxury automobile. Drive
through those pricey neighborhoods, imagining yourself walking
onto a spacious deck in the morning (when you decide to get up!).

   Love what you do. Remember **why** you are building this
business. You can do this in simple ways—by turning the key in

FOR SALE

your front door after coming home from a meeting, putting on a cup of hot tea, sitting down for a few moments and relishing the satisfaction of knowing that by building your own business, you are developing a wonderful lifestyle for you and your loved ones. Face it, few people are willing to make the sacrifices you are making, so pat yourself on the back from time to time.

A FINAL NOTE

As you build your business over the coming years, ask yourself continually:

How good am I challenging the process?

Am I getting better at inspiring a shared vision?

Can I enable others to act?

Am I modeling the way?

Do I consistently look for ways to encourage the heart?

You can see that a leader's responsibility extends beyond directing others. You must decide what you want. You must define what kind of life you want to have. You must determine what qualities or traits you desire. You need to even evaluate how you want others to treat you.

An old Chinese proverb goes like this:

If you want one year of prosperity,
*   grow grain.*
If you want ten years of prosperity,
*   grow trees*
If you want one hundred years of prosperity,
*   grow people.*

You must first define or decide how you would like things to be as a leader. Then you must build on those decisions.

We hope that building people is a major foundation of all your choices. If you want to be successful for the long-haul, then you must grow people—beginning with yourself.

You can learn to grow people
and become a great,
effective leader as you
BUILD YOUR OWN NETWORK
MARKETING BUSINESS.

BUILDING BLOCKS:

Perhaps the most important thing any coach can do is to make himself available to his players; to make them understand that his door is open, that he sees them as individuals as well as a team, that they can talk with him.[1]

BILL MCCARTNEY
Head Football Coach,
University of Colorado,
and Bestselling Author (USA)

There are so many great parts of this business that we mention--being with confident and successful people, going through both good and bad times, learning from winners, seeing dreams come true and being free.

These are wonderful, but as someone who has built this business as both married and single, I can tell you that there are so many benefits that we don't often talk about. For starters, as I experienced through the time of tragedy through my first husband's illness and death, people in this business are the most loving, caring and supportive you will ever find.

No dollar value can be placed on these unseen things!

PAT THORNTON
Homemaker
Diamond
Direct Distributor (USA)

---

1. Bill McCartney with Dave Diles, *From Ashes to Glory* (Nashville: Thomas Nelson, 1990), p. 245.

People don't want to be managed. They want to be led. Whoever heard of a world manager? World leader, yes. Educational leader. Political leader. Religious leader. Scout leader. Community leader. Labor leader. Business leader. They lead. They don't manage. The carrot always wins over the stick. Ask your horse. You can lead your horse to water, but you can't manage him to drink. If you want to manage somebody, manage yourself. Do that well and you'll be ready to stop managing. And start leading.[2]

WALL STREET JOURNAL

People succeed in this business when they learn certain principles. One is believing in the success system taught by the leaders in this business. The second is going the extra mile— being willing to go out of your way to help someone else make his or her dreams come true. The third is definiteness of purpose—setting a goal and sticking to it until you win.

DON KING
College Physics Professor
Diamond Direct
Distributor (USA)

I never teach my pupils; I only attempt to provide the conditions in which they can learn.

ALBERT EINSTEIN (1879-1955)
German Physicist
Nobel Prize Winner

---

2. *The Wall Street Journal*, November 27, 1984, p. 5.

People often ask what it takes to succeed in this business. Experience tells me that everyone's price tag is different, but experience in this business also tells me that you can know with great certainty that anyone who plugs into the success system can make it work—with lots of patience and great effort, of course. You really can reach your goals through this business-- including financial flexibility and a debt-free life.

JO CHATHAM
Former Veterinarian
Executive Diamond
Direct Distributor (Australia)

A house divided against itself cannot stand... Our cause must be intrusted to, and conducted by its own undoubted friends—whose hands are free, whose hearts are in the work— who do care for the result.[3]

ABRAHAM LINCOLN (1809-1865)
Sixteenth U.S. President

As an executive for a General Motors company, one of my biggest challenges was getting past the problem of worrying what others might think about the fact that Pilar and I were start- ing to build an Amway business. Though I was very careful not to take advantage of my position, some of my GM buddies found out about what I was doing and thought I had gone crazy.

But I somehow knew that if my dream of winning finan- cial flexibility was big enough, nothing else mattered. That helped me overcome any problems with status. The vision of winning my freedom continually motivated me to get out and share the dream with others.

MIGUEL AGUADO
Former Research &
Development Manager
Diamond Direct Distributor (Spain)

---

3. Remarks from "A House Divided"speech, in which he accepted the nomination for U.S. senator (June 16, 1858), quoted from Donald T. Phillips, *Lincoln on Leadership* (New York: Warner Books, 1992), p. 27.

But hard it is to learn the mind of any mortal, or the heart, till he be tried in chief authority. Power shows the man.[4]

SOPHOCLES (495-406 B.C.)
Greek Dramatist and Writer

All of the material rewards from this business are so much better than we could have ever imagined in the beginning, but the most rewarding thing of all is that no matter what goals you reach in this business, you get to help other people grow and achieve their dreams.

BARBARA WATERS
Former Mayor
Double Diamond
Direct Distributor (USA)
Past ADA Board President ('91-'92)

These are the hard times in which a genius would wish to live. Great necessities call forth great leaders.[5]

ABIGAIL ADAMS (1744-1818)
U.S. First Lady
Wife of President John Adams
(Second U.S. President)
Mother of President
John Quincy Adams (Sixth U.S.
President)
Chronicler of Her Times

---

4. From Sophocles' play, *Antigone.*
5. 1790, in a letter to Thomas Jefferson.

Success in this business is tied to commitment. The greatest rewards come only from the greatest commitments. With strong dedication, you really can be anything you want to be. You must have the determination to overcome any obstacle. This is the basis for any degree of success in this business.

ROSE KNICKMAN
Homemaker
Executive Diamond
Direct Distributor (USA)

The ultimate test of practical leadership is the realization of intended, real change that meets people's enduring needs.

JAMES MACGREGOR BURNS, Ph.D.
Author and Professor
of Government
at Williams College (USA)

There are so many opportunities in this business, but there are also responsibilities. If you want the people in your organization to read books, listen to tapes and attend meetings, you have to do it first. If you want the respect of your children, you have to do the things that win that respect.

Thankfully, with the system which is in place, anyone can learn to take responsibility for your own life.

SHARON DELISLE
Former Secretary
Triple Diamond
Direct Distributor (USA)

Tomorrow never waits. You must make your own tomorrows. If you want to join the achievers in this business, then you must begin today by making the right choices and using a system that works. Let me assure you—as someone who has seen both sides of life—this system works! I'm more excited about the growth of this business in the future than ever before, mostly because I know what it has done for me and my family as I learned to make the right choices.

JERRY MEADOWS
Former Textile Plant Manager
Double Diamond Direct Distributor (USA)
Past ADA Board President ('88-'89, '90-'91)

New Horizons

...Your View Toward the Future

Is success possible for you in network marketing? Yes!

We know with certainty that achievement is not the exclusive domain of a gifted few. No!

Instead, true success in this business is a process of self-development which can be used by many to bring forth the best from themselves and others.

What's more, tomorrow will require an entirely new breed of men and women who understand and model this kind of dynamic, innovative leadership.

Why?

Everything is changing! In Chapter Two, Marketing & Distribution Paradigms, we talked about the advent of new concepts that are changing the way we shop, play, learn and earn. During the past ten years, the world has experienced the most turbulent time in history. Two decades ago, noted futurist Alvin Toffler made this startling statement:

> *Change is avalanching upon our heads and most people are grotesquely unprepared to cope with it... For what is occurring now is, in all likelihood, bigger, deeper, and more important than the industrial revolution. Indeed, a growing body of reputable opinion asserts that the present movement represents nothing less than the second great divide in human history, comparable in magnitude only with that first great break in historic continuity, the shift from barbarism to civilization.*

More specifically, according to Toffler, these changes will happen at an accelerated rate:

> *This lifetime is also different from all others because of the astonishing expansion of the scale and scope of change... We have not merely extended the scope and scale of change, we have radically altered its pace. We have in our time released a totally new social force—a stream of change so accelerated that it influences our sense of time, revolutionizes the tempo of daily life, and affects the very way we "feel" the world around us.*

Time has proven that Toffler's predictions were hardly a collection of fictitious, book-selling ploys. Other business-oriented futurists, including John Naisbitt, Paul Zane Pilzer, Faith Popcorn, and Peter Drucker have since pointed to even more specific trends which will revolutionize most of our established foundations.

Leadership is changing! Leadership is one of the most challenged institutions in our society. No futurist is required to spot that direction.

In recent Lou Harris polls, public opinion concerning leadership continues to flounder. Of the adults questioned, 55%

expressed feelings of estrangement from leadership. Confidence in the United States Supreme Court has dropped from a high of 58% in 1966 to 28%. During the same time-frame, faith in the press has fallen from 38% to 18%, in college presidents from 58% to 34% and in Wall Street leaders from 26% to only 10%.

Similar declines in corporate confidence leave only 18% of those polled feeling that they can count on business leaders, while a much lower 14% express trust in labor union leaders.

During the coming years corporate leadership will be marked by a spreading more toward decentralization, and decisions will be increasingly made at the lowest possible level. As a result, leadership in these companies will be transformed into completely new patterns, and many of these people who have learned leadership skills in the corporate setting will be attracted to your business—especially during the increased climate of reengineering, restructuring and downsizing—because they can put their talents to better use by owning their own business.

Business is changing! The effect of such alienation among our work force has been disastrous through all levels of the marketplace. In surveys of the American work sector, the accelerated changes we have experienced are producing a number of upsetting consequences:

- More than 70% of the employees surveyed admitted that they seldom work at full capacity.

- Approximately 50% say they never do anything over and above that which is the most basic requirement for holding onto their jobs.

- The overwhelming majority, three out of every four respondents, admit that they could be considerably more efficient than they presently are.

- Nearly 65% of all employees in the survey believe that they used to work harder than they do now.

Perhaps related to this widespread lack of employee morale, of the top 100 companies on the original Fortune 500 list in 1955, only 46 remain in the top 100 today. If anything, those drop-out figures have accelerated during the past decade.

More importantly, **the network marketing and interactive distribution business is changing.**

We believe that this business is only going to get better and certainly bigger. According to the Direct selling association, the entire DSA, of which network marketing is considered a prime player, did approximately $13 billion. Amway already is doing 38% of that total industry figure and promises to continue to be a major force.

When asked by *Success* Magazine editors how big Amway could get, Co-founder Rich DeVos said:

> *I see no limit. I'm looking at $10 billion now. And here's why: This is a quote from Kaoru Nakajima, an Amway distributor in Japan: "I was a salaried man... Now I am my own boss. Now I am free. Now I am helping people in five different countries to own their own businesses. When I see so many people getting more abundant lives, I feel really excited. This is no job to me. It is more like play."* [1]

We are positioned for tremendous growth in the future. Rich DeVos says $10 billion as the next milepost. Analysts such as Paul Zane Pilzer are pointing to $20 or $30 billion. Frankly, with new interactive media and distribution methods already on the horizon, we envision this business growing to $50 billion or more and seriously competing with the world's top retailers and discounters.

Who knows what can happen? Take a look at Amway's growth and projection chart shown on the next page.

At first glance, there seems to be no comparison. But when you add several other factors, the idea that Amway can someday overtake and even pass Wall-Mart becomes more believable.

For starters, Amway has grown at an accelerated rate (25-27% a year), while Wal-Mart's growth, though still enviable, is tapering from highs of 25% in recent years to 19.5% for fiscal 1993. [2]

---

1. "The $4-Billion Man: Rich DeVos Bet on Capitalism and Won," *Success Selling*, May 1993, p.10
2. Associated Press Writers, "Experts Wonder About Price of Success: World's Largest Retailer Could Have Grown Past Its Roots," *High Point (NC) Enterprise*, August 8, 1993, p. 4D.

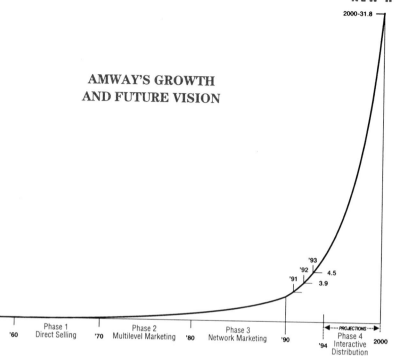

**AMWAY'S GROWTH
AND FUTURE VISION**

Now look at Wal-Mart's growth chart:

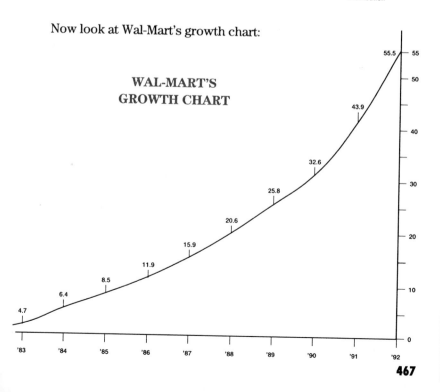

**WAL-MART'S
GROWTH CHART**

While Amway's communication and distribution methods are gearing up for the interactive media era, Wal-Mart is saddled with 1,900 stores (in 1993), up from one in 1962, 551 in 1983, and with 150 more being added annually. While Amway largely relies on its distributors' networks for sales and distribution, Wal-Mart now employs a whopping 470,000 people, up from 46,000 in 1983.[3] Multiply Wal-Mart's real estate, inventory and worker base with sharply rising fuel prices, local, state and national taxes, employee benefits and health care costs—it's a situation that points toward lower profit margins, at best.

Even Wall Street and industry analysts, including the United Shareholders Association, an investors' rights group with 65,000 members, are pointing to Wal-Mart's slowing growth rates. Wal-Mart has consistently placed at the top of the Association's 1,000-stock ratings, but slipped in 1993 to 145th.[4]

Says Ralph Whitworth, the association's president, "They're starting to mature in their industry, and starting to level off."[5]

If Wal-Mart is tapering in an industry that is facing increased competition and low-margin profits, then Amway's continued upswing in a emerging industry points toward future excitement for distributors.

Think about it: There were lots of disbelievers back in the 1960s, 1970s and even the 1980s when people began talking about Wal-Mart as a future contender for then gigantic Sears. Those critics were silenced in 1990, when Wal-Mart passed Sears to become the world's largest retailer.

Will history repeat itself? Will Amway someday compete in the Wal-Mart arena?

We don't know the future, but we do know that Amway continues to position itself for a new era of unparalleled hyper-growth and worldwide recognition. We believe Amway has positioned itself as a manufacturing, marketing and distribution force to begin to truly compete with such retail and discount giants as Wal-Mart and K-Mart during the next decade. Amway's

---

3. *Ibid.*
4. *Ibid.*
5. *Ibid.*

presence as a leader in this interactive distribution and network marketing industry continues to be cemented with sales now reaching $4.5 billion and distributorships rising to more than two million. Amway's international expansion already circles the globe, totalling 60 countries and territories.

What's next. Who knows.

WHAT IS AHEAD?

Decades ago, a few visionary leaders such as Rich DeVos and Jay Van Andel were pioneering new ideas which would bring a wave of creativity, flexibility and empowerment to the workplace. They were not alone.

Back in 1951, Clarence Randall, then head of Inland Steel, wrote:

> *We have come to worship production as an end in itself, which of course it is not. It is precisely there that the honest critic of our way of life makes his attack and finds us vulnerable. Sure there must be for each person some ultimate value, some purpose, some mode of self-expression that makes the experience we call life richer and deeper.*[6]

Even before Randall's statement, back in 1941 Mary Parker Follett, an economist and teacher, sketched an extraordinary, imaginary portrait of business and business leaders of the future:

> *...the most successful leader of all is one who sees another picture not yet actualized. He sees the things which belong in his present picture but which are not yet there... Above all, he should make his co-workers see that it is not his purpose which is to be achieved, but a common purpose, born of the desires and the activities of the group.*

Today, especially in the network marketing business, we

---

6. Clarence B. Randall, *A Creed for Free Enterprise* (Boston: Little, Brown and Company, 1952, p. 16.

are beginning to understand what yesterday's visionaries dreamed. What business better typifies such words as "self-expression" and "common purpose."

This business, quite frankly, is one of the greatest paradigm busters. It breaks the chains of traditional corporate thinking and allows us to participate in the wealth that we are creating through our interactive distribution systems.

The old way of thinking is no longer a viable option. It will survive, of course, for mediocrity will always be with us. It will not allow success, however, in the marketplace of tomorrow.

The network distribution model fits the future-view precisely. But it is not just a rehash of old systems; it is something bold and new.

The old paradigm places an inordinate concentration on position in the company and hierarchy. Its authority is founded on the boss/worker model. Initiative is stifled in favor of analytical thinking. Creativity and teamwork are talked about, but seldom promoted. Adding "new" systems on top of the old way of thinking actually builds resistance.

The new paradigm, as expressed throughout *The Business Handbook*, has dynamic, life-changing benefits for both individuals and organizations.

Based on trends we see on the horizon, we believe that during the coming decade the business environment will be more unpredictable than ever—much more so than most industry analysts are forecasting.

Many corporations, and the people within those organizations, which use outdated methods simply will not outlast the turbulence. Financial, technological, lifestyle and marketplace changes will come fast and furiously, and only the most flexible organizations, those which can learn to live with the turmoil, will survive.

Yet, during the coming chaos, there will also be a growing number of people and organizations who will flourish, despite the obstacles.

Naturally, we believe network marketing, especially Amway, will be at the forefront. We are not alone.

David M. La Buda, in an article which appeared in a recent issue of *Money Makers Magazine*, shared:

> *Network marketing is one of the most promising income opportunities in America today! It's an opportunity that has been tested and proven for more than 30 years, and today it represents a multi-billion dollar industry which is successfully providing income for hundreds of thousands of Americans from all walks of life. Almost anyone who has a true desire to be successful can do so in network marketing.*

More to the point, James Dale Davidson and Lord William Rees-Mogg, in their landmark book, *The Great Reckoning: How the World Will Change*, wrote favorably about network marketing businesses that will succeed during these changing times which they have labeled "The Amway Decade."

Leading economic futurist and businessman Paul Zane Pilzer has said:

> *The Amway Corporation is the number one network marketing company in the world, and there is no close second. Amway is at least a decade ahead of any other competitor. It is on the tip of the iceberg!*[7]

Clearly, as we have discussed throughout *The Business Handbook*, we have many great opportunities ahead.

CHALLENGES

Traditionally, we have expected each new generation to enjoy a better lifestyle than the previous one. But with the changes in our world coming so rapidly, a better life seems out of reach for so many people.

Why?

As jobs in service industries replace manufacturing jobs, many workers will be stuck with lower incomes. As many

---

7. From a speech at Weekend of Diamonds at the Charlotte (NC) Coliseum, May 24, 1992.

corporations continue mergers, closings and downsizings, the topsy-turvy marketplace will contribute to a rising tide of uncertainty, stress and confusion.

A lot of men and women will feel overwhelmed by forces seemingly beyond their control and find themselves directed more toward turf protecting than productivity boosting. Many more have simply fell victim to new waves of downsizings, layoffs and re-structurings. But so many today are deciding that they want to enter the world of personal business ownership in order to have more control over their future. These modern-day entrepreneurs represent the future of network marketing and interactive distribution.

This growing number of men and women want more than turbulence. They are committed to making a difference, both in business output, producing income and enjoying a better lifestyle. These network marketing champions also want all people to have the opportunity to own their own businesses and to view themselves as essential people in the personal and professional pursuit of a quality life.

You, too, can join this ongoing adventure!

A FINAL NOTE

The network marketing and interactive distribution business is attracting an influx of dynamic men and women to meet the demands of the future. But as we mentioned in Chapter Eighteen, network marketing leaders are not born; they are developed.

Simply stated, our purpose throughout this book has been to help get you started in the business-building process. Our goal has been to help you assess your strengths and weaknesses, then to assist as you learn how to inspire and motivate others toward shared goals.

The late Earl Nightingale, celebrated radio personality and positive-attitude speaker, said:

You can get anything in life you want, if you will help enough other people get what they want.

His words ring more true today than ever. Belief is the essence of leadership and achievement in this business.

Our friend Zig Ziglar says:

> *You build a big Amway business by prospecting one person at a time, by building your business all the time. You do it by thinking Diamond, Diamond, Diamond—all the time.*
>
> *I wrote a three-hundred and eighty four-page book that became a bestseller. I did it by writing 1.26 pages a day for ten months.*
>
> *It's what you do every day that makes the difference in your life.*

We face unprecedented challenges in today's marketplace. Without fresh solutions we are destined to slide downward. These needs are not new, but never before has there been such an urgent demand to continually create new and better solutions. You have the solutions!

We believe that you can look at problems differently, rather than "we've always done it this way around here." We believe that the tools we have offered can make a significant difference in the way you can build your own distribution business.

Catch the excitement of being your own boss. Turn your dreams into reality. It IS possible!

By joining the world of network marketing, you have linked yourself to a fantastic team—our Co-founders Rich DeVos and Jay Van Andel, our President Dick DeVos, our Chief Operating Officer Tom Eggleston, our Policy Board, the Amway Distributors Association and the ADA Council, the InterNet support system and, of course, your upline Diamonds (who are your link to this entire group).

All of your leaders are more excited about the business today than ever. There are many reasons for that enthusiasm, since the business is more profitable for everyone involved than at any time in the past.

The Amway Corporation is a one-of-a-kind enterprise, focusing on highly consumable, top-quality goods and services for you to use, retail and promote throughout your organization.

You are able to tap into an amazing network of business support materials, including audio and video cassettes, books, magazines and product literature. You can attend business-building meetings, seminars, rallies and other important functions.*

Best of all, this network has spread around the globe. It is the way business is being conducted today—through non-traditional, non-store marketing and distribution methods—and with a proven system to help and teach people just like you to operate their own business.

---

* These items are strongly recommended and available through your Upline. However, business support materials are optional and not required.

You have at your disposal the tools, the opportunity, the challenge and the availability to build one of the most exciting and profitable network marketing organizations in the world! What you do today has the potential of blessing your family— generation after generation—with additional income and security.

You CAN do it, but as we close out the final chapter of this book, that is no longer the question. The most pressing question is not "CAN you?" but "WILL you?"

You can do it, but will you? Will you begin to live your dreams? And when will you really make things happen?

Above all, we want you to know that we believe in you and your ability to make your dreams come true as you persist and stick with your action plan. When you really get down to the pro-verbial bottom line, dreams, persistence and stick-to-itiveness are what all of your successful Amway leaders have done. It's as simple as that. And we know you can become successful, too!

**Will you tap into
the power of the future today
as you BUILD YOUR OWN
SUCCESSFUL INTERACTIVE
DISTRIBUTION BUSINESS?**

BUILDING BLOCKS:

Life is a romantic business. It is painting a picture, not doing a sum; but you have to make the romance, and it will finally come to the question of how much fire you have in your belly.

OLIVER WENDELL HOLMES (1809-1894)
U.S. Essayist, Author and Poet
Dean of Harvard Medical School
Father of U.S. Supreme Court
Justice Oliver Wendell Holmes, Jr.

Tim and I dated to spend lots of time together, then after we got married, we were together less and less. This business has changed all that! We got involved in Amway for many reasons, but the best benefit of all is that our family actually spends time together.

CINDY KLINE
Homemaker
Diamond Direct
Distributor (USA)

One of the oldest axioms in the world revolves around the idea that whatever you plant, you will harvest. If you want people generally to treat you with respect and genuine concern, you must first deal with people that way.

CARL HENRY
Corporate Sales and
Customer Service Consultant
Author of *High Energy Selling* and
Everyone Serves... Everyone Sells (USA)

The secret to our Amway success is very simple. Lynne and I got a dream of financial flexibility. Once we set goals that would help us achieve our dream, we were willing to work harder than most other people to go forward. I really feel that success can be boiled down to three questions: What do you want? What will it take for you to get what you want? And are you willing to pay that price?

PETER MADDISON
Former Sales Representative
Diamond Direct Distributor (Australia)

Every day of our lives, we're telling our own futures. For it is what we think about, consciously and unconsciously, that becomes our compass, guiding us unrelentingly toward the destiny we have chosen for ourselves.

EARL NIGHTINGALE
Broadcaster, Author,
Speaker, Businessman and
Founder of Nightingale-Conant
Corporation (USA)

Both Bob and I lost our spouses tragically, so we know that overcoming obstacles—past, present or future—takes extraordinary amounts of courage. But we also know that a person who wants to succeed does what he or she must do, in spite of barriers, tragedies or pressures, especially when you are surrounded by the wonderful people in this business.

We can share this business with confidence because we have lived it. We know that all our dreams can come true, no matter what happens in life, because the system works.

NANCY STOUFFER
Former Registered Nurse
Diamond Direct Distributor (USA)

No es lo mismo hablar de toros, que estar en el redondel. *(It is not the same to talk of bulls as to be in the bullring.)*

SPANISH PROVERB

There are so many things this business offers. It gives an opportunity to live where I want, to drive whatever cars I choose, to be able to educate my children at the schools and colleges they desire and to travel to any country I choose. Sandee and I are living examples of how success can come to anyone who gets a big enough dream and the courage to commit to that dream—no matter what.

DICK MARKS
Former Policeman
Crown Ambassador
Direct Distributor (USA)
Past ADA Board President ('81-'82)

To produce more and more with less and less effort is merely treading water unless we thereby release time and energy for the cultivation of the mind and the spirit and for the achievement of those ends for which Providence placed us on this earth.[1]

CLARENCE B. RANDALL
Former President of
Inland Steel Company (USA)

"Whatever it takes!"

That's the key phrase to success in this business. Sure, it takes sacrifices. When we got involved, between my practice and my wife's responsibilities that included being mayor of our city, we had absolutely no time. Somehow, though, we found a way to leverage an hour here and there. Soon, we had a little more time. Eventually we were able to make choices which are based upon what we wanted to do, not what we had to do. We were so intent on winning financial flexibility that we were willing to do whatever it took. If you want to succeed in this business, I've got an idea that it will take that "whatever-it-takes" mentality for you, too.

LEE WATERS
Former Pediatrician
Double Diamond
Direct Distributor (USA)

What lies behind you and what lies before you pales in significance when compared to what lies within you.

RALPH WALDO EMERSON
(1803-1882)
U.S. Essayist,
Philosopher and Poet

---

1. Clarence B. Randall, *A Creed for Free Enterprise* (Boston: Little, Brown and Company, 1952), p. 16.

*Being a success in life is not easy because life is not easy,
and no rule for success will work if you don't.*

TONY RENARD
Former Music Teacher
and Entertainer
Diamond Direct
Distributor (USA)

*...striving for success becomes an experience of inner
growth, rather than just an effort to push, shove, and scramble
one's way to the top. Drive, ambition, intensity, and singleness
of purpose are certainly valuable qualities for the person who
wants to succeed. But perhaps the key lesson... is that achievement should never be an end in itself.*

*The idea is not just to work to finish a task but rather to
work well and to savor each step you take up the mountain
you've chosen. Then, when you reach the top, you won't feel
spent from all the effort. In fact, you won't even feel you've
arrived. Instead, you'll feel refreshed and invigorated by what
you've accomplished, and you'll find yourself looking for the
next peak to conquer.*[2]

GEORGE GALLUP, JR.
President of the Gallup Poll,
Co-Chairman of the
Gallup Organization
and Bestselling Author (USA)

---

2. George Gallup, Jr., and Alec M. Gallup with William Proctor, The Great American Success Story
(Homewood, IL: Dow Jones-Irwin, 1986), p. 200.

I believe you have to build this business from something deep inside. It's not just to buy the cars or merely for the money. It has to be more than those things. It must come from a decision, deep inside, to make things happen no matter what anyone else thinks or does.

PARKER GRABILL
Former Mechanical Draftsman
Diamond Direct
Distributor (USA)

The point is that I never wanted a traditional corporation, with each employee sitting robotically in his or her office. I tried to create a community for thinking, for I believe what inspires productivity the most is freedom, and freedom begets creativity. Having a free and flexible environment provides a place where people can work together to focus on the future.[3]

FAITH POPCORN
Futurist
Bestselling Author of
The Popcorn Report (USA)

There is so much potential in the Amway business. Once anyone begins to see how unlimited the possibilities are in this business, that person also becomes unlimited.

If we owe our success to anything, it is this: We treated our distributorship like a BIG business even when we only had a few people involved. We saw the potential. We stayed plugged into the tapes, books and functions. We are just a product of the Yager success pattern, and we are very thankful to be part of it!

KEN STEWART
Former Construction
Business Owner
Crown Direct Distributor (USA)
Past ADA Board Member

---

3. Faith Popcorn, *The Popcorn Report* (New York: HarperCollins, 1992) p. 11.

G*lossary*

In this book's introduction, we wrote, "Don't let your education end when you complete this book." We followed that phrase with a three-word suggestion: "Re-read the chapters."

Obviously, we don't believe for a moment that *The Business Handbook* is a be-all, end-all. One of the best parts of the system of books, tapes and meetings is the fact that you have a multitude of ways to learn about building your Amway business.

However, we have written this book precisely to offer you the best possible information to help you put together a growing organization. We desire for you to learn all you can, as fast as you can. That's why we say, "Re-read the chapters."

Repetition has always been one of the best ways to learn. This will certainly continue to be true as you build your own network marketing and interactive distribution business.

Reading is good, but **learning** and **understanding** are even better. Even more important than reading, learning or understanding is **acting on what you have read, learned and understood. Repetition** is the key to this entire process.

Naturally, as you plug into the system, you will probably develop a growing number of favorite cassettes that you enjoy listening to again and again. The same goes for positive books—you will want to visit familiar pages time after time.

Likewise, you will want to go back to the Eight Step Pattern in the front of the *Schedule Book Pocket Calendar.*

With those repetition patterns in mind, there is nothing that would make us feel better than for *The Business Handbook* which you are reading to be revisited and dog-eared in time.

We have written this book for people from various educational, sociological and economic backgrounds to use as both a reference manual and an inspirational source book. We have sought to focus on information and steps to help you at different stages of the business. Therefore, the material we have put together will undoubtedly gain new, deeper meaning for you at each new pin level.

That's what we mean when we suggest that you read and re-read each chapter. Your success is very important to your leaders, and we look forward to the times when we can see you onstage and be with you there.

May God bless you with wisdom as you pursue your dreams, achieve great goals and build your Amway business!

GLOSSARY OF TERMS

ADA

The Amway Distributors Association was formed even before Amway Corporation began. In 1959, it was known then as the American Way Association. It represents all Amway distributors worldwide.

The purpose of the association is to represent the distributors' interests to the corporation in all matters of policy relating to the development of their Amway businesses. Each year, the distributors elect a board of directors as representatives to the corporation. This balance of power and open line of communication has been the cornerstone of the mutual respect between the field and the corporation, as well as a monumental advantage over other industry competitors.

Any distributor can elect to join this association, and when you achieve the Direct Distributor pin level, you then earn the right to choose to become a voting member.

ADA COUNCIL

The ADA Council was established in June 1991 by the U.S. ADA Board of Directors. This council meets with Amway Corporation personnel in a cooperative effort to help determine business policies and overall direction of this business. The group of distributors achieve a broad representation throughout North America (U.S. and Canada) by an election of 30 distributors at the Diamond level and above, fifteen members elected by Direct Distributors and above, and fifteen council members nominated from a slate submitted by Amway Corporation, with a minimum of two members representing Canada.

AWARDS	The levels of recognition given to Distributors as they build their businesses identified by various pins.
	This distinguished group of men and women, whose backgrounds cut across lines of sponsorship, pin levels and geography, is dedicated to improving every facet of the Amway business. That fact that Amway Corporation has made this type of commitment to bring all proposed new policies or proposed policy changes to this legal body for discussion, evaluation, recommendation and approval is an additional factor why Amway has pioneered the way and remains a trendsetter in the network marketing business.
BURN	This refers to a dream that has become all-consuming—a burning desire or aspiration that compels you to achieve so much more than you ever thought possible. As we have said many times, if the dream if big enough, the facts don't count. That kind of dream is truly a burn!
CALL-IN	This is a designated time each week to receive telephone orders from your downline distributors, then to relay your organization's consolidated order to your upline.
	When you and/or your distributors reach approximately 2500 PV, your upline Direct may discuss having you order directly from your nearest Amway RDC (Regional Distribution Center).
COUNSELING	At least once a month during a pre-set session with an active upline (normally with a DD), you will spend valuable time discussing personal challenges, business successes and organizational growth.

CROSSLINE	This term refers to Amway distributors who are neither in your group or in your direct upline/downline line of sponsorship. For example, when you personally sponsor two distributors, they are "crossline" from each other.
CROSSLINING	"Crossline" distributors sometimes seek or attempt to acquire business-building information from each other. This practice is forbidden by Amway's policy standards.
CROWN	The Crown Direct Distributor has sponsored 18 groups, each of which qualifies at the 25% Performance Bonus level (7500 PV) for at least six months of Amway's fiscal year (September 1 through August 31).
CROWN AMBASSADOR	Amway's highest pin level, the Crown Ambassador Direct Distributor has sponsored 20 groups, each of which qualifies at the 25% Performance Bonus level for at least six months of Amway's fiscal year.
DEPTH	Anyone in your group is considered "downline" or in "depth." Building depth is the key to longevity in the network marketing and distribution business. The process by which you assist those whom you have sponsored to sponsor others is referred to as "building depth."
	When you sponsor someone, they are "one in depth" from you, and your organization is one level "deep." As you help personally-sponsored distributors get someone started in the business, the newest person is "two deep" from you or "two in depth."
DIAMOND	A Diamond Direct Distributor has sponsored six groups, each of which qualifies at the 25% Performance Bonus level for at least six months of Amway's fiscal year.

DIRECT	A Direct Distributor has built an organization that produces a minimum of 7500 PV six out of 12 months of Amway's fiscal year.
DOWNLINE	Anyone that is "downline" from you is in your organization or in your depth. Someone that is referred to as one of your "downline" is simply a distributor in your group.
DOUBLE DIAMOND	A Double Diamond Direct Distributor has sponsored 12 groups, each of which qualifies at the 25% Performance Bonus level for at least six months of Amway's fiscal year.
DREAM	In the context of building your network marketing and interactive distribution business, the "dream" refers to your vision of the future for yourself and those you love.

What are your hopes and aspirations for the years to come? In Chapter Five of *The Business Handbook*, you are given a roadmap for defining, clarifying and reaching your goals. Your dreams give you the energy and drive to reach those goals.

EDIFICATION AND LOYALTY	The business is built upon relationships which are founded on trust and mutual respect with both your upline and downline people. We believe that the most effective way to bring out the best in people is to concentrate and build on their strengths, as opposed to pointing toward weaknesses.

When you identify the positive qualities in your upline or downline associates, you nurture them through "edification" and help them become stronger.

Trust us—your upline and downline will

never be perfect, just as we aren't perfect, but when you are loyal to them and edify them in spite of their faults, people in your group will do the same for you.

EIGHT STEP PATTERN OF SUCCESS

You will find the Eight Step Pattern for Success in the front of the pocket calendar (TL-14) you should receive from your upline when you get started. This pattern relates eight essential activities you need to perform on your way to success in this business.

Read the Eight Step Pattern every day, especially during the first sixty days you are in this business. As you understand it, you will also want to teach it to new downline distributors.

EMERALD

An Emerald Direct Distributor has sponsored three groups, each of which qualifies at the 25% Performance Bonus level for at least six months of Amway's fiscal year.

EXECUTIVE DIAMOND

An Executive Diamond Direct Distributor (often referred to as an E.D.C., which points to membership on the Executive Diamond Council) has sponsored nine groups, each of which qualifies at the 25% Performance Bonus level for at least six months of Amway's fiscal year.

FOLLOW- THROUGH (FOLLOW-UP)

After showing the Amway Sales and Marketing Plan to a prospective distributor, leave an SA-4400 and other information for him or her to review. Your DD or upline will help you put together these FIRST NIGHT PACKS to use with follow-through.

You should get back with that prospect in person within 24-48 hours to retrieve your materials, answer any questions and preferably set up another time for the prospect to see the plan again.

Re-read Chapter Ten of *The Business Handbook* and study the follow-up section in the Eight Step Pattern. Remember, usually 80% of those who see the plan twice get involved.

FOSTER BONUS AND INTERNATIONAL LEADERSHIP BONUS   When an Internationally Sponsored Distributor reaches the maximum Performance Bonus level the Leadership Bonus is split with the Foster Line of Sponsorship receiving 2% (Foster Bonus) and an additional 2% (International Bonus) provided the minimum qualification requirements are met.

FOSTER SPONSOR   The recommended method for building international business is through foster sponsorship. Through the fostering method, your international group has a foster sponsor in the other country; that person takes full sponsorship responsibilities and works personally with a new distributor to insure a more successful start in building his or her own Amway business. For more information on this dual-sponsorship method, check with your upline Direct.

FRONTLINE   Someone that you personally sponsor is considered a "frontline" or "personal."

FUNCTION   Anytime a group of distributors get together for training and motivation, it is called a function. A get-together may be smaller (see SEMINAR and RALLY) or larger (see MAJOR FUNCTION).

GOALS   In Chapter Five, we feature a thorough discussion for writing your vision statement, setting your goals, defining your dreams and putting together an action plan.

We challenge you to set a target or goal each month to follow this process. How many times will you show the plan this month? How many people will you have at the next seminar? What will your PV be for the month? Use goals to help build your business in 30-day segments, based on daily, monthly, and yearly targets.

GO-GETTER A Go-Getter is someone who shows the plan at least 15 times and does 100 PV each month. Go-Getters who establish this pattern at least three months in succession are recognized at most seminars and rallies.

HOME MEETING After you get started building your business, your upline will want to schedule an introductory meeting in your or a prospect's home.

With your upline's help, write a list of prospective distributors. Use AD PACKS to prospect, then invite as many as possible to your first home meetings. Pack the house! Study the section in your calendar for more information on setting up your initial home meetings.

INTERACTIVE DISTRIBUTION A worldwide professional business development and distribution system, providing access to over 6,400 name-brand products and services with nearly 2,600 manufacturers, joint-venture distributors and service companies.

Building upon three decades of pioneering breakthroughs by tapping into the newest methods of networking both information and distribution.

By using their resources and experience, Amway stands alone in the network marketing industry in its ability to tap interactive distribution technologies.

These dramatic advancements now provide access to business-building information and communication systems. This has, in turn, revolutionized the process of getting goods and services to both distributors and customers throughout the worldwide network, and has set the stage for an era of unparalleled hypergrowth.

INTERACTIVE MEDIA
A relatively new form of in-home communication which combines the telephone, television and personal computers to offer the user instant access to such venues as shopping, publishing, education, banking and entertainment.

INTERNATIONAL SPONSOR
A Distributor who sponsors a prospect who lives in another country.

LEADERSHIP BONUS
A Bonus of 4% paid monthly on the Personal Group BV of any Personally Sponsored Direct Distributor at the maximum Performance Bonus level to the sponsor provided he/she meets the minimum qualification requirements.

LEG
Every personally-sponsored distributor and his or her group is sometimes called a "leg." The business works best when you build depth in three legs, at least three deep, then move on to building three more three-deep legs, until you reach at least nine personally-sponsored legs.

LINE OF SPONSORSHIP
Beginning with your sponsor, the "family tree or history" which links him or her to your upline Diamond and above is considered your line of sponsorship.

LIST
As soon as you begin making an initial commitment to building your Amway business,

you should begin developing a "Who Do You Know?" list of prospective distributors. Read your calendar and Eight Step Pattern for Success, for list-building guidelines.

When you get 50 people on your list, you are getting serious. When you get 100, you have set the stage for Diamondship. The longer your list, the less it matters when one out of that 50 or 100 people says "no" to the opportunity. It's hard to get too downtrodden over a rejection when you still have 49 or 99 people to go!

MAJOR FUNCTION

Several times during the year, your upline sponsorship will organize weekend conferences or seminars, generally held at resorts or large hotels. These usually feature in-depth training, powerful motivation, exciting speakers, special entertainment and relationship-building activities. One of the best benefits of major functions is the "big picture" of the business that most distributors see for the first time and a continued renewal of believing you can do it when you see others succeeding.

MAXIMUM PERFORMANCE BONUS LEVEL

The highest Performance Bonus percentage; 25% in the US and Canada, 21% in all other markets.

MINI SEMINAR

A "mini" is an upline local function, usually one day in length—Saturday afternoon and evening sessions—designed to educate a local group in basic skills and principles for developing an organization.

MULTIPLE DISTRIBUTOR-SHIP

A new Distributorship(s) established by a Distributor who already has an Amway Distributorship in another country. Each new business must have a Foster Sponsor in the country in which it is established. Multiple businesses must be established in compliance with all local government regulations and Amway rules. Usually the commitments require an Emerald business or above.

NEWSLETTER
Your upline may distribute a monthly publication which promotes dates and places for opens, seminars and rallies, upcoming functions and other important events. Often a newsletter will also recognize new pin winners.

Primarily, these monthly newsletters—both from your upline Diamonds and *Dreambuilders Review*—provide an opportunity to see where your downline distributors can "plug in" to activities in their areas.

NETWORK MARKETING
Network Marketing is derived from "**network**ing," and multi-level **marketing** when they were merged by us in 1983 to form this new term. The term, "Network Marketing," has been used to initially describe Amway's distribution system, and has since been adapted by an entire industry of competitors that seek to capitalize on Amway's success. Earlier, such terms as "direct sales" and "multi-level" were used. Today, this business approach is sometimes called "referral-based marketing" or "mutual-benefit marketing." Chapter Four provides a more thorough discussion of these terms.

NETWORKING
This concept first gained attention when John Naisbitt's bestselling book, *Megatrends*, featured the hottest trends of the 1980s. The term, "networking," pointed toward the then-revolutionary idea of developing loosely-knit groups of people to pro-

vide sources of information and to distribute that data. Led by our proven ability to capitalize on breakthrough trends, Amway Corporation followed as we together began applying it to the distribution of goods and services. A number of companies have since capitalized on this networking concept.

NUTS & BOLTS Many uplines—generally Directs or above—hold small, in-home or hotel sessions which cover areas of starting and building your business. These nuts & bolts forums are sometimes held after a home meeting, open meeting or a separate evening meeting.

ONE-ON-ONE Rather than inviting a prospect to join a group of people for a home or open opportunity meeting, you may decide to meet with a prospect for a shorter, more informal time of showing the plan. Most distributors usually get in the business as a result of this type meeting.

There are several variations of this, such as a one-on-two (when you show it to a couple) or a two-on-two (when you and your spouse show the plan to a couple). Often, a presentation book (TL 287)* is used for these smaller meetings initially.

OPEN or OPEN MEETING Often, and usually on a regular schedule your upline Direct will conduct an opportunity meeting in a hotel or public facility. Distributors are encouraged to bring prospects either to see the plan for the first time or as a follow-up meeting. It is referred to as an open, in the sense of an open invitation.

OUT-OF-TOWN GROUP Sometimes referred to as a "distance group" or "long-distance group," this term implies a leg that is at least four or more

* These items are strongly recommended and available through your upline. However, business support materials are optional and not required.

hours away, therefore usually requiring an overnight stay. It is best to work your distance groups on weekends. When you start an out-of-town leg, you should be willing to commit at least one weekend a month to them for at least a year. Be sure to counsel upline.

PARADIGM   A word used initially by behaviorists and sociologists to describe any idea or set of ideas that provides the basis for a person's framework of beliefs and actions. In today's terms, a paradigm is simply a controlling perception or your understanding of any given situation.

PEARL   A Pearl Direct Distributor has sponsored three groups, each of which qualifies at the 25% bonus level during the same month.

PICK UP   This is a time which is designated by your upline for you to pick up the product order you placed during "call in." Be considerate of your sponsor's time. Be prompt.

Also, bring a check, money order or cash. One of the nicest things about this business is that there are no accounts receivable. Therefore, don't embarrass your sponsor by asking for credit or by asking him or her to hold your check "for a few days."

PLUG IN   This term has three different meanings:

When you sign your Amway application, you "plug in" to the vast array of products and services which are made available to you as a distributor.

You can also "plug in" to a proven empowerment process of books, tapes, other business support materials, and meetings (refer to SYSTEM).

Also, "plugging in" sometimes refers to a term used when a distributor, often in an out-of-town group, who is allowed to attend opportunity meetings as well as seminars and rallies held by an upline who is not in that distributor's direct line of sponsorship. Always counsel with your upline before "plugging in" a new distributor.

POLICY BOARD Amway's Policy Board includes the Co-founders and their children: Dick, Dan, Cheri (VanderWeide) and Doug DeVos; Nan, Steve, Barb (Gaby) and Dave Van Andel. Both first and second generations of the DeVos and Van Andel families work official-ly as a corporate body responsible for all aspects of the Amway Corporation worldwide.

PROSPECT As a **noun**, this word means anyone whom you might consider to be a distributor. As a **verb**, the term refers to the active process of contacting and qualifying that person.

You can prospect (verb) a prospect (noun) through informal conversations, AD PACKS and/or in-depth interviews. Above all else, prospect your prospect by asking lots of questions.

PV/BV This refers to Amway's system of Point Value and Business Volume. This is the infla-tion protector in the sales and marketing plan. The PV accumulates and qualifies you for the Performance Bonus levels, which determines the percentage to be paid on your BV. For example, 100 PV equals 3% to be paid on your BV. Refer to Section 2 of the Amway Sales Review (SA-4400) or to your calendar for a detailed Performance Bonus schedule.

As prices change over the years, the PV remains constant, therefore requiring—at least in principle—that a person reaching Direct in the year 2001 will have to move the same amount of products as a person who reaches Direct this year. The BV, however, is tied to a market-based pricing index, so when prices climb or fall, so will the BV. With this system, inflation does not have a negative decreasing effect on your business, since an inflated BV means a larger Performance Bonus check.

QUALIFY

By asking questions and using the AD PACKS, you can often determine whether or not a prospect is looking for a better lifestyle and a way to make more money. This process of qualifying (some call it "pre-qualifying" before using an AD PACK) a prospect can save you time and energy before inviting that person to an opportunity meeting.

Let us offer you one note of caution: Qualify your prospects, but don't pre-judge them. A lot of people who appear to be uninterested or don't seem to need the Amway opportunity may actually be your best distributors someday. Look beyond the surface.

QUICKSILVER

"Quicksilver" is anyone who, during a 90-day period, sponsors five personal distributorships and has ten additional downline distributorships get involved in the business—making it a total of 15 new distributorships within the three-month period. Many uplines have Quicksilver promotions that include trips or get-togethers as rewards.

Going Quicksilver is advantageous anytime as you build your business, but it is good to remember that if you go Quicksilver during your first 90 days, you will be well on your way toward building your Directship, and you will begin acquiring some of the most prestigious pins in the business!

REGIONAL SEMINAR AND RALLY

A regional consolidates area mini-seminars into a larger training and motivational meeting, usually held on a Saturday afternoon (seminar) and evening (rally).

The regional generally draws from a several-hour driving radius, has a larger number in attendance and is conducted by an Emerald or Diamond.

REWARDS

The bonuses, trips and benefits earned by Distributors at different levels of achievement.

RUBY

A Ruby Direct Distributor has attained at least 15,000 personal group PV in one month.

SPONSOR

All persons who become Amway Distributors must be brought into the business, or sponsored by another Amway Distributor. This person is responsible for training and motivating and supplying those Distributors.

STP

In Amway, this definitely does not refer to a competitor's automotive engine additive! (After all, why buy **their** STP when you can buy **your** Freedom Fuel Additive and Amway Extra Oil Additive Concentrate?)

Instead, as you build the business, this term is an abbreviation for "Showing the Plan" or "Sharing the Plan."

When you STP, you expose the Amway Sales

and Marketing Plan to a prospect (refer to ONE-ON-ONE, HOME MEETING and OPEN).

Learn to show the plan as soon as possible. Get a presentation book (TL 287)* and go to work. Eventually you will also want to "get on the board" (using a white board, erasable markers and easel—available through your upline) to STP to groups of more than two or three.

SILVER PRODUCER
A Silver Producer has qualified for the 25% Performance Bonus level for at least one month.

SOT
As soon as you make a commitment to building this business, it is important for you to get on SOT (Standing Order Tape), which comes out once a week. Most leaders also receive the Go-Getter Tape, which also comes out once a week.

These audio cassettes contain the most current, powerful information and training to help you build a large organization. They also feature inspirational success-oriented stories of business heroes who have blazed the network marketing trail for you.

These tapes, available through your upline, are an important component of the proven books-tapes-meetings system.

SYSTEM
This term refers to an organized, time-tested program of books, tapes and get-togethers which has been carefully designed to help you and your distributors become informed and inspired as you build your own businesses.

Since ideally your business will grow into other areas and countries, it is important to "plug in" each new distributor to the system.

---

* These items are strongly recommended and available through your upline. However, business support materials are optional and not required.

The system represents the coordinated effort of hundreds of leaders working together to produce a process that provides possibly 90% of the encouragement and knowledge it will take for each of your distributors to succeed in network marketing and interactive distribution.

TOOLS OR BUSINESS SUPPORT MATERIALS

Every business has tools. Your network-building "tools" include such things as a board and easel, cassettes, videos, books, office and sales manuals, presentation books—anything that will help you develop a great organization.

TRIPLE DIAMOND

A Triple Diamond Direct Distributor has sponsored 15 groups, each of which qualifies at the 25% Performance Bonus level for at least six months of Amway's fiscal year.

UPLINE

Anyone who is in your direct line of sponsorship, from your sponsor up, is considered an "upline" or in your "upline." Edify them. Be loyal to them. As you become an upline to your downline, the positive seeds of loyalty and edification you plan in both directions will come back as a bountiful harvest of business growth and long-term relationships.

WIDTH

Your personally-sponsored distributors (the circles that are directly connected to your circle) are considered "width." If you have sponsored three distributors, for example, you are three "wide" or have three legs in "width."

To build a profitable, durable business, you must build both width and depth. a bountiful harvest of business growth and long-term relationships.

OTHER BOOKS
BY
DEXTER AND BIRDIE YAGER

Don't Let Anybody Steal Your Dream
Dexter Yager with Doug Wead

This classic in the field of motivational writing has sold more than a million copies and is selling as well today as it did in 1978 when it was first published. Dexter Yager has influenced millions with his forthright honesty, compassion and desire to see others succeed. Here is a man who has "made it" in all the right ways, and who is willing to pour out the ideas that make for successful living.

BK10 English Paperback
IBK1 Spanish Paperback
IBK7 French Paperback
IBK16 Dutch Paperback
IBK21 German Paperback

The Secret of Living Is Giving
Birdie Yager with Gloria Wead

Birdie Yager, wife of one of America's most famous and powerful businessmen, talks about:
- Marriage: How to make it work.
- Attitude: The way to popularity and self-esteem.
- Your Husband: How to make him rich!
- Children: When to say no, and when to say yes.
- Health and Beauty: They are result of our decisions, and are not automatic.
- Money: When it is bad; when it can be wonderful.
- Faith in God: Why you must deal with your guilt and inferiority, or self-destruct.

BK96 English Paperback
IBK24 Spanish Paperback
IBK22 French Paperback
IBK25 German Paperback

Becoming Rich
Dexter Yager and Doug Wead

Inspirational and moving stories of some of the world's greatest people and the eleven principles behind their success. Includes Walt Disney, Albert Einstein, Martin Luther King, Andrew Carnegie, Adolph Ochs, Jackie Robinson, Thomas Edison, Helen Keller, Harry Truman, Coco Chanel, Winston Churchill, Arturo Toscanini, and Douglas MacArthur.

BK97 English Paperback

Millionaire Mentality
Dexter Yager with Doug Wead

At last! A book on financial responsibility by one of America's financial wizards, Dexter Yager! Dexter gives freely of his remarkable business acumen, teaching you how to take inven-tory and plan for financial independence.

Here is a common sense, down-to-earth book about investments, shopping, credit and car buying, and budgeting time and money.

Included are anecdotes about other successful American business people—to give you ideas about where to go from here!

If you are serious about financial planning, this is the book for you!

BK206 English Paperback

A Millionaire's Common-Sense Approach to Wealth
Dexter Yager with Ron Ball

Financial principles on which to build your life and your dream. Based on Dexter Yager's own life-tested success secrets, this book provides valuable instruction and direction for those who are just beginning to get a vision for success. Learn common misconceptions people have about money and materialism; Discover the eleven reasons to be rich (some may surprise you!); read about the five keys to financial prosperity—the dream principle, work principle, perseverance principle, investment principle, and people principle; break down the budget barriers in your own life; and learn common sense perspectives on managing money. This book will help you turn your life around.

BK315 English Paperback

The Business Handbook
Dexter R. Yager, Sr. with Doyle Yager

This is it: The most comprehensive how-to-do-it book ever offered for building your Amway business!

Unleash the proven success system with this easy-to-read guide which details the way to CHART YOUR OWN PATH toward achievement.

The Business Handbook, now featuring over 500 pages filled with strategies, illustrations, quotations and proven patterns, brings you the finest, proven techniques for **anyone**—from a new distributor to a seasoned veteran—who desires to build a larger, more profitable, highly motivated organization.

Best of all, *The Business Handbook* helps provide you with the latest growth-oriented, validated information.

Understand the historic relationships between direct selling, network marketing and interactive distribution.

Learn the distinct, powerful differences between our corporate sponsor's time-proven sales and marketing plan and other "just-like-Amway-only-better" would-be companies.

Prepare to tap into the phenomenon known as interactive distribution.

Develop yourself for future success by learning about:

- Winning
- Leadership
- Goalsetting
- Dreambuilding
- Loyalty
- Mentor Relationships
- Paradigms
- Trends in Distribution
- International Sponsoring
- Using the Latest Tools
- Unity
- Prospecting
- Relationship Selling
- Making Presentations
- Developing Customers for Life

Above all, discover the powerful pattern for success, empowerment and fulfillment used by hundreds of Amway Diamonds!

BK247 English Paperback

Successful Family Ties: Developing Right Relationships for Lasting Success
Ron Ball with Dexter Yager

Right relationships with the people around you are fundamental to your success in life—emotionally, spiritually, and even in your work. This book will give you high-performance, practical guidelines for dealing with the many important issues that may be holding you back from experiencing success in your family relationships. You'll learn to recognize the signs of trouble and to take steps toward overcoming:
- ruptured relationships
- busy signals in communication
- sexual temptation
- stress
- negative people

And with principles founded on God-given, timeless truths you'll discover lasting success in all your challenges and be sure to have successful family ties.

BK310 English Paperback

Mark of a Millionaire
Dexter Yager and Ron Ball

Character principles that will change your life. Develop the traits that are common to successful business people. From becoming a dreamer to being hard-working, from overcoming fears to seeking good counsel, from becoming a pioneer to establishing yourself as a person of integrity—these classic character principles are the foundation for success.

BK334 English Paperback

Everything I Know at the Top I Learned at the Bottom
Dexter Yager and Ron Ball

Personal stories and lessons from the life of Dexter Yager provide insights into the keys to success. Read about Dexter Yager's early boyhood experiences selling soda pop to construction workers; learn the important business principle he picked up from his early days selling cars. Out of these personal accounts from the life of a successful leader, you can learn valuable lessons for use in your career and your life.
BK351 English Paperback

Ordinary Men, Extraordinary Heroes
Dexter Yager and Ron Ball

Essential advice for winning the war for your family. Discover how the forces of our culture are trying to destroy your relationship with your wife and kids. Learn how to avoid infidelity. Discover the strategies for hugging your kids. Read seven ways you can win in the battle for your business.
BK380 English Paperback

Available from your distributor, local bookstore, or write to:

Internet Services Corporation
P.O. Box 412080
Charlotte, NC 28241-2080